# On New Ground

# On New Ground

## Contemporary
## Hispanic-American Plays

edited by
M. Elizabeth Osborn

**Theatre Communications Group**
New York
1987

**Library of Congress Cataloging-in-Publication Data**

On new ground.

Contents: The guitarrón / Lynne Alvarez—
The conduct of life / Maria Irene Fornes—White water /
John Jesurun—[etc.]
1. American drama—Hispanic American authors.
2. American drama—20th century.   I. Osborn, M. Elizabeth.
PS628.H5705   1987   812'.54'0803520368   87-26734
ISBN 0-930452-68-21 (pbk.)

# Contents

# Preface

The most memorable lecture on American literature I ever heard was delivered by the noted black novelist Ralph Ellison, who began with this assertion: *Every American writer is a minority writer.* When he went on to talk about Mark Twain and William Faulkner, rather than the black artists we had expected him to discuss, we saw our entire literary heritage, Ralph Ellison and *ourselves* in a different light. Now, twenty-some years later, when the potential audience for any work of art is the global village, Ellison's point is truer than ever—and not just for Americans. But those of us who live in these United States are particularly fortunate to have among us many so-called minority artists who can, like Ellison, show us who we really are.

Clearly this anthology is catching a rising tide. In the past few weeks, while I have been finishing the editing of *On New Ground*, a front-page article in *The New York Times* announced that our Hispanic population is growing at a rate five times that of the rest of the United States. Pope John Paul II appeared before hundreds of thousands of Hispanic Catholics from Florida to California. *Newsweek* ran a major article on "Hispanic Art in the United States." *La Bamba* fills the airwaves and the movie screens. And just the other day many in this country were heartened when Costa Rica's president, Oscar Arias, won the Nobel Peace Prize.

This book grew out of Theatre Communications Group's Hispanic Translation Project, launched with the support of a leadership grant from the National Endowment for the Arts in 1984 to introduce both classic and brand-new plays from Hispanic cultures to English-speaking audiences. Though a program which includes reading and recommending plays from all Hispanic languages, co-commissioning English translations with American theatres looking to stage them, and publishing both translated scripts and information about Hispanic drama, TCG has set out to rectify our culture's neglect of this great body of work. At the same time, we wished to focus attention on at least some of the new plays written in English by Hispanic Americans.

It was far from easy to select the writers whose work would represent the range and the excellence of Hispanic-American drama. Even after we decided to limit the anthology to plays of the 1980s, written by people active in American theatre in

1987, there were many worthy plays by many talented playwrights to consider. *On New Ground* is the tip of the iceberg. We hope it can enhance the visibility of a much larger body of work as yet not widely known.

Every one of these six writers has won major national awards. Their names are known and respected and their plays often acclaimed by knowledgeable theatre people throughout the country. As yet few lovers of theatre have had the opportunity to see or to read their work. But these new worlds are beginning to be explored by American theatres and publishers. Writers and audiences alike have much to look forward to.

The widely divergent backgrounds of these six writers hint at the wondrous variety of cultures we too often clump together as "Hispanic." These writers are citizens of the modern world. They inhabit new ground—literally, linguistically, metaphorically, in art as well as in life. To suggest the rich heritage that lies behind each play, I have distilled a narrative autobiography from an interview with each playwright conducted during the summer of 1987. They have unhesitatingly shared with me the complexities that are their inheritance, their attempts to escape and to embrace their Hispanic roots, both the prejudices and the possibilities they have encountered. I hope readers will find in these brief narratives insights into the plays as well as the playwrights.

When Milcha Sanchez-Scott saw the cover illustration she exclaimed, "That looks just like the mountains in *Roosters*!" I discovered it in the course of an afternoon spent with Inverna Lockpez, curator of INTAR's art gallery, who enthusiastically showed me the work of a number of Hispanic-American artists until I happened upon a postcard depicting one of her own paintings, which proved to be exactly the kind of image we had in mind for *On New Ground*. The unselfish generosity of this Havana-born artist, as well as the strength and vivid color of her art, embody perfectly the spirit this book undertakes to honor.

*On New Ground* would be unthinkable without the work of Irene Fornes. Not only is she one of the preeminent playwrights of our theatre; the evidence increasingly suggests that she is the best teacher of playwriting we have. Half the plays in this anthology—*Roosters* and *Broken Eggs* as well as her own *Conduct of Life*—came directly out of her workshops. Even writers who avoid them for fear of falling under her spell testify to her power. José Rivera told me about a public forum, part of South Coast Repertory's 1987 Hispanic playwrights' project, during which Fornes was asked: "Do you think there's a danger in making people see Hispanic playwriting, Hispanic theatre?" According to Rivera, she smiled and said, "Yes, I think the danger is they'll never go back to American playwriting again." Anyone who experiences the best work of Hispanic-American playwrights could not conceivably entertain any notion of American theatre that excluded these voices, these visions.

A number of colleagues at Theatre Communications Group enabled me to bring my idea, conceived well before I became book editor, to fruition. Terry Nemeth and Jim Leverett have been especially helpful and encouraging. Roger Durling, our intern from Panama, provided invaluable assistance with the Spanish in the texts.

I am also grateful to my former student and longtime friend Caitlyn Johnson, who transcribed most of the interviews, and to literary managers at theatres across the country who recommended plays and supplied scripts, thereby making the selection process richer and more difficult. Most of all I wish to thank the playwrights themselves, who gave generously of their lives as well as their art, and who to a man and woman took advantage of the opportunity to make improvements in their already splendid plays published here.

M. Elizabeth Osborn
New York
October 1987

*On New Ground* and the Hispanic Translation Project have been supported by grants from Atlantic Richfield Foundation, AT&T Foundation, Consolidated Edison Company of New York, The Ford Foundation, National Endowment for the Arts and New York State Council on the Arts.

# The Guitarrón

Lynne Alvarez

# Lynne
# Alvarez

I was born in Portland, Oregon in 1947. My folks are from Córdoba, Argentina. Their families left independently in the '30s; they met in Florida. After they got married they lived in Detroit for a while. When my father was in the army he was sent out to Oregon.

We went back to Michigan when I was four or five. We lived in the country. My father was a good old-fashioned doctor, a GP. My mom wanted us kids to go to a good high school instead of a country school, so we moved into Detroit, just as a lot of other people were moving out.

In the country there were no Hispanic people around. My family was careful to speak English all the time, even in the house. But my grandmother lived with us for a long time—she spoke Spanish and we would answer in English. I understood Spanish, but I didn't want to study it. I studied French in high school. At that time if you had immigrant parents, you were always a little leery.

When I was quite young I went to the University of Michigan, in Ann Arbor, and majored in Italian and Romance languages and history. There I started meeting Latin Americans. At the end of college—I was about nineteen—I decided to go down to Mexico and visit relatives. I became a newspaper reporter in Veracruz and met my future husband, who is Mexican, there. I went down in '66 and stayed through '73.

That was a very political time. Even though my written Spanish was clumsy and it took me four hours to write what someone else would write in one, I worked as a regular reporter for *El Dictamen de Veracruz*, the major paper. I was also teaching journalism and English at the University of Veracruz. In 1970, right before the Olympic Games, students protesting government policies held a big event at a plaza in front of a middle-class apartment complex. The government sent in snipers who fired on them from helicopters and balconies. They killed five hundred. I was at the newspaper when the news came in on the ticker tape. We were all standing there and the head of the newspaper came by, ripped up the tape and said, "You never saw that."

I decided to create a column, "Youth's Podium." Some students and I called together leaders from the different colleges of the university for roundtable discussions which I would record. The sessions were infiltrated by the government, and people started turning on me, an American. Why was I there? Why was I asking these questions? The publisher of another paper said I was with the CIA. The cars of some of the students were stopped on the way to one of the meetings, and they were told, "Either you stop it or we'll make sure you stop it. We know who you are." It was very frightening. My husband had been picked up and thrown in jail without any reason at all. We thought it would be better to leave and went to Puebla. I decided I had better do graduate work in Latin American history because I didn't know what I had gotten into. That experience really politicized me.

When I returned to the States I went back to Detroit and was in the Urban Coalition there. My poetry became more important to me and I moved to New York. I raised money for the Puerto Rican Legal Defense Fund for a few years, then decided I had to write full time.

I always wrote poetry, ever since I can remember. In Mexico I could publish my own poetry. Somehow I didn't think I could be an artist, I thought the only artists were dead artists. Then I got something published in an obscure New York magazine and thought, "I'm a poet, that's why I've had all these problems." I started writing a lot and it kind of took over.

In 1978 the Puerto Rican Traveling Theatre started a playwriting workshop and invited published writers like me to join. There were maybe a hundred of us at the first meeting—Miriam Colón had called us together—but most dropped out. The workshop was run by Fred Hudson, who now heads the Frederick

4    Douglass Creative Arts Center. I'd never thought of writing a play, but I had this long narrative poem, and a piece that would later become *Guitarrón* that I couldn't fit into a poem. I tried them as short stories but that wasn't right. So I thought I'd try them as plays. Fred was a wonderful teacher—clear, supportive, patient. We were all from completely different backgrounds, and most of us had no idea how to write a play. We would bring in things that were just ludicrous, but Fred would keep a straight face and say, "Well now, have you thought. . . ." *The Guitarrón* came out of that workshop. I wrote three plays in two years there.

It took me a long time to get over feeling that I really belonged in Mexico. The first three plays I wrote were very Mexican. *The Wonderful Tower of Humbert Lavoignet*, for me, was really Mexican too, but I thought, "I'm not going through this again, I'd better start speaking through the culture where I am." I moved *The Wonderful Tower* to the Midwest, but it was incompletely transposed, I think. It's a transitional play. In *Thin Air* I try to speak through both the American voice and the kind of Hispanic voice of people who had gone to college in the States—voices I knew.

I found myself in a peculiar situation as a playwright. My experience with Hispanic culture was in Mexico, but I wasn't Mexican. The first plays I felt I had to write were about experiences in Mexico, because that time had been such a tremendous shock and awakening for me. I had nothing to say about regular daily life in the United States, or about the clash between cultures experienced by immigrant families. I had no stories to tell about that. I couldn't speak as a Mexican, so the Hispanic theatres didn't want to put my plays on. I couldn't be Argentinian, I'd never been to Argentina. And I couldn't speak about the urban Hispanic-American experience. It was hard to get productions.

Before I joined the workshop, I almost never went to the theatre. The big influences on me were poets—Mallarmé, Verlaine, Rimbaud, Dante. I used to read Lorca and Neruda constantly, obsessively. In Mexico what really influenced me theatrically were the popular concerts, the street. After I started writing plays I saw Peter Brook's *Conference of the Birds* and *The Ik* at La Mama, and was enthralled. I rewrote everything I could trying to include the kinds of things I saw in Brook's work.

Although it doesn't seem like it, *The Guitarrón* is very autobiographical. As a reporter in Mexico I was sent out to interview a very old man, a doctor, who was dying. Dr. Melo played the piano. He had studied with Pablo Casals in Paris; they were friends. When Casals came to Mexico he stayed with Dr. Melo. He told me stories about Casals—how he would walk along the beach with his cello.

At the same time, my husband had taken his life savings and invested in three fishing boats. We had very little money and lived right near the beach. In fact, the master boat builder lived with us, in the backyard. He was an alcoholic and a very gentle man, and he died. Antonio was one of the street beggars in the portales in the center of the city. He was a very handsome young man, very crippled, very bright. Around Veracruz there was a federal zone and the local police had no authority there. Local criminals would sleep on the beach, and to make money they would fish. I would imagine Casals walking out among brutal people, essentially outside the law. One of them was someone I knew who was nicknamed Calorías because they said he screwed around so much he burned up all his calories.

Three times a year schools of fish come by Veracruz. That year not one of them came through, which hadn't happened in forty years. The current shifted and the fish went to Cuba. We lost all our money. Everyone was wiped out. *The Guitarrón* is my innocent view of all this.

These experiences form the texture of *The Guitarrón*, but one moment was the key. I was in my kitchen washing dishes. Next door a house was being built. An Indian worker was singing a beautiful song that sounded like Bach—it was what they call a son huazteco. The house was all tile on the inside, so there was a wonderful echo. Something woke up in me, and I ran around asking, "What *is* that?" I *had* to know. In the play I tried to capture that feeling.

# Biographical Information

Lynne Alvarez's most recent plays are *Thin Air: Tales from a Revolution*, commissioned by Actors Theatre of Louisville, and *The Reincarnation of Jaimie Brown*, commissioned by the Ark Theatre. *The Wonderful Tower of Humbert Lavoignet*, selected by Albany's Capital Repertory Company as its 1985 winner of the FDG/CBS award, was co-winner of that year's national competition. *Hidden Parts* won the Kesselring Award in 1983. *Mundo* was staged in New York the previous year. Alvarez's translation of Arrabal's *Una doncella para un gorila*, commissioned by Theatre Communications Group's Hispanic Translation Project and INTAR, was produced in 1986.

Alvarez is the author of two volumes of poetry, *The Dreaming Man* and *Living with Numbers*. A former member of New Dramatists, she has been awarded the Le Compte du Noüy prize, a National Endowment for the Arts fellowship and a CAPS grant in poetry.

# About the Play

After readings at a number of theatres, including the Puerto Rican Traveling Theatre, American Place Theatre, INTAR, Circle Repertory Company, New Dramatists and Arizona Theatre Company, *The Guitarrón* was produced at St. Clement's in New York City in 1983, under the direction of Stephen Berwind.

# Characters

CALORIAS, a 45-year-old fisherman, powerful
JULIO, Calorías' friend and lover, high strung
MAESTRO, an eminent cellist who exists on several levels
GUICHO, 17-year-old fisherman and boat builder's apprentice
ANTONIO, 28-year-old street beggar, crippled, brash
MASTER BUILDER, 60-year-old alcoholic Cuban boat builder
MICAELA, 17-year-old prostitute

# Time and Place

The present. Along the beach, Veracruz, Mexico.

# The Play

# The Guitarrón

## ACT ONE

### Scene 1

*It is just before dawn on the beach of Veracruz in a makeshift fishing camp. The moon is out. We hear the waves.*

*Julio is squatting stage right looking offstage expectantly. We can barely make him out.*

*Suddenly the Maestro, an elderly cellist, is spotlighted on an elevated wooden square. He is in full concert attire. There is a music stand and a chair. Thunderous applause. He bows and smiles. He sits carefully in profile at first and tunes and adjusts his cello. There is a slight pause. He turns full face and begins to play.*

*After a few moments of vigorous playing, the lights come up on Julio. The sound of the sea becomes increasingly loud and Calorías emerges dripping wet. He has just stepped out of the ocean. He is laughing and slapping himself, shaking off the water.*

JULIO: Well? Well, mano?
CALORIAS: There's thousands of them. Thousands!
JULIO: Ahhhuuuuua!
CALORIAS (*Shaking water on Julio*): The sea's black with fish!
JULIO: Watch it!

7

CALORIAS: Coward!

JULIO: Bastard!

CALORIAS: Coward!

JULIO: It's cold.

CALORIAS (*Licks the salt from his skin*): I love the salt from the sea.

JULIO: And the sea—what did she say?

CALORIAS: She said albacore, tuna, bonito, bunker, snapper . . . sharks and dolphins swimmin' side by side . . .

JULIO: We'll be rich.

CALORIAS: You'll keep quiet.

JULIO: We'll be first. But if they see us leave?

CALORIAS: I'll leave at night. I'll fill the trawlers with ice in Alvarado.

JULIO: And where will you find the fish?

CALORIAS: At Villahermosa. They'll be at Villahermosa in three days.

JULIO: The sea tells you the time too, eh mano?

CALORIAS: Idiot. The sea tells me everything.

JULIO: You were born in the sea.

CALORIAS: I was born in the sea.

*The Maestro's music is heard sharply. Calorías looks around.*

What's that?! (*He shivers*)

JULIO: Are you all right?

CALORIAS: Yes!

JULIO: Are you cold?

CALORIAS: I'm not cold you fool.

JULIO: Sí.

CALORIAS: The sea keeps me warm. She loves me.

*Julio lights a cigarette and hands it to Calorías, who smokes.*

JULIO: And me?

CALORIAS: Don't be jealous of the sea.

JULIO: You're shaking.

CALORIAS: Come here. (*He throws the cigarette into the sea*)

JULIO: Don't throw out the butts.

CALORIAS: Cigarettes are for women. We'll buy black cigars as big as this. (*He holds himself and laughs*)

*Julio echoes his laugh, nervously. Calorías suddenly shivers.*

It's cold. Come here.

JULIO: I'm here.

CALORIAS: Good. (*He reaches out for him*) Kiss me.

*They kiss. The light on them fades. The Maestro turns his back.*

## *Scene 2*

*It is dawn the following morning. We hear gulls and the lighter sound of the morning tide.*

*A pair of feet stick out from underneath a large nearly finished shrimp boat on wooden barrels. There are tools scattered near it.*

*Guicho stumbles onstage, barely awake. He is wearing only a pair of dark trousers held up by a cord and rolled to the knee. He is dragging a net. He drapes it over a series of posts and examines it for holes. He takes out a needle and some thread and mends the holes.*

*Antonio enters in his cart, which is decorated with hubcaps and bottle caps. It is equipped with a horn and a handbrake. His hat is pushed back on his head. He checks under the boat, then wheels over to Guicho.*

ANTONIO: Pssst. *(Guicho doesn't hear)* Psssst. *(Honks his horn)*

GUICHO: Jesus Christ, Antonio! *(Indicates the boat)* Shut up.

MASTER BUILDER *(From under the boat)*: Goddammit it, motherfuckers, shut the fuck up!

ANTONIO: Whew!

GUICHO: I knew it. So you're grinnin' like an alligator. What's up?

ANTONIO: I did it mano . . . *(Waits dramatically)*

GUICHO: Sure. Great. All right. What did you do?

ANTONIO: Why Guicho. I did just what I promised. Sí señor. I've done the impossible!

GUICHO: Micaela!!

MASTER BUILDER: Will you two shut up!

GUICHO: Just ignore him.

*From under the boat a hand appears patting the ground. It finds a bottle and pulls it under.*

But what'd she say!

ANTONIO: She says she'll see you. Right now!

GUICHO: Right now?!

ANTONIO: You got it mano.

GUICHO: Right now . . . right now. Jeesus. How can I thank you. Right now?! You are terrific . . . superb—

ANTONIO: Excellent. I am excellent, right? *(Beaming)* Sí señor. Micaela took pity on this poor ruined street beggar.

GUICHO: Wait a minute. What do you mean she took pity on you?

ANTONIO: Well . . . I shouldn't tell you.

GUICHO: Wait a minute now—

ANTONIO: Well ya see . . . I was in the portales, making my rounds as usual, right?

GUICHO: Yeah, yeah. Go ahead.

ANTONIO: And Micaela was sittin' at that first table at the Diligencias where she always sits . . . so anyways, I made a sign to her that I wanted to talk . . . I kinda winked—

GUICHO: Coño, Antonio. Hurry up!

ANTONIO: So we went around the block and I tell her you want to fuck her, right?

GUICHO: Did you have to put it that way?!

ANTONIO: And she said no . . . but—

GUICHO: No?!

ANTONIO: Let me finish my story, coño! So she says no and then I give her my sorrowful look . . . ya know . . . like this . . . (He gives a very convincing sorrowful look) And then . . . (Long pause)

GUICHO: I don't want to hear this.

ANTONIO: So we did it mano. She thought I was a virgin, so she only took half my bag . . . fifty pesos, mano . . . (Holds up his money bag) I spent fifty pesos, a whole evening's work . . . all for you mano!

GUICHO: What do you mean all for me! How could you of done somethin' like that!

ANTONIO: Oye. She's gonna do it to you for nothin'! Free. You're a saint, mano . . . a saint makin' miracles.

GUICHO: What are you talkin' about. You knew how I felt about her. I mean, I thought it would be somethin' different. Special maybe . . . but shit. I'm not standin' in line for love. . . . What kind of friend are you anyways! (He walks away angrily)

ANTONIO: I'll tell you what kind of friend I am, little brother! You listen to me, 'cause I keep you from gettin' hurt! Do you hear?! I mean the world's like that. If Micaela's a pro, she's a pro. There's ways to enjoy that too. Do you hear me, little brother?

GUICHO: Yeah.

*The Maestro has appeared suddenly on a dune. He is playing in a short-sleeved shirt and wearing a straw hat. It is about 8:00 in the morning. He plays, stops, tunes and then plays again.*

ANTONIO: Don't feel down 'cause it ain't the romance of the century, right? So go on. Get ready . . . change your shirt or somethin' . . . (He catches a glimpse of the Maestro) Will you get a load of that.

GUICHO: What?

ANTONIO: That old músico up there.

GUICHO: We got music while we work.

ANTONIO (Inspecting closer): Hey no kidding. That old man's famous. His picture's plastered all over the zócalo, sí señor. That guitarrón must be worth a bundle. Yes indeedee. (Fishes around in his pockets) Speaking of which, manito. (He pulls out some bills) No woman'll look at you twice if you don't got money in your pockets.

GUICHO: Heyyy.

ANTONIO: Take it!

GUICHO: But I'll pay you back! I'm good for it.

ANTONIO: Yes sir, when the fish come in, right?

GUICHO: I mean it.

ANTONIO: Forget it.

GUICHO: You're a good friend, mano.

ANTONIO: Get outta here!

> *Guicho leaves. Antonio wheels closer until he is looking straight up at the Maestro. The Maestro nods and smiles. Antonio nods and smiles.*

ANTONIO (*Waving and smiling, but talking to himself*): You got a real nice guitarrón there, señor. Real nice.

*Antonio leaves. The Maestro plays. Lights dim.*

## Scene 3

> *The Maestro is seen playing in his shirt-sleeves on a dune, but he is almost off-stage or behind a scrim. His music cannot be heard.*
>
> *Micaela is sitting on the beach as if taking some sun. Her skirt is rolled up to her thighs and she is barefoot. Her shoes, pink high heels, are placed carefully next to her.*
>
> *Guicho enters. When he catches sight of her he tries to appear nonchalant.*

MICAELA: Hey Guicho. . . . Hi. How're ya doin'?

GUICHO: Oh hi, Micaela.

MICAELA: Lookin' for me?

GUICHO: Yeah sure . . . why not. (*Looks around*) Waitin' for . . . uh . . . someone special?

MICAELA: Of course.

GUICHO: Okay then . . . well . . . (*He starts to leave*)

MICAELA: I don't believe this. I'm waitin' for you. Didn't you talk to Antonio?

GUICHO: Yeah, I talked to him.

MICAELA: So? Well come on over.

GUICHO: Sure. (*He looks around nervously and sits down. He makes a grab for her and tries to kiss her*)

MICAELA (*Slapping him hard*): What's the matter with you. Animal! (*She stands up almost in tears*) You creep! I thought you were different from the rest!

GUICHO: Yeah. Well I sure as hell didn't think you were such a whore. . . . Makin' it with a cripple for Chrissakes!

MICAELA: Is that what Antonio told you?

GUICHO: Yeah. What'd you think? He'd keep it a secret? He's my friend you know.

MICAELA: Well your friend made it up. (*Pause*) Really. (*Pause*) All I did was give him a kiss . . . on the cheek . . . I was real glad you wanted to see me.

GUICHO: Yeah?

MICAELA: Yeah. I always thought you were cute.

GUICHO: I messed everything up, right?

MICAELA: So you were jealous?

GUICHO: Not jealous.

MICAELA (*Touching his arm seductively*): You were jealous and you haven't even laid a finger on me. . . . You are going to be some lover . . . ummmhmmm . . .

GUICHO: Look. Never mind.

MICAELA: What's the matter Guicho. Come on tell me. Am I so bad?

GUICHO: I just don't understand. One minute you're cold 'n' then you're all over me. Forget it.

MICAELA: You're scared.

GUICHO: Look. You're not dealing with . . . with a novice, you know. Chelito and I . . .

MICAELA: You don't got to be embarrassed with me, nene. Antonio told me everything.

GUICHO: I'll kill him.

MICAELA: Hey Guicho. It's simple. You're cute. You need a good woman to start you out. You get the wrong one manito and it'll put you off fucking for life. Believe me . . . I've seen a few and no matter what I've done . . .

GUICHO: Just don't talk about it.

MICAELA (*Giggling*): Oh yeah. You get jealous.

GUICHO: I ain't jealous. I just don't want you to be a—

MICAELA: A whore, right?

GUICHO: Not with me.

MICAELA: Oh I can see it now. Pretty soon, you'll say not with anyone else neither. You're really something.

GUICHO: Jesus. This definitely ain't going the way I thought. We'll do it another time. Okay?

MICAELA: Not so fast Guichito. You were my present too, you know. My special celebration. I had you all saved up. Somethin' sweet to remember when I go into La Falana's next week.

GUICHO: I've heard of her.

MICAELA: We don't got much time. Only a week.

GUICHO: I'll go see you there.

MICAELA: With all your money, right?

GUICHO: Right.

MICAELA: She's real expensive, Guicho. (*She looks into his eyes*) You'd pay to see me?

GUICHO: Yeah.

MICAELA: You don't have to pay now.

*They kiss.*

GUICHO: Don't go in. Stay like you are.

MICAELA: It's a big house. And she don't take just anyone, you know. She's got to send for you. Oh and you should see her, Guicho. She's got nails this long. And she's fat. But she smells like flowers. Doesn't use perfume either. They say her smell drives men crazy. They come and ask her to sleep on handkerchiefs and sheets for them.

GUICHO: Can you have a boyfriend?

MICAELA: You should see the dance floor. It's got beautiful tiles and there's jasmine and framboyán and little tiny lights laced through 'em enough to make you dizzy just standing there . . .

GUICHO: Come meet me outside. (*He kisses her again*)

MICAELA: And don't think for a minute I don't got a real future. 'Cause I do. I got it all planned out. I'm going to be a singer. La Falana likes my voice, she says I can sing sometimes.

GUICHO: I guess that's great Micaela.

MICAELA: Anyways, I'll leave there whenever I want to. You believe me don't you?

GUICHO: I believe you. (*He takes her hand*) Micaela can we go for a walk? I had it in my mind, we'd walk around or somethin'.

MICAELA: Sure. (*She stops*) Hey Guicho?

GUICHO: What?

*Micaela hugs him tightly. Lights dim.*

## Scene 4

*An afternoon. Master Builder and Guicho are sanding the hull of the boat.*
*Maestro is playing, but only a few notes can be heard now and then. The sea is loud.*
*Guicho puts down his tools and starts toward the Maestro.*

MASTER BUILDER (*Sharply*): Where are you going, chico?

GUICHO: Can't hear the music.

MASTER BUILDER: What, you think this is a dance floor? Get back here and work.

GUICHO: It's weird ain't it. Sometimes I catch a note and it sounds like a human voice.

MASTER BUILDER: Don't give me your back when I'm talking to you.

GUICHO: You said there's no hurry. I want to see where he's from, an old man like that.

MASTER BUILDER: He's from his mother's gut like the rest of us, chico. Now do me a favor and give the molding some blows around the rudder, eh? (*Guicho hesitates*) You can't hear this human voice neither?

*Guicho snatches the mallet sullenly and goes under the boat.*

Nothing weird about that. Just a guitarrón, the back's a little flat, uglier than most. Hey chico, go tell that músico I can make him a mother guitarrón with inlay and mother-of-pearl. You should go tell him that.

*Master Builder looks through his bottles as he talks, holds them up, sniffs them. Finally he douses his face and head with the contents of one. Guicho is striking the boat.*

Okay, okay chico, don't put a hole in her bottom!

*Guicho comes out scowling and hands him the mallet.*

Don't be looking at me like a chicken at a snake, boy. This is water, see! *(Pours some on him)*

GUICHO: You know how I feel about this.

MASTER BUILDER: No, no, no, no. Come here. Take a good look at her. She's a beauty . . . a beautiful seafarin' boat livelier than the fish theirselves. Damn! Once she hits the water, she'll be tight as a virgin. . . . *(Ruefully)* A virgin. Shit. I don't even remember. *(He laughs)*

GUICHO: Calorías been by today.

MASTER BUILDER: This boat'll never be for Calorías!

GUICHO: Keep it down, old man. He paid for the wood and the parts.

MASTER BUILDER: I can tell you where he can go with the wood and the parts! Wood and parts. Shit. I put life into them. Just look at her, the Seahawk. She'll swoop down on them fish like a wild thing. No way this'll be for Calorías, he's no fisherman. None of you Mexicans can fish. . . . This here masterpiece will be . . . *(Thinks for a moment)* for the Japanese, chico. Those motherfuckers know how to fish. They'll go clear to India for a catch. Not like you people, last as long as the weed does. Dope fiends!

GUICHO: So let's go. Let's leave, chinche. Take the damn boat and sail away. I hate it here.

MASTER BUILDER: What's gotten into you?

GUICHO: I'm seventeen. I got my whole life jumping inside of me and I ain't spendin' it here stinking of fish gut!

MASTER BUILDER: Well sure boy . . . sure, we'll leave . . . *(He looks around for a bottle with rum in it. He tries one and spits it out)* Acchhh. Water! *(He finds some rum, drinks and sighs)* You think I'm going to spend the rest of my life here. I'm with you, boy. Just you wait . . . we'll head off to Mother Cuba, yes we will and we'll find you a dark fragrant lady with sturdy legs. Wrap them around you till you forget your own name . . . ummhmmmm. And we'll take the bus to the Esquina del Pecado where the wind gusts in from the ocean . . . and we'll make this woman walk along in front of us. *(Laughs)* And you'll see how this famous wind makes the simplest man into a poet.

GUICHO: You're crazy, chinche.

MASTER BUILDER: No. No. I tell you, the finest poets in all Havana line up along the malecón and say sweet things to women as the wind blows and . . . lifts their skirts! *(Takes off his hat, as if he were bowing to a passing woman)* Blessed be the earth where they planted the seed . . .

GUICHO *(Joins in)*: . . . the seed from which the tree was born that was used to make the cradle of this beautiful Cuban rose . . . olé!

*They laugh and end with a flourish. The Master Builder takes a drink.*

MASTER BUILDER: You should have known me in better times. I was a man.

GUICHO: Don't drink.

MASTER BUILDER: No business of yours. A man's the master of his own body.

GUICHO *(Watches him)*: You're right.

MASTER BUILDER: What?

GUICHO: A man's the master of his own body.

MASTER BUILDER: Right.

GUICHO: I'm leaving.

MASTER BUILDER: What are you talking about?

GUICHO: I'm leaving . . . I'll climb that dune if I want to. *(Indicating the Maestro)* And keep going.

MASTER BUILDER: You got another job? *(Guicho shakes his head)* A woman? That's it, some woman put her spell on you . . . right, chico? Opened her legs and your brains fell out. I knew something made you lose your quiet. It'll pass.

GUICHO: I want to take her somewhere you know. Somewhere new, fresh, clean. You came from Cuba. Crossed the whole fuckin' ocean and never looked back!

MASTER BUILDER: But I was twenty-three. I was a master builder with eight boats to my name. I wasn't a punk kid chasing skirts. I sailed out of Havana with two shrimp boats and a fine blue boat to fish red snapper . . . I built them with these very hands . . . with not a single nail . . . every part cut and fitted from the finest woods . . . I was a master builder and only twenty-three. . . . But this rotten port . . . achhh . . . everything rots here. . . . We'll go back to Cuba, sí señor. We'll finish this Seahawk and sail back to Cuba . . . I'll take you down to the Esquina del Pecado and the Monument to Madrid . . .

*Calorías enters.*

GUICHO: You'll never leave.

CALORIAS: Who's leaving? *(Looks the boat over)* You're not done yet. But almost, eh? Another week should do it. What do you say, old man?

MASTER BUILDER: Maybe a week. Maybe more. Depends on the weather.

CALORIAS: Maybe it depends on the bottle too? I want this in the water in two weeks.

MASTER BUILDER *(Drinks)*: Creditors chasing you, eh chico?

CALORIAS *(Snatches the bottle from his hands)*: I want to take a pleasure cruise up the Papaloapán—so don't drink yourself to death before you finish!

GUICHO: Give it back to him Calorías. He ain't a child.

CALORIAS: And you neither.

GUICHO: I work like a man, I am a man. Give it back to him.

CALORIAS *(Pats the three knives at his belt)*: When I was sixteen, I was a man too. Had two of these three knives. Took each one from a dead man. Yes I did. *(Hands*

*Guicho the bottle)* So man to man—I leave him in your hands. Take care of him and we can all take a joyride and I'll buy barbacoa and mangoes and we'll dive for sweetwater clams. I like you Guichito. You're a good kid. *(To Master Builder)* And you, make me my Seahawk with wings spread out like so—and I'll rule the fuckin' ocean and you'll have money jingling in your pockets.

MASTER BUILDER: No fish. No money. No boat.

CALORIAS: I heard them sliding through the sea.

MASTER BUILDER: Well I know the sea whispers her secrets to you before she tells the rest of us . . . but I'm a practical man and the fact is . . . I ain't seen full payment on this boat and until I do, it's mine.

CALORIAS: It is?

MASTER BUILDER: You gave me a pile of sticks. I made the boat.

*Calorías calmly walks over to the boat. For a moment it seems he is caressing the hull, but he is looking for the edge of a plank. He finds one and suddenly pulls on it mightily until it comes off.*

CALORIAS: You're right. The boat is made of wood. The wood is mine. *(He takes off another plank)*

MASTER BUILDER: No!

GUICHO *(Grabs Calorías's arm to stop him)*: Bastard!

CALORIAS *(Shucks Guicho off easily)*: I'll take it down to killing, boy. Don't start what you can't finish. *(To Master Builder)* And if you want to see any money—have this ready. Soon. *(He leaves)*

MASTER BUILDER: How could I let someone speak to me like that? How? *(He picks up one board and tries to hold it to the hull, put it back. It slips. He tries again)* How have I come to this? Me? I thought this port would make me a millionaire. Three times a year I watched it fill black with fish. The air filled with birds . . . and I bought two new motors for my magnificent boats. I could go farther out to sea than anyone in Veracruz and I was only twenty-three! But now it's his turn. God toyed with me. I was his joke. The first school of fish never came and me waiting like an idiot . . . and so I lost one motor because I couldn't pay and then when I had no money to buy more marijuana for my crew—those perverts sank my other motor one night off the Bay of Tampico. . . . But I was a big man then and strong . . . and I jumped into the bay with one man under each arm. And I held them under until they *died!* They died.

*The boards keep slipping as he tries to fit them back into place. Guicho comes to help him.*

GUICHO: Not now, chinche. Later.

MASTER BUILDER: You! Go on. Leave. Go where you like. You treat me like he does. I don't exist. You don't hear me. You look through me.

GUICHO: No chinche. Hey.

MASTER BUILDER: Maybe I ain't here no more. What do I know. Those men took part of me down with them . . . in this bottle . . . and this . . . and hundreds more. They're trying to drown me too!

GUICHO (*Kneels near him*): And are you drowning, old man?

MASTER BUILDER: Shit, chico. I have my boat. It's become my lifeboat.

*Lights fade.*

## Scene 5

*That night. Calorías is asleep. He cries out, thrashing.*

*The Maestro is playing, spotlighted on a wooden square. He is in his tuxedo. He nods and smiles at Calorías as he plays. This time, he is so close they could almost touch him.*

*The Maestro stops playing and comes over with detached curiosity. He nudges Calorías with his bow several times.*

*Calorías moans louder.*

*Julio sits up and lights a cigarette. The lights around them brighten. Julio moves to Calorías and kneels by him, stroking his head as if he were a child.*

JULIO: Calorías. (*Calorías moves restlessly*) Wake up mano. Calorías.

*Calorías sits up suddenly. The Maestro returns to his seat, satisfied.*

CALORIAS: Julio mano, is that you?

JULIO: Yes man. Calm down . . . quiet.

CALORIAS: Jesus Christ. Are we home?

JULIO: You're all right mano.

*The music rises menacingly. Calorías jumps to his feet and pulls a knife. He stands right below the Maestro.*

CALORIAS: Where is that motherfucker?

JULIO: It was a dream.

CALORIAS: Shut up! (*He listens*)

JULIO: What is it?

*Calorías looks all around him. It's as if he looks through the Maestro.*

CALORIAS: Shut up! Listen.

JULIO: I don't hear nothin'.

CALORIAS: You idiot. Listen.

JULIO: It's the sea.

CALORIAS: No! I'll find the motherfucker!

JULIO: Come on back, it's another dream. (*Looks around*) There's no one here.

CALORIAS: I can hear it.

JULIO (*Listening*): Only the sea. Tell me the dream.

CALORIAS: What's that?

JULIO: The sea.

CALORIAS (*Squatting*): Ahhhhhh.

JULIO: Your dream's stuck in your head. Get it out.

CALORIAS: It was nothin'.

JULIO: Dreams mean somethin' . . . now tell me your dream, mano. You tell me 'cause it'll hit the air and eeeeva-po-rate . . . (*Whispers*) You keep it in and you go crazy.

CALORIAS: Is that so? (*Laughs*) It's the waitin's got me crazy.

JULIO: The dream.

CALORIAS: Massage my shoulders. . . . There . . . ahhhhh. . . . It was only a stupid old man.

JULIO (*Massaging*): Yeah?

CALORIAS: He had a stick that he moved. It made music.

JULIO: That's nothin'.

CALORIAS: But every time he moved this stick, it went into my heart and come out with blood on it. . . . Blood poured out *all over!*

JULIO (*Chanting*):
Aserrín, aserrán
Los maderos de San Juan . . .

CALORIAS: It's a bad dream. Something's wrong.

JULIO: Blood from the heart means a loss. It's bad luck. You'll lose something close to your heart.

CALORIAS: Is it death?

JULIO: No but maybe you should stay.

CALORIAS: Then I'd lose for sure. I'm leaving today . . . with that Japanese captain . . . Kirasawa . . . Kirasuga . . . on the other trawler . . . I can trust him . . .

JULIO (*Chanting*):
Piden pán
No les dán
Piden queso
Les dan un hueso . . .

CALORIAS: You wait for me in two days with ice . . . five tons . . . anchored offshore . . . don't tip off anyone at the market . . . we'll sell straight from the boat. Ahhh . . . I feel better.

*The Maestro has stopped playing. He is rosining his bow and listening to the conversation.*

JULIO: But something's wrong.

CALORIAS: The sea don't lie.

JULIO: No.

CALORIAS: I feel empty. (*Presses his hand to his heart*)

JULIO (*Massaging his shoulders*):
  Piden queso
  Les dan un hueso
  Para que se rasquen
  El pescuezo.

*Lights out.*

## Scene 6

*The next morning. Fresh, early. The Master Builder is working hard repairing the boat. He and Antonio are talking.*
  *Guicho walks out whistling, happy. He is carrying a pail, a minnow net and a hand net he can throw from shore.*

ANTONIO: Hey there Guichito, going to the river?

GUICHO: Well there ain't no fish in the sea.

ANTONIO (*Outlining a woman's body with his hands*): I hear the fishin' on land's been pretty good lately, right? (*He starts up after Guicho*) Hey wait up mano . . . wait up. (*Guicho waits for him*) Bet you're going to get oysters and clams. Am I right? . . . eh? Help you keep up with Micaela, right?

GUICHO (*Playfully tilting Antonio's cart*): I don't need no fish to keep up with her . . .

ANTONIO: Ooooooo manito's in love.

GUICHO (*Tilting the cart more*): You think so, eh?

ANTONIO (*Real fear*): Quit it. Quit it! Don't do that. I hate that.

GUICHO: I'm sorry.

*The Maestro appears suddenly on the dune. He is playing in his shirt-sleeves. The music is very distant.*

ANTONIO: It's okay.

GUICHO (*After an awkward silence*): Friends, right?

ANTONIO: Right. (*Pause*) Listen.

GUICHO: What?

ANTONIO: I need your help.

GUICHO: Sure, Antonio.

ANTONIO: You see that Maestro up there? The papers said his guitarrón's worth more than ten thousand dollars. And he's got maybe three or four of them someplace.

GUICHO: Yeah? So.

ANTONIO: Well, little brother. Obviously God planted him here on this beach for a purpose.

GUICHO: No schemes, Antonio. Absolutely not.

ANTONIO: All I need is a couple thousand pesos, that's it and I'll be set up.

GUICHO: Forget it.

ANTONIO: You'll get half.

GUICHO: No.

ANTONIO: Three-quarters. Hey manito. He wouldn't miss one. He got lots of them. We won't hurt him, an old man like that. You could just grab it away from him, push him over or something. Look. I know a politician's daughter who'd pay a lot for a guitarrón like that. One of his, you know. They don't grow on trees. Manito honest, he has at least eight or ten. He's world-famous, little brother. He'll never miss it. I promise. I swear to God.

GUICHO: Fishin' don't hurt nobody.

ANTONIO: Yeah. But it don't help anybody either, right? Sweating in the sun just to get up and do the same thing day after day. *(Guicho starts to walk away)* Hey wait, there. Just help me do a little research. Talk to him, mano. Look at that thing he's playing and tell me if it's worth anything. Look if you think he'd get hurt, I'd just forget about it. Just put my mind at rest, talk to him. It won't hurt to talk to him. He looks like a nice man.

GUICHO: I'll talk to him. That's it though.

ANTONIO: Sí señor. Whatever you say. *(Salutes)*

*Guicho climbs the dune and approaches the Maestro, who stops playing.*

GUICHO: Good morning.

MAESTRO: Good morning. *(He fishes in his pockets and pulls out some coins, holds them out)* Here you go.

*Guicho looks to see what they are, puzzled.*

GUICHO: I don't want your money.

MAESTRO: Is it too little?

*Guicho reaches out shyly to touch the cello.*

So you came to steal my cello, eh?

GUICHO: What? *(Retracts his hand quickly)*

MAESTRO: Well you certainly want something. You and your friend there. Unsightly bunch.

GUICHO: Ah, you saw us.

MAESTRO: Oh I see everything from here. The island there . . .

GUICHO: La Isla de Sacrificios.

MAESTRO: Yes, yes, and you people down there. I picked you out right away. Oh don't feel special now, you look just like the rest to me, you know. Perhaps I knew you'd be the one to come up. They always do.

GUICHO: Who?

MAESTRO: The natives. Great curiosity. But not for the music. Could you hear it?

GUICHO: No. A little sometimes. The wind brings it . . . like a voice.

MAESTRO: A voice, you say.

GUICHO: I seen a lot of músicos . . . the marimba in the plaza . . . the Indians come and fiddle during Carnaval by the docks . . . and play tin horns . . . but this guitarrón . . .

MAESTRO: It's a cello. A cello. This cello . . .

GUICHO: This cello, cello . . . has a human voice.

MAESTRO: Would you like to hear it talk? *(He plays a popular tune)*

GUICHO: Hey, I know that one.

MAESTRO: That's why I played it.

GUICHO: That was real nice and all . . . but there's something else I'd like to hear.

MAESTRO: Oh there is, is there?

GUICHO: Could you make it say a person's name? Like really talk.

MAESTRO: What name?

GUICHO: Micaela. Mii-caaa-ee-laaa.

MAESTRO: A musical name. Let me see. *(He tries one way and does it)*

GUICHO: Shit.

MAESTRO: I'll show you how to do it.

GUICHO: Me?

MAESTRO: Why not?

GUICHO: Sure.

MAESTRO: Your friend will think you've got it for sure now.

*He gets up and gives the cello to Guicho, who sits with it.*

GUICHO: Antonio don't mean nothing by it. He's always looking for a break, but he don't hurt nobody. He's got a good heart. *(He tries to hold the cello)* He says you're famous.

MAESTRO *(Adjusting Guicho's posture)*: Yes. Now grasp it between your knees so it doesn't move . . .

GUICHO: Why're you here then?

MAESTRO: Practicing. Now this is the bow. . . . Hold it . . . like so . . .

GUICHO: I mean here, on this beach.

MAESTRO: Oh, I have friends . . . *(Waves vaguely indicating the shore)* Now the trick is to be gentle, but firm . . . there is a trick you know. These are the notes . . .

*The Maestro moves Guicho's hand over the open strings, guiding the bow. They play three notes.*

Now let's add a little rhythm. Say the name again.

GUICHO *(Concentrating on moving the bow with the name)*: Mi-ca-e-la.

*The Maestro guides his hand.*

MAESTRO: There.

GUICHO: It's not the same as when you did it.

MAESTRO: Ahhhh, but this is a way you can do it. *(He moves Guicho's arm again)* Do you see. These three strings and back to the first. Try it alone.

*Guicho tries but the bow wobbles hopelessly. The Maestro grabs his arm.*

No. No. You'll strip the bow. Relax. Shoulders down. Smoothly.

*They do it again.*

Fill it with something beautiful. That's the trick.

*The Maestro frees Guicho's arm. Guicho tries it alone. He does it fairly well.*

GUICHO: Shit. I did it! *(He hands back the cello gingerly)*
MAESTRO: Now you know what you're stealing. It's not just a piece of wood.
GUICHO: I am good with my hands.
MAESTRO: Yes. You are. *(Sits and adjusts the cello)* Mi-ca-e-la.
GUICHO: I could bring her by. . . . Maybe I could show her what I did?
MAESTRO: I don't think so, young man.
GUICHO: Antonio'll be pissed. But don't worry.

*Guicho waits for a second. The Maestro is absorbed in his playing. Guicho starts off. Lights fade.*

### Scene 7

*Later that day. Guicho is lying on the beach. Micaela enters carrying her high heels and a large radio.*

GUICHO: It's about time.
MICAELA: How do you like the radio?
GUICHO: Come here.
MICAELA: I thought we could dance. I like to dance. Don't you?

*Guicho gets up and kisses her. They remain locked like that for a moment.*

GUICHO: Your hair smells like cigars.
MICAELA: Isn't it awful. Mmmmm you smell like the sea.
GUICHO: You've been drinking. I could taste it.
MICAELA: I stopped to get this radio. *(She finds a station she likes)*
GUICHO: You had a drink.
MICAELA: Yeah.
GUICHO: Where?
MICAELA: Villa del Mar.
GUICHO: Shit!
MICAELA: Let's dance. Can you dance? *(She takes his arm, but he won't move)* Oh come on. Don't spoil this.
GUICHO: I just got to know.

MICAELA: I met a friend. He had a radio. I asked if I could borrow it. He said never mind, keep it.

GUICHO: Quite a friend.

MICAELA: Yeah? Well, he's an old friend. Okay now. Let's dance.

*She turns up the radio. They dance together. He puts both arms around her. They kiss.*

Hey the kid can dance!

GUICHO: What'd you think.

MICAELA: You are toucheeee.

GUICHO: You think I'm a dumb kid who doesn't know what the fuck's going on, ain't that right?

MICAELA: Hey Guicho. Don't get your macho all riled up.

GUICHO: I know how you got that radio.

MICAELA: I thought we'd have fun. You know, dancing on the beach. I know you don't got any money.

GUICHO: Jesus!

MICAELA: I can't do anything right, can I?

GUICHO: You do everything right. That's the trouble. I get sick when I think of you with other men.

MICAELA: I warned you this would happen, didn't I?

GUICHO: I can't help it.

MICAELA: You're not like other men, mi amor. Believe me. You're special. My celebration. Anyways I told you this week was just for you. No one else.

GUICHO: Okay. All right. *(He fiddles with the radio)*

MICAELA: What're you doin'?

GUICHO: Finding something romantic. . . . There.

*He sits. She sits next to him.*

MICAELA: You want to go swimmin'?

GUICHO: No.

MICAELA: It's really a pisser . . . oh sorry. I mean it really gets me. I'm always near the ocean, but I never go in. Men always bother girls alone. I can't stand it.

GUICHO: I'll watch you if you like.

MICAELA: That's okay.

*They sit for a moment.*

GUICHO: So . . . how old are you?

MICAELA: You've been wanting to ask, right?

GUICHO: Yeah.

MICAELA: Why?

GUICHO: Well, I want to know something about you. I've seen you around but—

MICAELA: I'm seventeen.

GUICHO: Oh. I thought you were older.

MICAELA: I look that bad, eh?

GUICHO: No. You're beautiful. You just look . . . older.

MICAELA: More mature?

GUICHO: Right. *(Pause)* You know you could get married at seventeen. Even younger. . . . Does your father or brother think you should get married already?

MICAELA *(Laughs loudly and then stops)*: I shouldn't laugh should I?

GUICHO: I just want to find out about you.

MICAELA: No brothers and my father put me on the streets.

GUICHO: I'm sorry.

MICAELA: It's okay.

GUICHO: I was thinking . . . look there's no fish now and I'm broke. I live with an old man on the beach. He found me wandering around when I was four or five. I don't really know how old I am. . . . Maybe I'm eighteen already and don't know it . . . but I feel . . . I feel it's time I left. I feel like I'm on my way someplace. I don't know where exactly. Near the sea. I can fish and I'm good with my hands. When I leave I want you to come with me.

MICAELA: Seriously?

GUICHO: Yeah.

MICAELA: You don't know me. Maybe you wouldn't like me . . . after a while.

GUICHO: You're crazy. Kiss me. Come on.

*She gives him a quick shy kiss.*

That's the way you kiss a kid. Kiss me like you kiss the men.

MICAELA: I don't kiss them.

GUICHO: A real kiss then.

MICAELA: All right. You asked for it. Here. *(She kisses him hard)* This time open your mouth.

GUICHO *(Pulls back startled)*: You put your tongue in my mouth?

MICAELA *(Giggling)*: What a bobo. Now put your tongue in my mouth.

*They kiss.*

Did you like that?

*Guicho grabs her and kisses her. They fall to the ground and sit there laughing and out of breath.*

GUICHO: I'll see you every day, right? Then we'll go away together.

MICAELA: You're really sweet, Guicho. But I'm going to be a singer.

GUICHO: I take my hands wherever I go. You take your voice. You can sing anywheres.

MICAELA: I want to be a famous singer on the radio. I want men to . . . *(She thinks for a minute)* to fall dead in their tracks when they see me. I'm young now. Someone'll give me a break. I can't wander around little adobe villages. I got a future now. Pretty dresses. I won't even have to cook.

GUICHO: Just lie on your back.

MICAELA: We can get together after I make it. *(She turns the radio up)*

GUICHO: Sure.

MICAELA: Let's dance. Hold me close.

GUICHO: Would it make a difference if I had money?

MICAELA: Yeah. Maybe. *(She dances by herself)*

GUICHO: You're real pretty, Micaela. Beautiful. *(She gets shy and stops dancing)* Some man'll give you a break. You can bet on it. I better go.

MICAELA: Hey. We got time.

GUICHO: No. Life's too short.

MICAELA: Take the radio. I brought it for you.

GUICHO: I don't want your fuckin' radio! *(He turns away from her, wanting to go but unable to move)*

MICAELA: See, you're acting like a kid. You are a kid. I bet you're sixteen. Not seventeen. Christ. I couldn't just pick up and leave with a kid! *(She starts to stomp off with the radio on her shoulder blaring some popular instrumental the Maestro played)*

GUICHO: Micaela.

*He takes the radio from her and turns it off. He places it on the ground. He takes her arm and pulls her stage right. Lights dim.*


## Scene 8

*It is a few days later, late morning. We hear the sea.*

*The Maestro is playing softly, his back to the audience. As the scene progresses he turns more and more toward the audience, and the sound of the sea recedes as the music rises.*

*Julio is smoking nervously, cigarette after cigarette, staring out to sea.*

*Calorías comes up the beach toward him and stops some distance away. He is unkempt and obviously exhausted. Julio feels his presence.*

JULIO: Calorías, mano! What happened? You're three days late. *(Calorías stands staring at him)* I waited like you said offshore. But the ice melted in the sun. *(Calorías comes toward him)* And the fish? Mano? Were you wrong?

CALORIAS: I wasn't wrong. Fool! Idiot. The fish were there. Give me a smoke.

*Julio hands him a cigarette and lights one of his own.*

The sea doesn't lie. We sailed to Punto Verde. Nothing. The same at Boca Andrea. Rocks and water. But at Villahermosa, yes, we sighted them, just as she said! The sea was black with 'em. Bonitos, red snappers, sharks 'n' dolphins swimmin' side by side! *(He yells out)* Maldito sea. It was just like she said. But she betrayed me! They didn't come up the coast. They turned east at Villahermosa and swam towards Cuba!

JULIO: Nooo!

CALORIAS: She turned her back on me like I was a stranger, so I plowed the boats into the stream of them. We were three boats and we turned into the swarm of 'em, trying to turn them back, back to shore. And bone and gristle flew in our faces and we lost one motor and one boat sank, sharks diving after the men like they was tasty minnows. God, there was blood. (*Covers his face. Regains his composure*) They hauled me to Alvarado and I walked three days to get here.

JULIO: We'll lose everything.

CALORIAS: I walked day and night, thinking Why?

JULIO: They'll repossess everything.

CALORIAS: No. I will not let this be.

*The Maestro is now facing the audience, playing rapturously the music Calorías heard in his dream. Calorías is silent for a moment, listening.*

CALORIAS (*Gripping Julio*): That's it! Do you hear it?

JULIO: I hear what you're talkin' about. I hear a lot of things.

CALORIAS: The music. I heard that music before! (*He pulls out his knife*)

JULIO (*Jumps Calorías to restrain him*): Oh no you don't, mano. You're crazy. You can't be crazy now, you hear?! We got to do somethin' to protect ourselves, you know. We can grease the motors and sink 'em off port for a couple months. We can save them, right mano?

*Calorías struggles free and Julio grabs him again.*

No, Calorías!

CALORIAS: Idiot. Fool. Imbecile. He's toying with me. He's come here to laugh at me!

JULIO: I'm telling you, you're crazy.

CALORIAS: I ain't crazy. I heard that music before. That man was in my dream!

JULIO: He's just some old músico.

CALORIAS: He plays and she dances. But I challenge him! I challenge him!

JULIO: Fuck. You're getting me angry. Take a good look at him. Go on. Why're you botherin' with a pale skinny old músico like that? Eh?! We got things to do before the news comes in. We got to take the boat up the river to San Rafael, right?—'n' sink the motor 'n' keep good and clear so we can keep whatever the fuck we got!

CALORIAS: Her sides heaved up like an animal under my boats. She cast me off! I swear. I swear to God. He played and she danced. Yes. (*Starts up the dune*)

JULIO (*Forces him to his knees*): Listen to me, mano! You are not going crazy on me! Not now! Not ever!

*Julio massages him. Calorías lowers his head.*

Aserrín, aserrán
Los maderos de San Juan
Piden pán

No les dán
Piden queso
Les dan un hueso
Para que se rasquen
El pescuezo
Aserrín, aserrán . . . *(Keeps repeating the chant)*

CALORIAS: You're right. Okay. Okay. I just got thoughts, that's all. Just thoughts. *(He is quiet for a moment)* You got good hands, mano. I trust your hands.

JULIO:
Aserrín, aserrán
Los maderos de San Juan . . .

CALORIAS: And don't worry. I'm fine. I'll take care of everything.

*The Maestro gets up, walks right by Calorías and Julio, looking at them curiously. He exits.*

JULIO:
Piden pán
No les dán
Piden queso
Les dan un hueso
*(He fades out)*
Para que se rasquen
El pescuezo.

*Lights out.*

## END OF ACT ONE

## 28 | ACT TWO

### Scene 1

*Guicho is sprinting along the beach after seeing Micaela. He can hardly contain his excitement.*

*The Maestro is playing on top of a dune. It is midnight.*

*We can't hear the Maestro at first, but as Guicho approaches him the sound increases in volume. When Guicho addresses him, the Maestro stops.*

GUICHO: Maestro.

MAESTRO: Oh it's you.

GUICHO: An old man like you shouldn't be out here on the beach alone.

MAESTRO: And a young man like you?

GUICHO: This ain't a tourist beach. You could get yourself into trouble.

MAESTRO: Oh there's always the police, don't you think? I imagine a scream or two would bring them running.

GUICHO: The police won't come here. It's a federal zone. Only the army can come and they don't bother with us . . . unless they want dope. What you doing out here anyways? It's dangerous.

MAESTRO: I agree. But it wouldn't be quite so beautiful without danger, don't you think? Soft waves, a sea breeze, salt in the air . . . utterly forgettable without that sharp edge of malice. Brings me alive, reminds me one never knows what will happen next! Delightful.

GUICHO: I'll walk you to the street if you like. I ain't tired at all.

MAESTRO: And I'm not tired either. We're in the same mood, no doubt. In love.

GUICHO: You got a girlfriend?

MAESTRO: Don't be so incredulous, young man. *(Holds out the cello)* Isn't this shaped like a woman? And I make her tremble when I touch her so. *(He passes the bow over the strings)*

GUICHO: I thought you were talking about a girl . . . a woman.

MAESTRO: There are loves beyond women.

GUICHO: Not for me, señor. And it's more than love. It's passion!

MAESTRO: Passion. Of course, she's beautiful, wonderful, a cornucopia of delights!

GUICHO: She can kill me with a look!

MAESTRO: Well, well, well, we have a common language. Passion is my daily bread.

GUICHO: An old man like you.

MAESTRO: I measure passion by foolhardiness, young man. And what could be more foolhardy than a rich old man sneaking out to play alone at midnight on a beach infested with . . . criminals! You may feel you're risking your heart for a mere glance from this girl, but I am risking my life for one moment of beautiful music on a beach at midnight! That's passion.

*Guicho laughs and sits down at the Maestro's feet.*

GUICHO: You can keep playing if you like. It's nice out.

MAESTRO: You'll stand guard, eh?

GUICHO: Sure.

MAESTRO: Thank you. But you had better leave.

GUICHO: I like it here.

MAESTRO: It's dangerous. *(Guicho laughs)* I'm dangerous.

GUICHO: Are you kidding? I could snap you in two like a twig, old man . . .

MAESTRO: Of course, you see danger as clubbing someone on the head, don't you. Go away and be happy with your young woman!

GUICHO: There's no way you could be dangerous to me. No way!

MAESTRO: Then why are you up in arms, your back bristling, your heart pumping fire? *(He laughs)* When I say something you don't understand, you feel threatened, look at you.

GUICHO: I was just wondering.

MAESTRO: You'll do more than wonder. You'll remember.

GUICHO: How do you know? You can't see into my mind. You got no idea what I'll remember. You ain't no witch.

MAESTRO: Of course I'm a witch and music is my magic. I wave my magic bow like so . . . *(He draws it across the strings)* and the stars appear *(The stars become bright. Guicho looks up startled)* like so . . . *(He plays again)* and the tides rise up . . . *(The noise of the sea increases. Guicho looks out to sea)* and sooo . . .

GUICHO: Don't joke like that!

MAESTRO: Ahhhh you're superstitious. I'm sorry. I'm just a crotchety old man on the beach and this is just a bow. Here. Take it. *(Guicho steps back)* Are you afraid?

GUICHO *(Grasps it too quickly)*: No!

MAESTRO: Do you want to play again? Perhaps the name of your young woman . . . Micaela . . . is that correct?

GUICHO *(Hastily returns the bow)*: No.

MAESTRO: I'll tell you what, I'll play it, then.

GUICHO: No. *(He reaches out to stop him)*

MAESTRO: You needn't worry. Nothing will happen to her. Well then I'll play something soothing. Do you care for merengues? I especially like those huazteco songs, don't you?

GUICHO: That's okay. *(Starts to leave)*

MAESTRO: I thought you wanted to stay.

GUICHO: I've changed my mind.

MAESTRO: You mean *I've* changed your mind.

*Guicho exits. Maestro lifts his bow to play.*

And so it goes.

*The Maestro plays sonorously. Lights out.*

## Scene 2

*It is a nice hazy morning along the beach. Perhaps we see the edge of some moorings in the background.*

*The Maestro seems to be very far away stage left. We cannot hear him and can barely see him.*

*Julio and Calorías are moving a huge object, one of their new motors wrapped in canvas and tied to some poles in sledlike fashion. Julio pulls from the front and Calorías pushes from behind. It is slow difficult work.*

JULIO *(Stumbling)*: Hey, hey, hey. Watch it. You're runnin' me over. Shit! That's it. I quit. *(He sits)* Let them have their fuckin' motor.

CALORIAS: What are you talkin' about. It's almost paid for. I'd slit their throats before I'd let them take it back. For three payments, you fool.

JULIO: Okayyyy. Okayyy.

CALORIAS: Now get movin'. The sun's up!

JULIO: I'm resting.

CALORIAS *(Paces)*: Fuckin' delicate. I want this sunk and us halfway up the river before noon!

JULIO *(Looks toward the sun)*: They ain't even dreamin' about getting up yet.

*Antonio wheels in, out of breath.*

ANTONIO: Hey there. Good morning. Good morning. How do you do, gentlemen?

JULIO: I need a drink.

ANTONIO: Well what do you know, señor. I search around in my magic box and . . . *(He feels around, pulls out a bottle. Julio pounces on it)* Burn a hole in your brain and let the sunlight in, señor.

CALORIAS: What do you want, cripple?

ANTONIO: What makes you think I want somethin'? Perhaps I only wanted to greet you fine gentlemen.

CALORIAS: Don't bullshit me, cripple. I ain't in the mood.

ANTONIO: Fine, right, correct. Well now. Down to business. I hear you and Julio are skipping off.

CALORIAS: You're wrong.

ANTONIO: I see. *(He turns to go)* Well then I'll just keep my little going-away present. *(He holds up two bags of marijuana)*

JULIO: I'll just keep mine, little brother. *(He giggles and holds up the bottle)*

CALORIAS *(Laughs and steps in front of Julio)*: If it happens that we were going on a little trip, what did you want from us?

ANTONIO: There is a trip, right?

CALORIAS: Let me see what you got. *(He opens one bag, smells and tastes the contents)*

ANTONIO: Well let me tell you about these two bags. They are worth four, sí señor. The finest dope, straight from Sonora with a little mixed in from Guatemala. It got two tribes of Indians high just picking it. And all for the slightest favor.

CALORIAS: We're in a hurry, cripple.

ANTONIO: Barely a moment out of your way.

CALORIAS: So?

ANTONIO: You see the Maestro there?

CALORIAS: What about him?!

ANTONIO: I need his guitarrón.

JULIO: It's too big for you, mano. You need a fiddle.

CALORIAS: The Maestro, eh?! Why do you want it?

ANTONIO: I like music.

CALORIAS: Fuck you.

ANTONIO: I got a friend who likes music. A lady. I want to impress her, all right?

CALORIAS: I don't believe you.

ANTONIO: Just grab it. What can he do? You could snap him in half.

JULIO: Snap him in a minute, like dry wood. Must be close to a hundred years old.

ANTONIO: You'll do it?

CALORIAS: For you? Of course. I'd be glad to pay my respects. (Holds out his hand) The dope.

ANTONIO: You forget. I'm a businessman. A paid musician plays a bad tune.

CALORIAS (Holds Antonio easily while he takes the other bag): And you forget, mi cuate. You ain't a businessman. You're a cripple. (Opens the second bag and tastes the dope)

ANTONIO: You bastard.

CALORIAS: Don't worry, little brother. I'll take care of it for you.

JULIO: Me too.

CALORIAS: Andale, Julio. You idiot. Let's sink the motor. Move it!

*Julio and Calorías move off. Antonio wheels in the opposite direction. The Maestro turns to face the audience, enraptured in his music. Lights fade.*

## Scene 3

*Another part of the beach later that morning. The Maestro is seated far away, stage right. We can hear only trails of music now and then, as if carried by the wind.*
*Guicho and Micaela enter. Guicho is carrying some varnish. Micaela is fanning herself.*

GUICHO: I like the way you look with nothing on your face.

MICAELA: Thanks.

GUICHO: Without all that gook you look seventeen like you said.

MICAELA: Fifteen.

GUICHO: I thought you said seventeen.

MICAELA: Oh no. Fifteen.

GUICHO: Well whatever. You look like a kid. And you love me.

MICAELA: Uhmmmm.

GUICHO: Amazing. I can hardly believe it. Go ahead. Say it. Look straight in my eyes and tell me.

MICAELA (Mugging, putting her face next to his): I love you.

GUICHO: Amazing.

MICAELA: I told you you were my celebration.

GUICHO: Yeah, I know. *(They walk a little)* Don't think I forgot about our future. I got it all figured out.

MICAELA: By yourself?

GUICHO: Come on Micaela. I don't like it when you make fun of me. You got to stop being fresh like that.

*Micaela walks away. The music comes up. She is irritated.*

MICAELA: I wish that old man would get out of here. He gets my nerves on edge.

GUICHO: Listen to me. I'll go to Villahermosa and get a job in the oil fields. They give you a brick room and a stove of your own . . . if you're married.

MICAELA: Great.

GUICHO: It ain't that I'm putting pressure on you. I just mentioned it.

MICAELA: It sounds nice.

GUICHO: There's thousands of people. French, gringos. You could sing there.

*Micaela takes out a mirror and puts on rouge and then lipstick.*

Why're you putting that stuff on?

MICAELA: Well, you got to work, right?

GUICHO: Yeah.

MICAELA: My brother's going to give me a loan.

GUICHO: I thought you didn't have any brothers.

MICAELA: A half brother. My dad got around.

GUICHO: Micaela.

MICAELA: You got to look good. Can't look like you need it too bad.

GUICHO: I'll meet you this afternoon. When the varnish is drying?

MICAELA: You got any money? If you had, it would sure save me a trip. *(Guicho can't look at her)* I'll see you.

GUICHO: This afternoon.

MICAELA: I do love you.

*Guicho holds her and kisses her. She walks away, swaying on her heels. Lights dim.*

## Scene 4

*The Maestro is drinking water from a thermos and cooling off.*
*Antonio is trying to get the Master Builder up.*

ANTONIO: Hey old man. Your luck's changing. Get up!

MASTER BUILDER: You're right chico. My luck's changing. I dreamt the sea was black and there was music, Cuban music, far away.

ANTONIO: This boat'll be yours, señor. Can you hear me? Julio and Calorías are leaving.

MASTER BUILDER: They'll be back.

ANTONIO: Finish this and you can sail awaaayyyy.

MASTER BUILDER: I'll be gone. Give me a drink.

ANTONIO: But keep it quiet. Not a word about it. Keep the lid on and the water won't boil away, right? Hey are you okay?

MASTER BUILDER: I can't see anything. Are my eyes open, chico?

ANTONIO: They're closed, old man.

MASTER BUILDER: Give me a drink. I can't see.

ANTONIO: You stupid old man. You don't want a drink. *(He looks through the bottles)* How will you work on your boat? I'll get you some water. *(He opens a bottle and smells it)* You got any water here?

MASTER BUILDER: A man like me shouldn't be reduced to drinking water.

ANTONIO: Here. Try this.

*Antonio tries to make the Master Builder drink but he spits out the water.*

Don't be so stubborn. An old captain like you ain't afraid of a little water.

MASTER BUILDER *(Grabbing Antonio's hand)*: I feel very bad.

ANTONIO *(Afraid himself and looking around for someone)*: Where's Guicho? *(The Master Builder makes a weak gesture)* Has he seen you like this? You're overworking, my friend. Do you need more water?

MASTER BUILDER: I need all the water this alcohol has sucked from me these thirty years . . . an ocean of water . . . *(His mind wandering)* beautiful seafaring boats.

ANTONIO: What?

MASTER BUILDER: Guicho?

ANTONIO: No. It's me. Antonio. *(Giving him more water)* Hey. That's better. You kept some water down. Sí señor.

MASTER BUILDER: My feet are swollen. I can't walk. I'm dying.

ANTONIO: No you ain't. You're just tired. Just tired. *(Tries to soothe him)*

MASTER BUILDER: Guicho?

ANTONIO: I ain't Guicho.

*Calorías and Julio enter. The Maestro plays Calorías's theme.*

CALORIAS: Hey there cripple. Master Builder. Hot today.

JULIO: Hey there chinche. *(Kneels next to the Master Builder)*

*Calorías shades his eyes and studies the Maestro, who nods at him.*

He's nodding at me. He knows.

ANTONIO: Not a hint. He's smiling.

CALORIAS: Well. I'm a man of my word.

*Calorías strides up the dune. The Maestro watches his approach nodding and smiling.*

MASTER BUILDER: Is that Calorías? *(He reaches out for Antonio's hand)*

JULIO: Calorías and me, Julio.

ANTONIO: Don't worry, chinche.

MASTER BUILDER: He wants the boat!

ANTONIO: He don't want nothing with you. It's okay. Everything's fine. Don't you worry, right?

*Calorías stands by the Maestro.*

CALORIAS *(Softly)*: It's time for you to go now.

MAESTRO *(Stops)*: Ahh well. *(Irritated, he looks up but has to shade his eyes)* Step over here. I can't see you.

CALORIAS: Why don't you tell me who you are, eh?

MAESTRO: You are a perfect stranger.

CALORIAS: Who are you?

MAESTRO: An old man.

CALORIAS: I saw you before.

MAESTRO: There are so many posters.

CALORIAS: No. Not that way.

MAESTRO *(Tiredly)*: I have been here for days and days. An eternity. It's very hot. *(He wipes his face with a kerchief)* I must be going.

CALORIAS: You were in my dream.

MAESTRO: Perhaps you are right. It's time to go.

CALORIAS: It was you in my dream and your music. You know me, don't you?

MAESTRO: I know many men.

CALORIAS: You played with that . . . thing and my blood spilled and my boats sank! You sank my boats! You'll pay!

MAESTRO: I've annoyed you, haven't I? *(He stands carefully and turns out his pockets)* I don't have any money. Nothing. Look!

CALORIAS: You were in my dream . . . and the guitarrón.

MAESTRO *(Holding the cello)*: This? You want this then?

CALORIAS *(Jumping back)*: Don't wave that thing at me.

MAESTRO *(Gathering his things)*: It's beautiful here. The sea. But I'll leave.

CALORIAS: Give me the guitarrón.

MAESTRO: No.

CALORIAS: A simple request, old man. The guitarrón.

MAESTRO: I'm sorry. I can't do that. *(Holds it tightly)*

CALORIAS: You're stronger than you look, cabrón.

MAESTRO: And you're weaker. You see, I'm still a man of pride. I know what matters.

CALORIAS: So you want it man-to-man . . . eh? *(He pulls harder, but the Maestro clings to it)* Idiot! Imbecile! Don't cross me! *(He pulls out his black knife)* Not man-to-man. See this? This is my gutting knife. . . . Black and silver. See it? Now let go of that guitarrón before I cut you away from it.

MAESTRO: Man-to-man? Not with a knife. You are a beast and an animal. *(He starts to leave)*

CALORIAS (*Grabbing him*): Give me that guitarrón. Give it to me! Give it to me!

*They struggle.*

Hijo de la chingada . . . give it to me. . . . No old man is going to get the best of me!

*Calorías grabs the Maestro by the hair, pulls back his head and slits his throat.*

Not *me!*

*Julio runs to the top of the dune.*

ANTONIO (*Seeing what Calorías has done*): No! No! Nooo.
MASTER BUILDER: What? What is it?
JULIO: Oh my God. What have you done?
CALORIAS (*Staggering with the cello and bow*): I don't know. I'm sticky.
JULIO: Let's go . . . (*Calorías looks back*) Drop that thing. (*Pulls Calorías down the dune*)
CALORIAS: I can't.
ANTONIO: Calorías, mano . . . (*Going to him*) You didn't have to kill him.
CALORIAS: But I did.
JULIO: God help us.
ANTONIO: The guitarrón. (*He clings to Calorías*) Give it to me.
CALORIAS (*Tips Antonio over*): Stupid! (*Throws him the bow*) Here.
ANTONIO: Puto, bastard!
MASTER BUILDER: What is it? What's he done?
JULIO: Let's go. Let's get outta here. Now! Andale!

*Julio and Calorías run off.*

MASTER BUILDER: What?
ANTONIO: He killed the old músico. Bastard! Help me! Help me!

*Master Builder struggles to get up but can't. Lights fade.*

## Scene 5

*A short while later. The Master Builder is asleep. Antonio is sprawled, exhausted from trying to pull himself into his cart, which is turned over on its side, some distance from him.*
    *Guicho enters near the dune. He sees the overturned chair and crumpled figure of the Maestro. He climbs up and stands looking down at him. He kneels, touches him, takes off his shirt and covers his face. He stands up and looks down at Antonio and the Master Builder, then out along the beach. Antonio catches sight of him.*

ANTONIO: Guicho. Guicho mano. Guicho, help me.
GUICHO: He's dead. Poor old man.

ANTONIO: Guicho.

GUICHO: Poor old man.

*Guicho starts searching near the boat and finds a knife, examines it for sharpness and slips it through his belt. Master Builder stirs.*

MASTER BUILDER: Is that Calorías?

ANTONIO: Hey mano, what you doin'? Help me will you. Guicho. Hey mano, don't make me beg. *(He is almost crying)*

GUICHO *(Helping Antonio into the cart)*: It was Calorías, wasn't it?

ANTONIO: He didn't have to kill him. My God.

MASTER BUILDER: Guicho?

ANTONIO: He stole the guitarrón.

MASTER BUILDER: I can't see. I've gone blind.

GUICHO: Did they go to the river?

ANTONIO: Leave them alone. They're gone.

MASTER BUILDER: What are you doing? Are you going after them? Chico? *(He is guiding himself along the boat toward the voices)*

GUICHO: Yes.

ANTONIO *(To Master Builder)*: He's got a knife. But you ain't goin' to use it, right little brother? Correct? That would be highly stupid.

*Guicho starts off. The Master Builder catches hold of him.*

MASTER BUILDER: Stay here, chico. Calorías likes to kill. He's crazy. Don't go. Think about me too.

GUICHO: Let me go, old man.

MASTER BUILDER: He's a stranger, an old man ready to die. What do you care about a stranger?

GUICHO: He was old. But he was a man. To get what he loved away from him, they had to rip open his throat!

*Guicho pushes the Master Builder away. The Master Builder stumbles.*

And you? You fall away like rotten fruit.

MASTER BUILDER: I am a man!

GUICHO: Would a man let them walk away with his boat and fish? Would a real man let them smile and fuck him over again and again as if nothing happened? Shit. *(He leaves)*

MASTER BUILDER *(Sits on the sand)*: I am a man. Still. Inside.

ANTONIO *(Finds the bow and holds it up examining it for cracks)*: Ahhhhhh.

MASTER BUILDER: Guicho?

ANTONIO: You okay, old man?

MASTER BUILDER: Go in my shoe, Antonio. Under the boat. I got some money there.

*Antonio looks, finds it.*

ANTONIO: Twenty-five pesitos, manitos. Not much.

MASTER BUILDER: Get me a pint or two of something . . . anything . . . that won't kill me right off.

ANTONIO: Not me. I ain't going to help you kill yourself, old man. *(He wheels away)* Get some sleep. *(He exits)*

*The Master Builder sits and then drags himself to his boat. He finds some iron tools, gets a long one and sticks it under a board like a lever. With great effort, he pries a board loose. He tries another.*

MASTER BUILDER: Ah my beauty, my Seahawk. I won't betray you. No. I am a man. See. I am a Master Builder with forty boats to my name, shaped and fitted from the finest . . . *(He loosens another board)* woods! Did you think I would finish you and make you go to Calorías? My beauty? My masterpiece. . . . My lifeboat?

*Lights dim.*

## Scene 6

*It is nearly dusk. The sound of the sea is strong. Guicho is sitting on one of several huge cement breakwaters. They are shaped like giant jacks thrown up against the shore.*

*Micaela climbs out to Guicho.*

MICAELA: There you are. *(She sits with him)* You okay? *(He's silent)* Talk to me.

GUICHO: What do you want?

MICAELA: You can hide with me for a few days. I heard about Chinche . . . and that Maestro. I'm sorry.

GUICHO: Go away.

MICAELA: I can help you, you know.

GUICHO: I just let things pass. Everything. So I got nothing.

MICAELA: Let me hold you. I can help.

GUICHO: I don't get it Miki. I can't seem to do nothin' I want, but Calorías, he can do anything he fuckin' likes. I'm a coward. *(Takes out the knife)* You know, I ain't stuck anyone in my life.

MICAELA *(Caresses his arm, takes the knife from him and puts it down)*: I was thinking. The oil fields might not be too bad. I could just not show up at La Falana's tomorrow morning. Pack a few things. Like an adventure, you know. Maybe I'll learn to say something in French or something. I'd like that. *(She holds him)*

GUICHO: It'll be the same there.

MICAELA: Oh no, manito. Americans, French, Arab people. All different. Everyone likes oil. I could learn all different kinds of music. That might make me famous. "Micaela of the thousand tongues," how does that sound? *(Laughs)* They might get the wrong idea from "tongues" though. Right? Hey Guicho, come on. Laugh a little.

GUICHO: I can't.

MICAELA: Forget Calorías. He's crazy.

GUICHO: He has the guitarrón—its wood's so thin, delicate, like you. Not glittery. And it sings . . . like you . . . it makes your name sound like music. I'll play your name for you, Micaela.

MICAELA: Make love to me.

GUICHO: I'll get it back.

MICAELA *(Picks up the knife)*: With this? I heard they slit the Maestro's throat. Antonio told me.

GUICHO *(Takes it back)*: With this, if I have to. *(He studies it, puts it away, takes a moment preparing himself and gets up)* Okay, so I'll see you later.

MICAELA: Stay here with me. Let me make you feel better.

GUICHO: If I stayed, you wouldn't love me.

MICAELA: I do love you.

GUICHO: If he ever did anything to you, you'd want his heart out.

MICAELA: But he didn't. He hasn't. He won't. Guicho, Guichito. This is different.

GUICHO: I'll be back.

MICAELA: I see. You'd rather kill than make love. Is that it, little brother? You want to kill, like Calorías. Feel that thrill of a knife entering. Muy macho. Go around with knives in your belt. I've seen it a thousand times. Yeah. You pull out a knife—and guys turn cold . . . and girls turn hot. Is that it?

GUICHO: Don't talk like that.

MICAELA: Why? You want me to always talk sweet poetry to you? I can do that, if that's what you want. Maybe you want me to act like a hooker, maybe that's what you really want, right? Say all those phony things to you. I was mistaken. I thought I could act like myself with you. Say what I really feel.

GUICHO: Miki—don't take it like that. We'll talk later.

MICAELA: No. You'll be different later. Listen to me now. I'm telling you, we can leave. You and me. Go away. We'll be so sweet together. *(She starts kissing him)*

GUICHO: I got too many things in my head.

MICAELA: You don't got to do nothing with your head. *(She tries to pull him down)* I'll make you forget the old man, Calorías, knives, everything. Come here.

GUICHO: I can't do it, Micaela. I can't.

MICAELA: You can do it, papacito. Mi amorcito. You're young, healthy, handsome, strong. And I'll do everything for you. Anything you want . . . papacito.

GUICHO: Not that way. Not like a fucking whore! *(He breaks free and exits)*

MICAELA: Don't you dare look down on me. Not with blood dripping off your knife. Stinking lousy fisherman. Don't you ever come near me. Do you hear. Idiot. My last free night and I waste it on this idiot! *(She is crying. She starts after him)* Hey Guicho. What's the matter? *(She stops)* Don't you like me? Don't you like me?

*Lights dim.*

## *Scene 7*

*The stage is empty except for a few pale stars.*
*Calorías and Julio enter. Calorías carries the cello on his shoulder.*

GUICHO *(Out of sight)*: CA-LO-RIIIIAAS! CAAA-LOOOO-RIIIIAAS!

*Guicho appears over a dune. Calorías and Julio stand looking at each other.*
*Guicho takes out his knife.*

JULIO: Hey Guichito.

CALORIAS: Why Guicho, you comin' with us?

GUICHO: No.

CALORIAS: Ah yes. I see now. You have a knife. *(Approaching)* Perhaps you're angry.
Did I hurt a friend of yours? *(He laughs)* Have you come to kill me, little boy?

*Guicho shakes his head. He is terrified.*

GUICHO: I want the guitarrón.

JULIO: Ay Guichito. Go away.

CALORIAS *(Picking up the cello)*: This. Ah yes. It is this you want.

GUICHO: Just give it to me.

CALORIAS: If only it were so simple . . . eh? But I can't give it to you. I have to destroy
it.

*Calorías turns toward the fire which Julio is building.*

GUICHO: Please Calorías.

CALORIAS: Please? *(He laughs)*

GUICHO: *You animal!*

JULIO: Leave him alone, Guicho.

GUICHO: Give me the guitarrón, Calorías.

JULIO *(Trying to keep Guicho from approaching)*: Manito. You got to understand. Calorías he got a thing about it. I'm beggin' you.

GUICHO: Turn and look at me Calorías. *(He brushes by Julio)* You killed the Maestro!
*You slit his throat!*

*Guicho lunges at Calorías, who turns. The knife is imbedded in Calorías's*
*shoulder. He staggers with the blow. He drops the cello. Julio rushes to pull the*
*knife out.*

CALORIAS: Stay away you fool. If you take it out, I'll bleed to death!

JULIO *(To Guicho)*: Run. Shit! Get away from here.

*Guicho is too frightened to move.*

CALORIAS: You see Guichito. You see why I must burn this guitarrón. You see how it works little brother? It has changed everything, everyone. Even you. *(He takes out his black knife)* Now I have to kill you too.

*Julio stands blocking Calorías.*

JULIO: What terrible luck. Guicho run, for God's sake. *(He throws up his hands to Calorías)* Remember your dream. The blood!

CALORIAS: Burn it!

JULIO: Throw it into the ocean, mano.

*Calorías is trying to stalk Guicho.*

Then I'll throw it away for you. I'll break it into a thousand pieces. Let's get out of here.

*Calorías slashes Julio across the hands.*

CALORIAS: Move!

JULIO: Ayyyy, my hands. My hands.

*Calorías walks toward Guicho.*

GUICHO: You can't kill me, Calorías. Look at you. You're a dying man.

CALORIAS: It takes more than a little boy's knife to do me in. *(He starts circling)*

GUICHO: I'll never let you keep that guitarrón, Calorías.

CALORIAS: Ay Guichito. Why have you done this? Eh? When I love you. If you go now . . . I might let you leave.

GUICHO: I want the guitarrón.

*He tries to get it and Calorías blocks him laughing.*

CALORIAS: You don't even have a knife now, Guichito.

GUICHO *(Circling him)*: And if I reach out and take back my knife? You'll spill your blood all over the sand.

CALORIAS: You won't . . .

*Guicho lunges and taps his knife hard. Calorías shudders.*

GUICHO: You see how easy?

CALORIAS: Ayyy.

GUICHO: Shall I do it again? And you'll shake and bleed? *(He taps it again)* See?

*Calorías shudders violently in pain. Julio approaches with one hand bound in his shirt.*

GUICHO: Give me the guitarrón.

JULIO: Andale . . . give him the pinche guitarrón, mano. We'll leave . . . go to Villahermosa . . . andale.

CALORIAS *(Bellows)*: NOOOOO!

GUICHO: Give me that guitarrón!

JULIO (*Picks up the cello and holds it above his head*): You two is crazy. Fightin' about a fuckin' piece of wood. Will you die for a lousy piece of wood?!

CALORIAS: There's death in its stomach!

GUICHO: There's life. I felt it.

*Calorías lunges at Guicho and nearly lands a blow with his knife.*

GUICHO: And I will feel it whenever I want! (*He grabs the handle of the knife in Calorías's shoulder and pulls it out with great effort*)

JULIO: Dios mío.

*Calorías staggers. Julio drops the cello and catches him, desperately trying to stop the bleeding.*

CALORIAS: Julio . . . Julio. . . . Take me to the sea.

JULIO: Quiet. Quiet.

*Julio leads Calorías off. Guicho slowly picks up the cello. He places it on its metal tail and sinks to the ground center stage. The cello remains upright above him. The light darkens gradually. The stars shine. Blackout.*

## Scene 8

*Very early the next morning. There is still a moon. We hear the ocean.*
*Guicho is sitting as before. He has fallen asleep with the cello propped upright.*
*He is dimly spotlighted so that we can only just make out his shape.*
*Antonio wheels in. He approaches cautiously, not sure if Guicho is alive.*

ANTONIO (*Whispering*): Guicho? Hey manito?

GUICHO (*Stirs*): What? . . . Ay. It's only you.

ANTONIO: Are you all right?

GUICHO: No. (*He sighs*) Yes.

ANTONIO: I see you got the guitarrón. . . . Way to go, mano . . . (*He looks around curiously. He finds Calorías's knife and holds it up*) And Calorías?

GUICHO: I don't know . . . yes. He went (*Motions*) to the sea.

ANTONIO: You all right, manito?

GUICHO: Yes. (*He gets up*)

ANTONIO: Heyy okayyyy . . . (*He pauses*)

*Guicho shakes the sand from his clothing. He examines the cello.*

Nice instrument, right? . . . Well. Guess what I have for you, little brother?

GUICHO: What?

ANTONIO: Look! (*He pulls out the bow from his cart*) I kept the little stick that goes with it!

GUICHO: That's great Antonio! I didn't even have time to think about it. You are excellent, su-perb!

ANTONIO: Wait a minute. It's mine now too.

GUICHO: What do you mean "yours"?

ANTONIO: I saved it for you didn't I?

GUICHO: What are you talkin' about?

ANTONIO: We're partners, ya know. Part of the guitarrón belongs to me.

GUICHO: What the fuck are you talkin' about?! I'm the one who was close to the Maestro. I'm the one who played the fuckin' thing!

ANTONIO: I'm not talkin' about playin' it, manito.

GUICHO: I'm keepin' it with me.

ANTONIO: Well now Guicho. I'm goin' to do you a favor, see? I'm goin' to teach you a little business sense. We're goin' to sell this guitarrón for a few hundred pesos, right, mano? And then we're goin' to buy some grass and double our money. Go into business.

GUICHO: Sell the Maestro's guitarrón for grass? What the fuck do you think I am?

ANTONIO: You can buy a little prime time with Micaela, right? The full treatment!

GUICHO: You mean, all you can think of is to sell this for a fuck and a ten-minute smoke for some hijo-de-puta murderer?! I got stupid bloody death hangin' all over me and that's all you can think of?!

ANTONIO: Hey mano. Cool down a minute. I got to think about my future. Yours too.

GUICHO: Don't bother.

ANTONIO: Oh, I see. You're going to give concerts on the street, right. Shit. You can't play that thing and the Maestro's gone. He's dead as lead, señor.

GUICHO: I'll get him back. With a wave of that little stick.

ANTONIO: You ain't no músico, little brother. 'N' no magician neither.

GUICHO: Well I ain't no street beggar. That's all you are . . . a beggar!

ANTONIO: I do what I can, mano. You forget, I'm a cripple.

GUICHO: You never said that before!

ANTONIO: Why do I have to say it? Don't you got eyes, manito? Didn't you see me turned on my back like a fuckin' turtle? I couldn't get up without your help.

GUICHO: I never thought of you as a cripple before.

ANTONIO: Well my head ain't crippled, right? I can make my way good enough.

GUICHO (Snatches the bow from Antonio): No. Not good enough!

ANTONIO: Oye!

GUICHO: Not everythin' in this world is ugly!

ANTONIO: Part of that guitarrón is mine!

GUICHO: How could it ever be yours! You don't even know its fuckin' name. It's a cello! A cello! Do you hear me?! (Menaces Antonio) Now get outta here before I turn you over again! (He walks toward the cart) Andale!

ANTONIO (Leaving): You'll be alone. You'll see!

GUICHO: I am alone.

*Guicho sits for a moment. The light brightens. It is noon. It fades to late afternoon. Then, three bright stars appear.*

*The Maestro walks out. He watches Guicho curiously. His shirt is stained with blood.*

*Guicho walks a bit with the cello and finds one of the giant jacks. The Maestro follows.*

*Guicho sits on the breakwater and checks the cello. He tightens the strings. We hear the ocean crash. Guicho strokes the cello, looking out to sea. Then the boy sits in imitation of the Maestro and places the cello between his knees. He holds the bow crudely.*

*The Maestro takes off his shirt, cleans himself off, rolls up his pantlegs, removes his shoes, puts on a bandana. He looks like a fisherman.*

*Guicho moves the bow across the strings. They are out of tune and the bow bounces on them or makes them squeal.*

*Guicho stops. He tries again, this time trying for the rhythm of Micaela's name. The sounds are terrible. He tries again slower—it is worse—then faster. He rests his head against the neck of the cello.*

Maestro?

*Light comes up on a place above Guicho, perhaps on a breakwater situated higher up. The Maestro walks there. He finds a net and examines it, getting comfortable with it.*

Micaela. Mi-ca-e-laa.

*Guicho accompanies the name with the bow across the strings. He does it lightly but successfully. He does it harder. We hear the waves. The stars glitter. The sounds are off-key. He continues one more time with the full rhythm and then finds the last note and plays it over and over again.*

*The Maestro casts the net. He gathers in the stars and the lights dim, then black out.*

## END OF PLAY

# The Conduct
of Life

Maria Irene Fornes

# Maria Irene
# Fornes

I was born in Havana in 1930. My father was a bureaucrat, he had government jobs. He was very bright and completely self-educated, even though his mother owned a prestigious school. Classes were taught in English, because my grandmother had spent time in the United States. She attended a Catholic school in Baltimore—the daughter of the President went there, and my grandmother spent a weekend in the White House.

My father hated school. It was hard for him to be disciplined about it because he was at home; the family lived at the school. As a boy my father spent a number of years in Ocala, Florida. He joined the American army and was in Hawaii. He traveled through California as a hobo. He spoke English without an accent. When he went back to Cuba he married my mother, a teacher at his mother's school. He was a bohemian by nature. He read constantly, and spent hours telling us about the books. He loved to cook—he always cooked dinner.

We were very poor. I am the youngest of six children, and I was born right into the Depression. My sister who's only one year older and I went to grammar school when there was money for it. My mother didn't want us to go to public school. She and my oldest sister taught us some at home. It never occurred to me to go to high school. I had a boring childhood—I was like a vegetable, practically. I always had to play with my sister; like a soldier, I was supposed to do exactly what she said. My mother was constantly watching to make sure we didn't learn what she called bad things.

I came to New York when I was fifteen, with my mother and sister. My father died, and my mother had always wanted to live in the United States. It was quite a liberation. I sat in the back of a sixth-grade classroom at St. Joseph's Academy for a few weeks—the nuns gave me *Little Women* to read and I couldn't begin to understand it. I was bored to death and got a job before it was legal for me to work.

You really begin to develop as a person when you start to have your own little adventures, when you do things on your own initiative. For this reason I think my life in Cuba has not been an important influence on my work. But *the* life in Cuba had a strong effect on me. In many ways I still think like a Cuban, or maybe just a Latin, or maybe like a European. In 1945 Cuba was much closer to Europe than to the United States—in the sense of values, the order of things, what you were and were not allowed to do. I have a strong accent, and I think it's because there's a part of me I don't want to eradicate.

For many years I insisted that the Hispanic theatre in this country could never develop, could never be called a serious institution, unless it had its own playwrights. No theatre can become strong if it does only classics or plays from other countries. Eventually INTAR's artistic director, Max Ferra, said he wanted to start a playwrights' project and asked me to help create a format.

I told him that first of all the writers need a stipend. What makes all artists want to work is in part the art itself, the pleasure of making something, of discovering new forms, of accomplishing something. It is an enormous pleasure, but it is not enough; you need also to think that what you're doing could become important to people, could have an impact. Some people also need to feel that they could be rich and famous, or need to earn a living, need to have respect from the community. Hispanic playwrights don't have any of this. They have no one to look to and think, "Oh, I could be a playwright like so-and-so." I thought too that the writers should participate in all the readings, not just come to their own, and should have a say in what is done. The pilot project, which Max conducted, was based on these ideas.

When a more elaborate workshop was proposed and I was asked for suggestions I said playwrights should come and work every day, just as if they were going to an office. When INTAR got the funding I had to create a detailed plan. I asked myself, "If there were a Buddhist temple for playwrights what would it be

like?" Then it was easy for me to set the whole thing up. The first year I brought in guest speakers, which isn't a bad idea but takes away from the writing time. The first two years I had someone lead the physical exercises, but when I thought I understood which were most beneficial for writers I started leading them myself. The writing exercises have developed enormously since that first year but the format has remained the same.

Although I see a lot of interesting writing when I do workshops in other places, I do find that the writing coming out of the INTAR workshop is unique. There's no doubt that it is Hispanic, that it is different, and that it is interesting. It is important to replenish the American theatre.

My plays come out of my workshops now. *The Conduct of Life* began with an exercise. What came to me was mostly an image. I saw a girl—a mulatto girl—wearing a little pink slip and a soldier who was wearing an undershirt, military breeches and boots. They were in a hotel room, and she was being sweet to him. I think I wrote what was happening rather than dialogue. The girl's boyfriend had been arrested and she had met and seduced this captain to see whether through him she could get her boyfriend freed. The pink slip was exactly like the slip that Sheila Dabney wore in *Sarita*. It was just a little scene but it had a strong impact on me.

Until this year I have been spending my summers with the Padua Hills Playwrights' Festival, teaching and staging my own pieces. The first version of *Conduct of Life* was developed the year we were at California Institute of the Arts. It was mostly a visual piece. I used a big terrace which is actually the roof of an apartment building. Three stories down is a field with a little tree, beyond it a road, then a housing development that looks like a little village. The terrace was Orlando's house. He and his wife and three sisters were having lunch at a big table and being crazy and neurotic. Downstairs a peasant girl was getting married. She had a white goat, which she brought to the wedding ceremony under the tree.

After another scene on the terrace, the girl and the goat and the groom—carrying a little suitcase—walked across the field. The little goat was almost buried in the tall grass. Later you saw the girl on the road, being followed by a car. It went very slowly and she ran and ran until she went off into the grass and fell down. Four thugs got out of the car, picked her up while she hung on to the grass and tore her free.

In the next scene, Orlando was down in the field, interrogating, kicking, torturing the girl's husband. Then you saw the girl lying on the big table, naked, covered with a sheet. She was on her side with her back to the audience when Orlando took the sheet off and recited a romantic ode to her beauty. He mounted her and she turned face up and you saw that she was still clutching fistfuls of grass. When Orlando left, the girl got up and started asking her husband how he was, addressing her questions to the sky over the audience, implying she'd been driven mad.

A Gary Cooper type of American sat in the field reading an irrigation pamphlet as lepers appeared, who walked very slowly and looked up at the audience and asked for money. Two men dragged the body of the boy to the tree, and the girl came running down, sobbing and screaming. She clung to the body while the irrigation speech was still going on.

It was wonderful, but none of it would work at Theater for the New City. It wouldn't even work on a big stage—it would become a Martha Graham ballet. When you're on a real terrace looking down at a real field, you can believe what you see. For TNC I had to write a lot of dialogue; what little there was in the original version got changed completely. I wrote some speeches—those in which Orlando talks about sadism—after the TNC production, because I knew the play needed that aspect. I have never seen those speeches done.

# Biographical Information

Maria Irene Fornes is the author of more than two dozen works for the stage. She began painting at nineteen and spent part of her twenties in Paris, where she was profoundly affected by Roger Blin's production of *Waiting for Godot*. Her first play, *Tango Palace*, was produced in 1963; before long she was directing all of her own work. Among her many plays are *Promenade*, *Fefu and Her Friends*, *The Danube*, *Mud*, *Sarita* and *Abingdon Square*.

*Cold Air*, Fornes's translation and adaptation of Virgilio Piñera's *Aire frío*, was commissioned by Theatre Communications Group's Hispanic Translation Project and INTAR, and published in TCG's *New Plays USA 3*, winning her a Playwrights USA Award. Fornes has also been the recipient of a Guggenheim fellowship, a National Endowment for the Arts two-year playwriting fellowship, a Rockefeller Foundation grant, an award from the American Academy and Institute of Arts and Letters, and numerous Obies, including one for sustained achievement.

*Maria Irene Fornes: Plays*, a volume containing four recent works, was published last year by PAJ Publications, which has also reprinted *Promenade and Other Plays*, a collection of earlier pieces. *Lovers and Keepers*, a musical play written with Tito Puente and Fernando Rivas, was part of TCG's *Plays in Process* script circulation series last season. In addition to directing the INTAR Hispanic Playwrights-in-Residence Laboratory in New York, Fornes conducts playwriting workshops across the country.

# About the Play

*The Conduct of Life*, developed at the Padua Hills Playwrights' Festival in 1984, premiered at Theater for the New City in New York in 1985, in a production directed by the author. It won an Obie for best play and was included in the *Maria Irene Fornes: Plays* collection.

# Characters

ORLANDO, an army lieutenant at the start of the play. A lieutenant commander soon after.
LETICIA, his wife, ten years his elder.
ALEJO, a lieutenant commander. Their friend.
NENA, a destitute girl of twelve.
OLIMPIA, a middle-aged, somewhat retarded servant.

# Time and Place

The present. A Latin American country.

# The Play

# The Conduct of Life

*To Julian Beck
in memory of his courageous life
(1925–1985)*

*The floor is divided in four horizontal planes. Downstage is the living room, which is about ten feet deep. Center stage, eighteen inches high, is the dining room, which is about ten feet deep. Further upstage, eighteen inches high, is a hallway which is about four feet deep. At each end of the hallway there is a door. The one to the right leads to the servants' quarters, the one to the left to the cellar. Upstage, three feet lower than the hallway (the same level as the living room), is the cellar, which is twenty feet wide and sixteen feet deep. Most of the cellar is occupied by two platforms, which are eight feet wide, eight feet deep, and three feet high. There is a space four feet wide around each platform. Upstage of the cellar are steps leading upstairs. Approximately ten feet above the cellar is another level, extending from the extreme left to the extreme right, which represents a warehouse. There is a door on the left of the warehouse. On the left and the right of the living room there are archways that lead to hallways or antechambers. The floors of these hallways are the same level as the dining room. On the left and the right of the dining room there is a second set of archways that lead to hallways or antechambers, the floors of which are the same level as the hallways. All along the edge of each level there is a step that leads to the next level. All floors and steps are black marble. In the living room there are two chairs. One is to the left, next to a table with a telephone on it. The other is to the right. In the dining room there are a large green marble table and three chairs. On the right cellar platform there is a mattress, on the left cellar platform there is a chair. In the warehouse there is a table and a chair to the left, and a chair and some crates and boxes to the right.*

## Scene 1

*Before the lights come up one hears Orlando doing jumping-jacks. He is in the upper left corner of the dining room. A light slowly comes up on him. He wears military breeches held by suspenders, and riding boots. He continues doing jumping-jacks as long as the actor can endure it. When he stops, the lights come up on the center area. There is a chair upstage of the table. There is a linen towel on the left side of the table. Orlando dries his face with the towel and sits as he puts the towel around his neck.*

ORLANDO: Thirty-three and I'm still a lieutenant. In two years I'll receive a promotion or I'll leave the military. I promise I will not spend time feeling sorry for myself. – Instead I will study the situation and draw an effective plan of action. I must eliminate all obstacles. – I will make the acquaintance of people in high power. If I cannot achieve this on my own merit, I will marry a woman in high circles. Leticia must not be an obstacle. – Man must have an ideal, mine is to achieve maximum power. That is my destiny. – No other interest will deter me from this. – My sexual drive is detrimental to my ideals. I must no longer be overwhelmed by sexual passion or I will be degraded beyond hope of recovery.

*Lights fade to black.*

## Scene 2

*Alejo sits to the right of the dining-room table. Orlando stands to Alejo's left. He is now a lieutenant commander. He wears an army tunic, breeches, and boots. Leticia stands to the left. She wears a dress that suggests 1940s fashion.*

LETICIA: What! Me go hunting? Do you think I'm going to shoot a deer, the most beautiful animal in the world? Do you think I'm going to destroy a deer? On the contrary, I would run in the field and scream and wave my arms like a mad woman and try to scare them away so the hunters could not reach them. I'd run in front of the bullets and let the mad hunters kill me – stand in the way of the bullets – stop the bullets with my body. I don't see how anyone can shoot a deer.

ORLANDO *(To Alejo)*: Do you understand that? You, who are her friend, can you understand that? You don't think that is madness? She's mad. Tell her that – she'll think it's you who's mad. *(To Leticia)* Hunting is a sport! A skill! Don't talk about something you know nothing about. Must you have an opinion about every damn thing! Can't you keep your mouth shut when you don't know what you're talking about? *(He exits right)*

LETICIA: He told me that he didn't love me, and that his sole relationship to me was simply a marital one. What he means is that I am to keep this house, and he is to provide for it. That's what he said. That explains why he treats me the way he treats me. I never understood why he did, but now it's clear. He doesn't love me. I thought he loved me and that he stayed with me because he loved me and that's why I didn't understand his behavior. But now I know, because he told me that he sees me as a person who runs the house. I never understood that because I would have never – if he had said, "Would you marry me to run my house even if I don't love you." I would have never – I would have never believed what I was hearing. I would have never believed that these words were coming out of his mouth. Because I loved him.

*Orlando has reentered. Leticia sees him and exits left. Orlando sits center.*

ORLANDO: I didn't say any of that. I told her that she's not my heir. That's what I said. I told her that she's not in my will, and she will not receive a penny of my money if I die. That's what I said. I didn't say anything about running the house. I said she will not inherit a penny from me because I would be humiliated by how she'd put it to use. She is capable of foolishness beyond belief. Ask her what she would do if she were rich and could do anything she wants with her money.

*Leticia reenters.*

LETICIA: I would distribute it among the poor.

ORLANDO: She has no respect for money.

LETICIA: That is not true. If I had money I would give it to those who need it. I know what money is, what money can do. It can feed people, it can put a roof over their heads. Money can do that. It can clothe them. What do you know about money? What does it mean to you? What do you do with money? Buy rifles? To shoot deer?

ORLANDO: You're foolish! – You're foolish! You're a foolish woman! *(He exits. His voice becomes faint as he walks into the distance)* Foolish! Foolish! Foolish!

LETICIA: He has no respect for me. He is insensitive. He doesn't listen. You cannot reach him. He is deaf. He is an animal. Nothing touches him except sensuality. He responds to food, to the flesh. To music sometimes, if it is romantic. To the moon. He is romantic but he is not aware of what you are feeling. I can't change him. – I'll tell you why I asked you to come. Because I want something from you. – I want you to educate me. I want to study. I want to study so I am not an ignorant person. I want to go to the university. I want to be knowledgeable. I'm tired of being ignored. I want to study political science. Is political science what diplomats study? Is that what it is? You have to teach me elemental things because I never finished grammar school. I would have to study a great deal. A great deal so I could enter the university. I would have to go through all the subjects. I would like to be a woman who speaks in a group and have others listen.

ALEJO: Why do you want to worry about any of that? What's the use? Do you think you can change anything? Do you think anyone can change anything?

LETICIA: Why not? (*Pause*) Do you think I'm crazy? – He can't help it. – Do you think I'm crazy? – Because I love him?

*He looks away. Lights fade to black.*

## Scene 3

*Orlando enters the warehouse holding Nena close to him. She wears a gray over-large uniform. She is barefoot. She resists him. She is tearful and frightened. She pulls away and runs to the right wall. He follows her.*

ORLANDO (*Softly*): You called me a snake.
NENA: No, I didn't.

*He tries to reach her. She pushes his hands away from her.*

I was kidding. – I swear I was kidding.

*He grabs her and pushes her against the wall. He pushes his pelvis against her. He moves to the chair dragging her with him. She gets away from him and crawls to the left. He goes after her. She goes behind the table. He goes after her. She goes under the table. He grabs her foot and pulls her out toward the downstage side. He opens his fly and pushes his pelvis against her. She screams. Lights fade to black.*

## Scene 4

*Olimpia is wiping crumbs off the dining-room table. She wears a plain gray uniform. Leticia sits to the left of the table facing front. She wears a dressing gown. She writes in a notebook. There is some silverware on the table. Olimpia has a speech defect.*

LETICIA: Let's do this.
OLIMPIA: Okay. (*She continues wiping the table*)
LETICIA (*Still writing*): What are you doing?
OLIMPIA: I'm doing what I always do.
LETICIA: Let's do this.
OLIMPIA (*In a mumble*): As soon as I finish doing this. You can't just ask me to do what you want me to do, and interrupt what I'm doing. I don't stop from the time I wake up in the morning to the time I go to sleep. You can't interrupt me whenever you want, not if you want me to get to the end of my work. I wake up at 5:30. I wash. I put on my clothes and make my bed. I go to the kitchen. I get the milk and the bread from outside and I put them on the counter. I open the icebox. I put one bottle in and take the butter out. I leave the other bottle on the counter. I shut the refrigerator door. I take the pan that I use for water and put water in it. I know how much. I put the pan on the stove, light

the stove, cover it. I take the top off the milk and pour it in the milk pan except for a little. *(Indicating with her finger)* Like this. For the cat. I put the pan on the stove, light the stove. I put coffee in the thing. I know how much. I light the oven and put bread in it. I come here, get the tablecloth and I lay it on the table. I shout "Breakfast." I get the napkins. I take the cups, the saucers, and the silver out and set the table. I go to the kitchen. I put the tray on the counter, put the butter on the tray. The water and the milk are getting hot. I pick up the cat's dish. I wash it. I pour the milk I left in the bottle in the milk dish. I put it on the floor for the cat. I shout "Breakfast." The water boils. I pour it in the thing. When the milk boils I turn off the gas and cover the milk. I get the bread from the oven. I slice it down the middle and butter it. Then I cut it in pieces *(Indicating)* this big. I set a piece aside for me. I put the rest of the bread in the bread dish and shout "Breakfast." I pour the coffee in the coffee pot and the milk in the milk pitcher, except I leave *(Indicating)* this much for me. I put them on the tray and bring them here. If you're not in the dining room I call again. "Breakfast." I go to the kitchen, I fill the milk pan with water and let it soak. I pour my coffee, sit at the counter and eat my breakfast. I go upstairs to make your bed and clean your bathroom. I come down here to meet you and figure out what you want for lunch and dinner. And try to get you to think quickly so I can run to the market and get it bought before all the fresh stuff is bought up. Then, I start the day.

LETICIA: So?

OLIMPIA: So I need a steam pot.

LETICIA: What is a steam pot?

OLIMPIA: A pressure cooker.

LETICIA: And you want a steam pot? Don't you have enough pots?

OLIMPIA: No.

LETICIA: Why do you want a steam pot?

OLIMPIA: It cooks faster.

LETICIA: How much is it?

OLIMPIA: Expensive.

LETICIA: How much?

OLIMPIA: Twenty.

LETICIA: Too expensive.

*Olimpia throws the silver on the floor. Leticia turns her eyes up to the ceiling.*

Why do you want one more pot?

OLIMPIA: I don't have a steam pot.

LETICIA: A pressure cooker.

OLIMPIA: A pressure cooker.

LETICIA: You have too many pots.

*Olimpia goes to the kitchen and returns with an aluminum pan. She shows it to Leticia.*

OLIMPIA: Look at this.

*Leticia looks at it.*

LETICIA: What?

*Olimpia hits the pan against the back of a chair, breaking off a piece of it.*

OLIMPIA: It's no good.
LETICIA: All right! (*She takes money from her pocket and gives it to Olimpia*) Here. Buy it! – What are we having for lunch?
OLIMPIA: Fish.
LETICIA: I don't like fish. – What else?
OLIMPIA: Boiled plantains.
LETICIA: Make something I like.
OLIMPIA: Avocados.

*Leticia looks at Olimpia with resentment.*

LETICIA: Why can't you make something I like?
OLIMPIA: Avocados.
LETICIA: Something that needs cooking.
OLIMPIA: Bread pudding.
LETICIA: And for dinner?
OLIMPIA: Pot roast.
LETICIA: What else?
OLIMPIA: Rice.
LETICIA: What else?
OLIMPIA: Salad.
LETICIA: What kind?
OLIMPIA: Avocado.
LETICIA: Again.

*Olimpia looks at Leticia.*

OLIMPIA: You like avocados.
LETICIA: Not again. – Tomatoes. (*Olimpia mumbles*) What's wrong with tomatoes besides that you don't like them? (*Olimpia mumbles*) Get some. (*Olimpia mumbles*) What does that mean? (*Olimpia doesn't answer*) Buy tomatoes. – What else?
OLIMPIA: That's all.
LETICIA: We need a green.
OLIMPIA: Watercress.
LETICIA: What else.
OLIMPIA: Nothing.
LETICIA: For dessert.
OLIMPIA: Bread pudding.
LETICIA: Again.

OLIMPIA: Why not?

LETICIA: Make a flan.

OLIMPIA: No flan.

LETICIA: Why not?

OLIMPIA: No good.

LETICIA: Why no good? – Buy some fruit then.

OLIMPIA: What kind?

LETICIA: Pineapple. *(Olimpia shakes her head)* Why not? *(Olimpia shakes her head)* Mango.

OLIMPIA: No mango.

LETICIA: Buy some fruit! That's all. Don't forget bread.

*Leticia hands Olimpia money. Olimpia holds her hand out for more. Leticia hands her one more bill. Lights fade to black.*

## Scene 5

*The warehouse table is propped against the door. The chair on the left faces right. The door is pushed and the table falls to the floor. Orlando enters. He wears an undershirt with short sleeves, breeches with suspenders and boots. He looks around the room for Nena. Believing she has escaped, he becomes still and downcast. He turns to the door and stands there for a moment. He takes a few steps to the right and stands there for a moment staring fixedly. He hears a sound from behind the boxes, walks to them and takes a box off. Nena is there. Her head is covered with a blanket. He pulls the blanket off. Nena is motionless and staring into space. He looks at her for a while, then walks to the chair and sits facing right staring into space. A few moments pass. Lights fade to black.*

## Scene 6

*Leticia speaks on the telephone to Mona.*

LETICIA: Since they moved him to the new department he's different. *(Brief pause)* He's distracted. I don't know where he goes in his mind. He doesn't listen to me. He worries. When I talk to him he doesn't listen. He's thinking about the job. He says he worries. What is there to worry about? Do you think there is anything to worry about? *(Brief pause)* What meeting? *(Brief pause)* Oh, sure. When is it? *(Brief pause)* At what time? What do you mean I knew? No one told me. – I don't remember. Would you pick me up? *(Brief pause)* At 1:00? Isn't 1:00 early? *(Brief pause)* Orlando may still be home at 1:00. Sometimes he's here a little longer than usual. After lunch he sits and smokes. Don't you think 1:30 will give us enough time? *(Brief pause)* No. I can't leave while he's smoking . . . I'd rather not. I'd rather wait till he leaves. *(Brief pause)* 1:30, then. Thank you, Mona. *(Brief pause)* See you then. Bye.

*Leticia puts down the receiver and walks to the stage right area. Orlando's voice is heard offstage left. He and Alejo enter halfway through the following speech.*

ORLANDO: He made loud sounds, not high-pitched like a horse. He sounded like a whale, like a wounded whale. He was pouring liquid from everywhere, his mouth, his nose, his eyes. He was not a horse but a sexual organ. – Helpless. A viscera. – Screaming. Making strange sounds. He collapsed on top of her. She wanted him off but he collapsed on top of her and stayed there on top of her. Like gum. He looked more like a whale than a horse. A seal. His muscles were soft. What does it feel like to be without shape like that. Without pride. She was indifferent. He stayed there for a while and then lifted himself off her and to the ground. *(Pause)* He looked like a horse again.

LETICIA: Alejo, how are you?

*Alejo kisses Leticia's hand.*

ORLANDO *(As he walks to the living room)*: Alejo is staying for dinner. *(He sits left facing front)*

LETICIA: Would you like some coffee?

ALEJO: Yes, thank you.

LETICIA: Would you like some coffee, Orlando?

ORLANDO: Yes, thank you.

LETICIA *(In a loud voice towards the kitchen)*: Olimpia . . .

OLIMPIA: What?

LETICIA: Coffee . . .

*Leticia sits to the right of the table. Alejo sits center.*

ALEJO: Have you heard?

LETICIA: Yes, he's dead and I'm glad he's dead. An evil man. I knew he'd be killed. Who killed him?

ALEJO: Someone who knew him.

LETICIA: What is there to gain? So he's murdered. Someone else will do the job. Nothing will change. To destroy them all is to say we destroy us all.

ALEJO: Do you think we're all rotten?

LETICIA: Yes.

ORLANDO: A bad germ?

LETICIA: Yes.

ORLANDO: In our hearts?

LETICIA: Yes. – In our eyes.

ORLANDO: You're silly.

LETICIA: We're blind. We can't see beyond an arm's reach. We don't believe our life will last beyond the day. We only know what we have in our hand to put in our mouth, to put in our stomach, and to put in our pocket. We take care of our pocket, but not of our country. We take care of our stomachs but not of our hungry. We are primitive. We don't believe in the future. Each night when the sun goes down we think that's the end of life – so we have one last fling. We don't think we have a future. We don't think we have a country. Ask anybody, "Do you have a country?" They'll say, "Yes." Ask them, "What is your country?" They'll say, "My bed, my dinner plate." But, things can change. They can. I have changed. You have changed. He has changed.

ALEJO: Look at me. I used to be an idealist. Now I don't have any feeling for anything. I used to be strong, healthy, I looked at the future with hope.

LETICIA: Now you don't?

ALEJO: Now I don't. I know what viciousness is.

ORLANDO: What is viciousness?

ALEJO: You.

ORLANDO: Me?

ALEJO: The way you tortured Felo.

ORLANDO: I never tortured Felo.

ALEJO: You did.

ORLANDO: Boys play that way. You did too.

ALEJO: I didn't.

ORLANDO: He was repulsive to us.

ALEJO: I never hurt him.

ORLANDO: Well, you never stopped me.

ALEJO: I didn't know how to stop you. I didn't know anyone could behave the way you did. It frightened me. It changed me. I became hopeless.

*Orlando walks to the dining room.*

ORLANDO: You were always hopeless.

*Orlando exits. Olimpia enters carrying three demitasse coffees on a tray. She places them on the table and exits.*

ALEJO: I am sexually impotent. I have no feelings. Things pass through me which resemble feelings but I know they are not. I'm impotent.

LETICIA: Nonsense.

ALEJO: It's not nonsense. How can you say it's nonsense? – How can one live in a world that festers the way ours does and take any pleasure in life?

*Lights fade to black.*

## Scene 7

*Nena and Orlando stand against the wall in the warehouse. She is fully dressed. He is barechested. He pushes his pelvis against her gently. His lips touch her face as he speaks. The words are inaudible to the audience. On the table there is a tin plate with food and a tin cup with milk.*

ORLANDO: Look this way. I'm going to do something to you.

*She makes a move away from him.*

Don't do that. Don't move away. *(As he slides his hand along her side)* I just want to put my hand here like this. *(He puts his lips on hers softly and speaks at the same time)* Don't hold your lips so tight. Make them soft. Let them loose. So I can do this. *(She whimpers)* Don't cry. I won't hurt you. This is all I'm going to do to you. Just hold your lips soft. Be nice. Be a nice girl. *(He pushes against her and reaches an orgasm. He remains motionless for a moment, then steps away from her still leaning his hand on the wall)* Go eat. I brought you food.

*She goes to the table. He sits on the floor and watches her eat. She eats voraciously. She looks at the milk.*

Drink it. It's milk. It's good for you.

*She drinks the milk, then continues eating. Lights fade to black.*

## Scene 8

*Leticia stands left of the dining-room table. She speaks words she has memorized. Olimpia sits to the left of the table. She holds a book close to her eyes. Her head moves from left to right along the written words as she mumbles the sound of imaginary words. She continues doing this through the rest of the scene.*

LETICIA: The impact of war is felt particularly in the economic realm. The destruction of property, private as well as public, may paralyze the country. Foreign investment is virtually . . . *(To Olimpia)* Is that right? *(Pause)* Is that right!
OLIMPIA: Wait a moment. *(She continues mumbling and moving her head)*
LETICIA: What for? *(Pause)* You can't read. *(Pause)* You can't read!
OLIMPIA: Wait a moment. *(She continues mumbling and moving her head)*
LETICIA *(Slapping the book out of Olimpia's hand)*: Why are you pretending you can read?

*Olimpia slaps Leticia's hands. They slap each other's hands. Lights fade to black.*

## Scene 9

*Orlando sits in the living room. He smokes. He faces front and is thoughtful. Leticia and Olimpia are in the dining room. Leticia wears a hat and jacket. She tries to put a leather strap through the loops of a suitcase. There is a smaller piece of luggage on the floor.*

LETICIA: This strap is too wide. It doesn't fit through the loop. *(Orlando doesn't reply)* Is this the right strap? Is this the strap that came with this suitcase? Did the strap that came with the suitcase break? If so, where is it? And when did it break? Why doesn't this strap fit the suitcase and how did it get here? Did you buy this strap, Orlando?

ORLANDO: I may have.

LETICIA: It doesn't fit.

ORLANDO: Hm.

LETICIA: It doesn't fit through the loops.

ORLANDO: Just strap it outside the loops.

*Leticia stands. Olimpia tries to put the strap through the loop.*

LETICIA: No. You're supposed to put it through the loops. That's what the loops are for. What happened to the other strap?

ORLANDO: It broke.

LETICIA: How?

ORLANDO: I used it for something.

LETICIA: What! *(He looks at her)* You should have gotten me one that fit. What did you use it for? – Look at that.

ORLANDO: Strap it outside the loops.

LETICIA: That wouldn't look right.

ORLANDO *(Going to look at the suitcase)*: Why do you need the straps?

LETICIA: Because they come with it.

ORLANDO: You don't need them.

LETICIA: And travel like this?

ORLANDO: Use another suitcase.

LETICIA: What other suitcase. I don't have another.

*Orlando looks at his watch.*

ORLANDO: You're going to miss your plane.

LETICIA: I'm not going. I'm not traveling like this.

ORLANDO: Go without it. I'll send it to you.

LETICIA: You'll get new luggage, repack it and send it to me? – All right. *(She starts to exit left)* It's nice to travel light. *(Offstage)* Do I have everything? – Come, Olimpia.

*Olimpia follows with the suitcases. Orlando takes the larger suitcase from Olimpia. She exits. Orlando puts the suitcase down on the floor. He goes up the hallway and exits through the left door. A moment later he enters holding Nena close to him. She is pale, disheveled and has black circles around her eyes. She has a high fever and is almost unconscious. Her dress is torn and soiled. She is barefoot. He carries a new cotton dress on his arm. He takes her to the chair in the living room. He takes off the soiled dress and puts the new dress on her over a soiled slip.*

ORLANDO: That's nice. You look nice.

*Leticia's voice is heard. He hurriedly takes Nena out the door, closes it, and leans on it.*

LETICIA *(Offstage)*: It would take but a second. You run to the garage and get the little suitcase and I'll take out the things I need.

*Leticia and Olimpia reenter left. Olimpia exits right.*

Hurry. Hurry. It would take but a second. *(Seeing Orlando)* Orlando, I came back because I couldn't leave without anything at all. I came to get a few things because I have a smaller suitcase where I can take a few things.

*Leticia puts the suitcase she left behind on the table and opens it. Olimpia reenters right with a small suitcase.*

OLIMPIA: Here.

LETICIA *(Taking out the things she mentions)*: A pair of shoes. A nightgown. A robe. Underwear. A dress. A sweater.

OLIMPIA *(Overlapping Leticia's lines, packing the things she mentions in the small suit-case)*: A robe. A dress. A nightgown. Underwear. A sweater. A pair of shoes.

*Leticia closes the large suitcase. Olimpia closes the small suitcase.*

LETICIA *(Starting to exit)*: Good-bye.

OLIMPIA *(Following Leticia)*: Good-bye.

ORLANDO: Good-bye.

*Lights fade to black.*


## Scene 10

*In the cellar, Nena is curled up on the mattress. Orlando sits on the mattress using Nena as a back support. Alejo sits on the chair. He holds a green paper in his hand. Olimpia sweeps the floor.*

ORLANDO: Tell them to check him. See if there's a scratch on him. There's not a scratch on that body. Why the fuss! Who was he and who's making a fuss? Why is he so important.

ALEJO: He was in deep. He knew names.

ORLANDO: I was never told that. But it wouldn't have mattered if they had because he died before I touched him.

ALEJO: You have to go to headquarters. They want you there.

ORLANDO: He came in screaming and he wouldn't stop. I had to wait for him to stop screaming before I could even pose a question to him. He wouldn't stop. I had put the poker to his neck to see if he would stop. Just to see if he would shut up. He just opened his eyes wide and started shaking and screamed even louder and fell over dead. Maybe he took something. I didn't do anything to him. If I didn't get anything from him it's because he died before I could get to him. He died of fear, not from anything I did to him. Tell them to do an autopsy. I'm telling you the truth. That's the truth. Why the fuss.

ALEJO *(Starting to put the paper in his pocket)*: I'll tell them what you said.

ORLANDO: Let me see that.

*Alejo takes it to him. Orlando looks at it and puts it back in Alejo's hands.*

Okay so it's a trap. So what side are you on? (*Pause. Alejo says nothing*) So what do they want? (*Pause*) Who's going to question me? That's funny. That's very funny. They want to question me. They want to punch my eyes out? I knew something was wrong because they were getting nervous. Antonio was getting nervous. I went to him and I asked him if something was wrong. He said, no, nothing was wrong. But I could tell something was wrong. He looked at Vélez and Vélez looked back at him. They are stupid. They want to conceal something from me and they look at each other right in front of me, as if I'm blind, as if I can't tell that they are worried about something. As if there's something happening right in frong of my nose but I'm blind and I can't see it. (*He grabs the paper from Alejo's hand*) You understand? (*He goes up the steps*)

OLIMPIA: Like an alligator, big mouth and no brains. Lots of teeth but no brains. All tongue.

*Orlando enters through the left hallway door, and sits at the dining-room table. Alejo enters a few moments later. He stands to the right.*

ORLANDO: What kind of way is this to treat me? – After what I've done for them? – Is this a way to treat me? – I'll come up . . . as soon as I can – I haven't been well. – Okay. I'll come up. I get depressed because things are bad and they are not going to improve. There's something malignant in the world. Destructiveness, aggressiveness. – Greed. People take what is not theirs. There is greed. I am depressed, disillusioned . . . with life . . . with work . . . family. I don't see hope. (*He sits. He speaks more to himself than to Alejo*) Some people get a cut in a finger and die. Because their veins are right next to their skin. There are people who, if you punch them in their stomach, the skin around the stomach bursts and the bowels fall out. Other people, you cut them open and you don't see any veins. You can't find their intestines. There are people who don't even bleed. There are people who bleed like pigs. There are people who have the nerves right on their skins. You touch them and they scream. They have their vital organs close to the surface. You hit them and they burst an organ. I didn't even touch this one and he died. He died of fear.

*Lights fade to black.*

## Scene 11

*Nena, Alejo and Olimpia sit cross-legged on the mattress. Nena sits right, Alejo center, Olimpia left. Nena and Olimpia play patty-cake. Orlando enters. He goes close to them.*

ORLANDO: What are you doing?

OLIMPIA: I'm playing with her.

ORLANDO *(To Alejo)*: What are you doing here? *(Alejo looks at him as a reply. He speaks sarcastically)* They're playing patty-cake. *(He goes near Nena)* So? *(Short pause. Nena giggles)* Stop laughing!

*Nena is frightened. Olimpia holds her.*

OLIMPIA: Why do you have to spoil everything. We were having a good time.

ORLANDO: Shut up! *(Nena whimpers)* Stop whimpering. I can't stand your whimpering. I can't stand it. *(Timidly, she tries to speak words as she whimpers)* Speak up. I can't hear you! She's crazy! Take her to the crazy house!

OLIMPIA: She's not crazy! She's a baby!

ORLANDO: She's not a baby! She's crazy! You think she's a baby? She's older than you think! How old do you think she is. – Don't tell me that.

OLIMPIA: She's sick. Don't you see she's sick? Let her cry! *(To Nena)* Cry!

ORLANDO: You drive me crazy too with your . . .

*Orlando imitates Olimpia's speech defect. She punches him repeatedly..*

OLIMPIA: You drive me crazy! *(He pushes her off)* You drive me crazy! You are a bastard! One day I'm going to kill you when you're asleep! I'm going to open you up and cut your entrails and feed them to the snakes. *(She tries to strangle him)* I'm going to tear your heart out and feed it to the dogs! I'm going to cut your head open and have the cats eat your brain! *(Reaching for his fly)* I'm going to cut your peepee and hang it on a tree and feed it to the birds!

ORLANDO: Get off me! I'm getting rid of you too! *(He starts to exit)* I can't stand you!

OLIMPIA: Oh, yeah! I'm getting rid of you.

ORLANDO: I can't stand you!

OLIMPIA: I can't stand you!

ORLANDO: Meddler! *(To Alejo)* I can't stand you either. *(He exits)*

OLIMPIA *(Going to the stairs)*: Tell the boss! Tell her! She won't get rid of me! She'll get rid of you! What good are you! Tell her! *(She goes to Nena)* Don't pay any attention to him. He's a coward. – You're pretty.

*Orlando enters through the hallway left door. He sits center at the dining-room table and leans his head on it. Leticia enters. He turns to look at her.*

LETICIA: You didn't send it.

*Lights fade to black.*

### Scene 12

*Leticia sits next to the phone. Without holding the phone, she speaks to an imaginary Mona.*

LETICIA: I walk through the house and I know where he's made love to her I think I hear his voice making love to her. Saying the same things he says to me, the same words. *(There is a pause)* There is someone here. He keeps someone here in the house. *(Pause)* I don't dare look. *(Pause)* No, there's nothing I can do. I can't do anything.

*Leticia walks to the hallway. She hears footsteps. She moves rapidly to the left and hides behind a pillar. Olimpia enters from right. She takes a few steps down the hallway. She carries a plate of food. She sees Leticia and stops. She takes a few steps in various directions, then stops.*

OLIMPIA: Here kitty, kitty.

*Leticia walks to Olimpia, looks closely at the plate, then up at her.*

LETICIA: What is it?
OLIMPIA: Food.
LETICIA: Who is it for?

*Olimpia turns her eyes away and doesn't answer. Leticia decides to go to the cellar door. She stops halfway there.*

Who is it?
OLIMPIA: A cat.

*Leticia opens the cellar door.*

LETICIA: It's not a cat. I'm going down. *(She opens the door to the cellar and starts to go down)* I want to see who is there.
ORLANDO *(Offstage from the cellar)*: What is it you want?

*Lights fade to black.*

## Scene 13

*Orlando lies back in the chair in the cellar. His legs are outstretched. His eyes are bloodshot. His tunic is open. Nena is curled on the floor. Orlando speaks quietly. He is deeply absorbed.*

ORLANDO: What I do to you is out of love. Out of want. It's not what you think. I wish you didn't have to be hurt. I don't do it out of hatred. It is not out of rage. It is love. It is a quiet feeling. It's a pleasure. It is quiet and it pierces my insides in the most internal way. It is my most private self. And this I give to you. – Don't be afraid. – It is a desire to destroy and to see things destroyed and to see the inside of them. – It's my nature. I must hide this from others. But I don't feel remorse. I was born this way and I must have this. – I need love. I wish you did not feel hurt and recoil from me.

*Lights fade to black.*

## Scene 14

*Orlando sits to the right and Leticia sits to the left of the table.*

LETICIA: Don't make her scream.

*There is a pause.*

ORLANDO: You're crazy.

LETICIA: Don't I give you enough?

ORLANDO *(He's calm):* Don't start.

LETICIA: How long is she going to be here?

ORLANDO: Not long.

LETICIA: Don't make her cry. *(He looks at her)* I can't stand it. *(Pause)*Why do you make her scream?

ORLANDO: I don't make her scream.

LETICIA: She screams.

ORLANDO: I can't help it.

*Pause.*

LETICIA: I tell you I can't stand it. I'm going to ask Mona to come and stay with me.

ORLANDO: No.

LETICIA: I want someone here with me.

ORLANDO: I don't want her here.

LETICIA: Why not?

ORLANDO: I don't.

LETICIA: I need someone here with me.

ORLANDO: Not now.

LETICIA: When?

ORLANDO: Soon enough. – She's going to stay here for a while. She's going to work for us. She'll be a servant here.

LETICIA: ... No.

ORLANDO: She's going to be a servant here.

*Lights fade to black.*

## Scene 15

*Olimpia and Nena are sitting at the dining-room table. They are separating stones and other matter from dried beans.*

NENA: I used to clean beans when I was in the home. And also string beans. I also pressed clothes. The days were long. Some girls did hand sewing. They spent the day doing that. I didn't like it. When I did that, the day was even longer and there were times when I couldn't move even if I tried. And they said I couldn't go there anymore, that I had to stay in the yard. I didn't mind sitting in the yard looking at the birds. I went to the laundry room and watched the women work. They let me go in and sit there. And they showed me how to press. I like to press because my mind wanders and I find satisfaction. I can iron all day. I like the way the wrinkles come out and things look nice. It's a miracle isn't it? I could earn a living pressing clothes. And I could find my grandpa and take care of him.

OLIMPIA: Where is your grandpa?

NENA: I don't know.

*They work a little in silence.*

He sleeps in the streets. Because he's too old to remember where he lives. He needs a person to take care of him. And I can take care of him. But I don't know where he is. – He doesn't know where I am. – He doesn't know who he is. He's too old. He doesn't know anything about himself. He only knows how to beg. And he knows that only because he's hungry. He walks around and begs for food. He forgets to go home. He lives in the camp for the homeless and he has his own box. It's not an ugly box like the others. It is a real box. I used to live there with him. He took me with him when my mother died till they took me to the home. It is a big box. It's big enough for two. I could sleep in the front where it's cold. And he could sleep in the back where it's warmer. And he could lean on me. The floor is hard for him because he's skinny and it's hard on his poor bones. He could sleep on top of me if that would make him feel comfortable. I wouldn't mind. Except that he may pee on me because he pees in his pants. He doesn't know not to. He is incontinent. He can't hold it. His box was a little smelly. But that doesn't matter because I could clean it. All I would need is some soap. I could get plenty of water from the public faucet. And I could borrow a brush. You know how clean I could get it? As clean as new. You know what I would do? I would make holes in the floor so the pee would go down to the ground. And you know what else I would do?

OLIMPIA: What?

NENA: I would get straw and put it on the floor for him and for me and it would make it comfortable and clean and warm. How do you like that? Just as I did for my goat.

OLIMPIA: You have a goat?

NENA: . . . I did.

OLIMPIA: What happened to him?

NENA: He died. They killed him and ate him. Just like they did Christ.

OLIMPIA: Nobody ate Christ.

NENA: . . . I thought they did. My goat was eaten though. – In the home we had clean sheets. But that doesn't help. You can't sleep on clean sheets, not if there isn't someone watching over you while you sleep. And since my ma died there just wasn't anyone watching over me. Except you. – Aren't you? In the home they said guardian angels watch your sleep, but I didn't see any there. There weren't any. One day I heard my grandpa calling me and I went to look for him. And I didn't find him. I got tired and I slept in the street, and I was hungry and I was crying. And then he came to me and he spoke to me very softly so as not to scare me and he said he would give me something to eat and he said he would help me look for my grandpa. And he put me in the back of his van. . . . And he took me to a place. And he hurt me. I fought with him but I stopped fighting – because I couldn't fight anymore and he did things to me. And he locked me in. And sometimes he brought me food and sometimes he didn't. And he did things to me. And he beat me. And he hung me on the wall. And I got sick. And sometimes he brought me medicine. And then he said he had to take me somewhere. And he brought me here. And I am glad to be here because you are here. I only wish my grandpa were here too. He doesn't beat me so much anymore.

OLIMPIA: Why does he beat you? I hear him at night. He goes down the steps and I hear you cry. Why does he beat you?

NENA: Because I'm dirty.

OLIMPIA: You are not dirty.

NENA: I am. That's why he beats me. The dirt won't go away from inside me. – He comes downstairs when I'm sleeping and I hear him coming and it frightens me. And he takes the covers off me and I don't move because I'm frightened and because I feel cold and I think I'm going to die. And he puts his hand on me and he recites poetry. And he is almost naked. He wears a robe but he leaves it open and he feels himself as he recites. He touches himself and he touches his stomach and his breast and his behind. He puts his fingers in my parts and he keeps reciting. Then he turns me on my stomach and puts himself inside me. And he says I belong to him. (*There is a pause*) I want to conduct each day of my life in the best possible way. I should value the things I have. And I should value all those who are near me. And I should value the kindness that others bestow upon me. And if someone should treat me unkindly, I should not blind myself with rage, but I should see them and receive them, since maybe they are in worse pain than me.

*Lights fade to black.*


## Scene 16

*Leticia speaks on the telephone with Mona. She speaks rapidly.*

LETICIA: He is violent. He has become more so. I sense it. I feel it in him. – I understand his thoughts. I know what he thinks. – I raised him. I practically did.

He was a boy when I met him. I saw him grow. I was the first woman he loved. That's how young he was. I have to look after him, make sure he doesn't get into trouble. He's not wise. He's trusting. They are changing him. – He tor-. tures people. I know he does. He tells me he doesn't but I know he does. I know it. How could I not. Sometimes he comes from headquarters and his hands are shaking. Why should he shake? What do they do there? – He should transfer. Why do that? He says he doesn't do it himself. That the officers don't do it. He says that people are not being tortured. That that is questionable. – Everybody knows it. How could he not know it when everybody knows it. Sometimes you see blood in the streets. Haven't you seen it? Why do they leave the bodies in the streets – how evil, to frighten people? They tear their finger-nails off and their poor hands are bloody and destroyed. And they mangle their genitals and expose them and they tear their eyes out and you can see the empty eyesockets in the skull. How awful, Mona. He mustn't do it. I don't care if I don't have anything! What's money! I don't need a house as big as this! He's doing it for money! What other reason could he have! What other reason could he have!! He shouldn't do it. I cannot look at him without thinking of it. He's doing it. I know he's doing it. – Shhhh! I hear steps. I'll call you later. Bye, Mona. I'll talk to you.

*She hangs up the receiver. Lights fade to black.*

## Scene 17

*The living room. Olimpia sits to the right, Nena to the left.*

OLIMPIA: I don't wear high heels because they hurt my feet. I used to have a pair but they hurt my feet and also *(Pointing to her calf)* here in my legs. So I don't wear them anymore even if they were pretty. Did you ever wear high heels? *(Nena shakes her head)* Do you have ingrown nails? *(Nena looks at her questioningly)* Nails that grow twisted into the flesh. *(Nena shakes her head)* I don't either. Do you have sugar in the blood? *(Nena shakes her head)* My mother had sugar in the blood and that's what she died of but she lived to be eighty-six which is very old even if she had many things wrong with her. She had glaucoma and high blood pressure.

*Leticia enters and sits center at the table. Nena starts to get up. Olimpia signals her to be still. Leticia is not concerned with them.*

LETICIA: So, what are you talking about?
OLIMPIA: Ingrown nails.

*Nena turns to Leticia to make sure she may remain seated there. Leticia is involved with her own thoughts. Nena turns front. Lights fade to black.*

### Scene 18

*Orlando is sleeping on the dining-room table. The telephone rings. He speaks as someone having a nightmare.*

ORLANDO: Ah! Ah! Ah! Get off me! Get off! I said get off!

*Leticia enters.*

LETICIA *(Going to him)*: Orlando! What's the matter! What are you doing here!
ORLANDO: Get off me! Ah! Ah! Ah! Get off me!
LETICIA: Why are you sleeping here! On the table. *(Holding him close to her)* Wake up.
ORLANDO: Let go of me. *(He slaps her hands as she tries to reach him)* Get away from me. *(He goes to the floor on his knees. He staggers to the telephone)* Yes. Yes, it's me. – You did? – So? – It's true then. – What's the name? – Yes, sure. – Thanks. – Sure.

*Orlando hangs up the receiver. He turns to look at Leticia. Lights fade to black.*

### Scene 19

*Two chairs are placed side by side facing front in the center of the living room. Leticia sits on the right. Orlando stands in the down left corner. Nena sits to the left of the dining-room table facing front. She covers her face. Olimpia stands behind her, holding Nena and leaning her head on her.*

ORLANDO: Talk.
LETICIA: I can't talk like this.
ORLANDO: Why not?
LETICIA: In front of everyone.
ORLANDO: Why not?
LETICIA: It is personal. I don't need the whole world to know.
ORLANDO: Why not?
LETICIA: Because it's private. My life is private.
ORLANDO: Are you ashamed?
LETICIA: Yes, I am ashamed!
ORLANDO: What of . . . ? What of . . . ? – I want you to tell us – about your lover.
LETICIA: I don't have a lover.

*Orlando grabs Leticia by the hair. Olimpia holds on to Nena. Olimpia and Nena hide their faces.*

ORLANDO: You have a lover.
LETICIA: That's a lie.
ORLANDO *(Moving closer to Leticia)*: It's not a lie. Come on tell us. *(He pulls her hair)* What's his name? *(Leticia emits a sound of pain. He pulls harder, leans toward her and speaks in a low tone)* What's his name?

LETICIA: Albertico.

*Orlando takes a moment to release Leticia.*

ORLANDO: Tell us about it.

*There is silence. Orlando pulls Leticia's hair.*

LETICIA: All right.

*Orlando releases Leticia.*

ORLANDO: What's his name?
LETICIA: Albertico.
ORLANDO: Go on. *(Pause)* Sit up! *(She does)* Albertico what?
LETICIA: Estévez.

*Orlando sits next to Leticia.*

ORLANDO: Go on. *(Silence)* Where did you first meet him?
LETICIA: At . . . I . . .
ORLANDO *(He grabs Leticia by the hair)*: In my office.
LETICIA: Yes.
ORLANDO: Don't lie. – When?
LETICIA: You know when.
ORLANDO: When! *(Silence)* How did you meet him?
LETICIA: You introduced him to me.

*Orlando lets Leticia go.*

ORLANDO: What else? *(Silence)* Who is he!
LETICIA: He's a lieutenant.
ORLANDO *(He stands)*: When did you meet with him?
LETICIA: Last week.
ORLANDO: When!
LETICIA: Last week.
ORLANDO: When!
LETICIA: Last week. I said last week.
ORLANDO: Where did you meet him?
LETICIA: . . . In a house of rendezvous . . .
ORLANDO: How did you arrange it?
LETICIA: . . . I wrote to him . . . !
ORLANDO: Did he approach you?
LETICIA: No.
ORLANDO: Did he!
LETICIA: No.
ORLANDO *(He grabs Leticia's hair again)*: He did! How!

LETICIA: *I* approached him.

ORLANDO: How!

LETICIA *(Aggressively)*: I looked at him! I looked at him! I looked at him!

*Orlando lets Leticia go.*

ORLANDO: When did you look at him?

LETICIA: Please stop . . . !

ORLANDO: Where! When!

LETICIA: In your office!

ORLANDO: When?

LETICIA: I asked him to meet me!

ORLANDO: What did he say?

LETICIA *(Aggressively)*: He walked away. He walked away! He walked away! I asked him to meet me.

ORLANDO: What was he like?

LETICIA: . . . Oh . . .

ORLANDO: Was he tender? Was he tender to you!

*Leticia doesn't answer. Orlando put his hand inside her blouse. She lets out an excruciating scream. He lets her go and walks to the right of the dining room. She goes to the telephone table, opens the drawer, takes a gun and shoots Orlando. Orlando falls dead. Nena runs to downstage of the table. Leticia is disconcerted, then puts the revolver in Nena's hand, hoping she will take the blame. Leticia steps away from Nena.*

LETICIA: Please . . .

*Nena is in a state of terror and numb acceptance. She looks at the gun. Then, up. The lights fade.*

# END OF PLAY

# White Water

## John Jesurun

# John
# Jesurun

I was born in 1951 in Battle Creek, Michigan. My parents were born in Puerto Rico—both grew up in San Juan—although my father's family is from Curaçao. His father worked for a shipping company. There was certainly more Spanish than English spoken in the house. My parents spoke Spanish to each other and to us—I have a sister and two brothers—and we would answer in English, although they encouraged us to speak Spanish as much as we could.

My father was an army doctor, so we moved every few years. We went to Puerto Rico when I was four. We lived on base, inside the walls of El Morro, the big castle you see in the Bacardi ads. Our house was right on the edge of a cliff, with the water down below. When I was seven we moved to San Francisco, then, four or five years later, to Frankfurt, West Germany. By my last year in high school, my father had retired and we were in South Orange, New Jersey.

I studied sculpture at the Philadelphia College of Art, and in graduate school at Yale. Drawing was always something I did, but never really well. It was just too much trouble in a way. Painting was much easier. I started painting when I was in Germany. I dismantled one of those paint-by-number kits—cut the canvas up and mixed up all the paints—and made my own painting of a bullfighter.

In about eighth grade, we had to write one-page stories in English class. I wrote one about a bullfighter, one about two very old people, one set in a concentration camp. The teacher loved them, and I had fun writing them. I didn't think much about writing after that. Throughout high school I was constantly painting.

I've always read a lot, mostly nonfiction. History is very important to me. When we were in Europe I'd find out all I could about places we were going to visit and report to the family. My interest in history goes back to playing inside El Morro. You were sure people had been killed there, which was kind of exciting and sort of spooky. There was a great sense of history, and, because of the jungle-like atmosphere, something that went further back, before history. In Puerto Rico you sense the way things grow and rot and grow and rot—and nobody seems to worry about it.

I was an altar boy for years, starting when I was seven or eight. In San Francisco I went to a Catholic school. I rode across town in a bus and served mass at 7:00 A.M. I don't have painful memories about it at all; I liked the sense of discipline mixed with religion and school and learning. I never felt I was being indoctrinated; it was a rich experience, including plenty of humor. A mass is as symmetrical as possible—a candlestick on each side, an altar boy on each side, a priest in the middle, everything balanced to give the audience a sense of unity and a focal point. It was visually interesting to me that everything was set up to focus into one little spot—the Host.

I got to where I am today by way of film. At Yale when I started to make sculptures that moved, I got a camera to make a record. I had a lot of stuffed birds flying around a room and realized, as I was filming them, that each one took on within the frame its own character, its own inner presence. I just transferred that to people. I thought, "This is great, I can film people and I won't have to draw them"—something I had always found difficult. I wanted to add in sound, but didn't want music. I preferred having the poeple speak. I was seeing any kind of film I could, all day long. People like Buñuel, Bergman, Godard, Fellini interested me, and I learned that they had written quite a bit. Under the influence especially of Buñuel I started writing and shooting short filmscripts.

In New York I worked for a film company, then for CBS, watching TV for three years as part of a sociological study. Then I worked for Dick Cavett for three years. When Cavett was taken off the air, I was out of a job and I had no money to make films. I thought, "I have everything I need to make a film except the film, so I'll let the audience be the camera. Their eyes will be the film and it will happen once."

We did the first half-hour of *Chang in a Void Moon* and I thought, "This is a great idea. I have actors and I can write a script every week." That year I educated myself into writing. The *Chang* schedule was connected to the schedule I'd been on with Cavett. I just used that type of energy. My mind is always going anyway. Everything had to be quick and it had to be logical. We couldn't waste time and we couldn't waste money because we didn't have any. Everybody was in a state of wonderful hysteria. We were doing *Chang* in a rock club, a very chaotic place. To make order out of all this interested me; to focus onto a paper was great. I don't think anybody ever thought *Chang* was a play, nobody was calling it theatre. I don't know what we thought we were doing. We did almost forty episodes that year. From there I went to La Mama and started making plays or whatever they are—pieces in spaces.

*White Water* seems to have started in several different corners of my head simultaneously. Part of it was an idea of the talk-show host. In *Chang* there was always a television set on the stage, and in the very first episode I had a live person talking back and forth with a person on TV. This became something locked in my head. I kept wondering how to make TVs talk to each other and to people, how to do it right instead of crudely. I was fascinated by the talk-show business, by all those jumbled questions and answers and facts and lies, with the questioner at the center. I imagined the talk-show host as a district attorney or a lawyer.

In another corner was an idea about seeing visions, an idea going back to my Catholic childhood. We'd gone to Lourdes when I was in Europe. This strange mysticism that attacks twelve- and thirteen-year-old children always interested me, as a contrast to TV evangelism.

I envisioned in a third corner another type of questioner, a kind of hysteric. I wanted to put all these things together in a verbal boxing ring, to let them at each other more than at the audience. *White Water* took me a little longer than usual to write down—about two weeks—and for the first time I ended up with a lot I didn't use. As I'm writing at the typewriter I know who's going to say what, but I don't slow down to put in the speakers' names. When I go back and put the names in, sometimes I switch lines between speakers. The whole thing is one voice to me anyway, with several poeple speaking it who sometimes are characters and sometimes are not, who switch their identities back and forth.

From the first I wanted a trinity of people. I had Larry Tighe and Valerie Charles, two of my strongest performers since *Chang* days. Larry's son Michael has been acting for me since he was nine. Now he was twelve; I knew I had to write this piece I'd been thinking about for a long time before he got any older. I wanted the six characters to merge into the three actors to merge into one thing—I saw perspective lines meeting at the end. That was the goal to get to in one way or another.

*White Water* has to do with someone's thinking processes, constantly whizzing around. The piece starts off quietly, even slowly, and then twists around more and more, becomes more and more claustrophobic, until the boy sees a way out. It is like a beam of light that comes in after everything gets very dark, like a pinhole that he could escape through, that the audience could escape through. I really like that part, and the actors liked it too. The whole thing is a question mark. Questions are always more interesting than answers—nobody believes the answers anyway. In the end *White Water* focuses back on the audience, I think, when Kirsten asks Mack how many people are in the room and the answer goes from six to three to two to one. This represents my feeling of being in an audience. I'm always wondering if I'm seeing something, if I'm the only one who's seeing it in exactly that way. Even in the midst of other people, everybody's locked inside his own head.

# Biographical Information

Between June 1982 and the following June, John Jesurun wrote, designed and directed thirty-six half-hour episodes of his "living film serial" *Chang in a Void Moon* at the Pyramid Club in New York. Fourteen more episodes were presented in various venues between 1984 and 1986; the entire work won a Bessie award in 1985. Jesurun's other pieces, which include *Bird's Eye View, Dog's Eye View, Number Minus One, Red House, Shatterhand Massacree/Riderless Horse, Deep Sleep* and *Black Maria*, have been staged in New York at La Mama, The Performing Garage and The Kitchen, as well as in performance-art spaces across the country and throughout Europe.

    *Deep Sleep*, the winner of an Obie award for best play in 1986, has been published by PAJ Publications in *Wordplays 5*. Jesurun's work has been supported by several National Endowment for the Arts grants, and he holds a First Level Award for American playwrights from the Rockefeller Foundation for 1987.

# About the Play

*White Water* was commissioned by the Institute of Contemporary Art in Boston, and premiered there in the fall of 1986. It was subsequently presented at The Kitchen and at the Mickery in Amsterdam. The production was designed and directed by the author.

# Characters

ACTOR #1 plays PRODUCER and MACK
ACTOR #2 plays KIRSTEN and PEGEEN
ACTOR #3 plays DOC and CORTEZ

*Layout showing positioning and duplicating of 20 monitors*

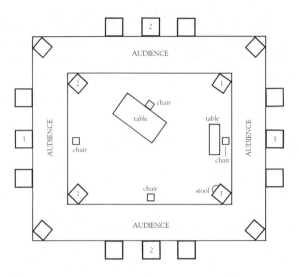

# Setting

The playing space is rectangular, 18 feet by 36 feet. It is raked from floor level on one end to 3 feet in height at the other, and covered by an industrial gray carpet.

At each corner of the space is an upended television monitor (19″) on a black boxlike pedestal 3½ feet in height. Each of these monitors faces inward toward the playing area. From scene to scene talking heads appear on these monitors, as well as various images. The audience sits surrounding the playing space.

Surrounding the audience are 16 additional upended monitors, each on a 15-foot pedestal. These monitors display numerous ambient images throughout the performance. The image on each of the 3 main floor monitors is duplicated so that a specific talking head can be seen from all sides. Images and heads shift from monitor to monitor as the piece progresses.

The following items are preset: paper and pens on the tables, a glass of water on the large table, cigarettes and an ashtray on the small table, a toreador jacket on the back of a chair.

# About the Text

In the text the prerecorded dialogue spoken by the talking heads on the monitors appears in italic type. Lines spoken live appear in roman type.

# The Play

# White Water

*Kirsten sits at large table.*

PRODUCER: *What was that?*

KIRSTEN: I saw something last night.

PRODUCER: *And what was that? What was it?*

KIRSTEN: I'm not sure really. It was floating up in the sky and then it went down into the gutter. A glowing ball.

PRODUCER: *It was probably a soap bubble.*

KIRSTEN: No. No it wasn't. It didn't shine like that. It shone from the inside.

PRODUCER: *Oh dear. And then what?*

KIRSTEN: Well, it disappeared.

PRODUCER: *So what. Then forget about it.*

KIRSTEN: I can't. I keep thinking about it.

PRODUCER: *Well don't. Can we get on with this?*

KIRSTEN: Who is the first guest?

PRODUCER: *It's Jimmy Jam.*

KIRSTEN: Jimmy Jam.

PRODUCER: *The singer.*

KIRSTEN: Can he talk?

PRODUCER: *He can sing.*

KIRSTEN: But can he talk?

PRODUCER: *Probably not.*

KIRSTEN: No.

PRODUCER: *Then you'll have to pre-interview him and see if he can talk.*

KIRSTEN: And what if he can't?

PRODUCER: *If he can't talk then we make him sing a lot and then cut him off so that it looks like we don't have any time left and he can't talk and if he can't talk then that's perfect, no love lost.*

KIRSTEN: What if he can talk?

PRODUCER: *Too bad.*

KIRSTEN: Too bad then. What if he wants to talk?

PRODUCER: *He's not here to talk he's here to sing. Tell him that.*

KIRSTEN: But he wants to talk.

PRODUCER: *How do you know that?*

KIRSTEN: All the press says that.

PRODUCER: *Then tell him we don't have enough time to talk and if he wants to talk he can talk to someone else. We don't have any time to talk so tell him to talk to someone else.*

KIRSTEN: But he can sing.

PRODUCER: *So let him sing. Let him sing his heart out.*

KIRSTEN: What if he has something interesting to say?

PRODUCER: *Do you think he does?*

KIRSTEN: I think so.

PRODUCER: *Why?*

KIRSTEN: Because I've heard him talk before.

PRODUCER: *Where?*

KIRSTEN: On TV.

PRODUCER: *Do you have a tape of it?*

KIRSTEN: No, can't get one.

PRODUCER: *Do you have any print interviews of him?*

KIRSTEN: Yes, here's one or two.

PRODUCER: *What does he say?*

KIRSTEN: Read it.

PRODUCER: *I don't have any time to read it.*

KIRSTEN: Oh, there's blood on this paper, ugh, I cut myself.

PRODUCER: *Well, what does he say?*

KIRSTEN: Oh, he talks about his childhood in Ireland and all that stuff.

PRODUCER: *Anything political?*

KIRSTEN: No.

PRODUCER: *Well then that's good. Any good stories?*

KIRSTEN: Yes, once he saw a leprechaun or a holy mouse or vidioon or something. It was all in the papers.

PRODUCER: *And then what happened?*

KIRSTEN: Then he didn't see it anymore and that was it. They never talked about it again.

PRODUCER: *Well, we could ask him about that.*
KIRSTEN: We don't want to get too specific, he's just a singer.
PRODUCER: *Can he sing "Danny Boy"?*
KIRSTEN: Can I sing with him?
PRODUCER: *I don't think so. He's pretty serious.*
KIRSTEN: If he sings, I sing. If I talk, he talks. If he doesn't talk, I talk anyway.
PRODUCER: *Does he tell jokes?*
KIRSTEN: I don't know.
PRODUCER: *Can he talk? Is he a talker?*
KIRSTEN: He seems to be.
PRODUCER: *Seems isn't enough. Find out.*
KIRSTEN: He's touring in Canada or something. Find him and call him and book him tomorrow if he can talk.
PRODUCER: *What if he can't talk?*
KIRSTEN: Book him anyway. He can sing. Book him anyway. He's popular isn't he?
PRODUCER: *Oh yes, very.*
KIRSTEN: Fine, then book him anyway.
PRODUCER: *How old is he?*
KIRSTEN: Twenty-five.
PRODUCER: *Perfect age.*
KIRSTEN: For what?
PRODUCER: *For anything.*
KIRSTEN: We can ask him about the queen of England and all that.
PRODUCER: *What's his name again?*
KIRSTEN: Jimmy Jam.
PRODUCER: *Jimmy Jam? What kind of a name is that?*
KIRSTEN: I don't know.
PRODUCER: *Doesn't sound Irish to me.*
KIRSTEN: Did he change it? Is it a fake name?
PRODUCER: *They usually are.*
KIRSTEN: Find out. Then we can nail him with his real name.
PRODUCER: *But why?*
KIRSTEN: In case he can't talk.
PRODUCER: *Sounds like a fake name.*
KIRSTEN: Isn't Bob Dylan a fake name?
PRODUCER: *We'll talk about Bob Dylan first and then—*
KIRSTEN: —nail him with his fake name.
PRODUCER: *Did you get all that?*
KIRSTEN: Yes.
PRODUCER: *Anything else?*
KIRSTEN: Anyone else?
PRODUCER: *There's the bishop and the mayor of Constantinople.*
KIRSTEN: Cancel the mayor. I don't think that'll be interesting.

PRODUCER: *He can talk. He can really talk.*

KIRSTEN: Who cares. Does he have anything interesting to say.

PRODUCER: *Probably not.*

KIRSTEN: Who else?

PRODUCER: *Tina Turner, Irene Dunne and Marie Curie.*

KIRSTEN: I thought she was dead?

PRODUCER: *So did I.*

KIRSTEN: She's alive.

PRODUCER: *I can't bear the sight of another movie star and their stupid stories about the shores of Babylon.*

KIRSTEN: Book her.

PRODUCER: *Can I finish telling you what I saw last night?*

KIRSTEN: No, that's it. Call me tomorrow with the results.

PRODUCER: *Resultata. Go, you are dismissed, go in peace.*

KIRSTEN: Thanks be to God.


(Cut)


*Mack seated, Kirsten and Doc at tables. On monitors, daytime shot of window, full of light.*

MACK: I know you're going to be upset but I know what I'm saying. It's the truth and I don't mean maybe.

PRODUCER: *And what is it exactly that you saw?*

MACK: First I saw a light in the sky.

PEGEEN: *Flashing?*

MACK: Like a cigarette glowing in the dark except it was daylight.

DOC: Was it an angel or something?

MACK: Oh no it wasn't an angel it was something better.

KIRSTEN: How do you know it wasn't the devil trying to trick you?

MACK: Trick me into what?

PRODUCER: *Trick you into thinking you saw something incredible.*

MACK: Why would he do that?

DOC: To confuse you. Lead you on the wrong path so he could destroy you.

MACK: No.

PEGEEN: *Do you see these things often?*

MACK: No.

KIRSTEN: Have you ever seen anything like this before?

MACK: Never.

DOC: Have you ever had a daydream that was so strong you thought it was really happening?

MACK: I never daydream I only see what's there. If it isn't there I don't see it. If I don't see it it's not there and that's why I'm sure that I saw this and that it was really there and if I saw it, it was really there.

PEGEEN: *Doesn't it seem foolish to you?*

PRODUCER: *Had you been reading any religious comic books or anything?*

MACK: No.

KIRSTEN: Have you ever read the Bible or anything which could be of any influence to what you saw?

MACK: No, I never read anything religious.

DOC: Have you been seeing any religious programs on TV?

MACK: No.

PEGEEN: *Have you ever seen any of them?*

PRODUCER: *Which ones?*

MACK: I don't know they're all the same to me.

KIRSTEN: Do you watch them often?

MACK: No, I just saw a few by mistake when I was switching channels.

DOC: So you think they could have influenced you into seeing anything?

MACK: No, because those people don't really see anything like this.

PEGEEN: *What do you think of these shows?*

PRODUCER: *You don't think anything at all about them? You don't have any feelings about them?*

MACK: No, not at all.

KIRSTEN: Were you brought up religiously?

MACK: No.

DOC: Did your parents ever have you memorize any prayers?

MACK: One or two.

PEGEEN: *Which ones?*

MACK: Our Father.

PRODUCER: *Can you repeat it?*

MACK: Our Father who art in heaven, hallowed by thy name. Thy kingdom come, thy will be done on earth as it is in heaven. Give us this day our daily bread and forgive us our trespasses as we forgive those who trespass against us and lead us not into temptation but deliver us from evil. For thine is the power and the kingdom and the glory now and forever. Amen.

KIRSTEN: What do you think of that prayer?

MACK: Nothing really.

DOC: Do you believe it?

MACK: Not really.

PEGEEN: *Do you think there is a God?*

PRODUCER: *Why?*

MACK: I just don't think there is anything there.

KIRSTEN: Did anyone tell you this?

MACK: No.

DOC: Do you talk about God much with other people?

MACK: No, the subject never comes up.

PEGEEN: *Are you interested in God?*

MACK: No.

PRODUCER: *What exactly do you think this thing is that you saw? Something from outer space?*

MACK: Maybe.

KIRSTEN: But not a God.

MACK: Maybe. It might be, but not a Bible God.

DOC: If it's not a Bible God then what kind of God could it be?

MACK: Something from the sky or universe.

KIRSTEN: A form of energy?

PEGEEN: *A form of energy.*

PRODUCER: *How do you know you just didn't experience it in your mind?*

MACK: Because I know I saw it.

KIRSTEN: But no one else saw it.

MACK: I know they didn't see it but it really is there.

DOC: How can you explain the fact that no one else saw it and you did?

MACK: Because I've seen it a few times already and it's speaking to me.

PEGEEN: *It?*

MACK: She.

PRODUCER: *Who is she?*

MACK: We've gone through this before. I don't know.

KIRSTEN: Do you listen to a lot of loud music?

MACK: Sort of.

DOC: What kind?

MACK: Just what's on the radio.

PEGEEN: *Do you have earphones?*

PRODUCER: *Do you play them very loud?*

MACK: Sometimes.

KIRSTEN: Do you think that you had them on when you experienced this vision?

MACK: It wasn't a vision she was there.

DOC: Now we have a transcript of what she said.

PEGEEN: *And she doesn't say much.*

MACK: She's the quiet type I guess.

KIRSTEN: Do you believe in the devil?

MACK: No.

DOC: Do you think the devil might have had anything to do with this?

MACK: I don't believe in the devil.

PEGEEN: *What do you think the devil is?*

MACK: The devil is what people think is bad and they think it's a person that is personified in all this evil and tempts them to do bad things so they can blame all the bad things on the devil.

PRODUCER: *Have you ever been in a Catholic church?*

MACK: No.

KIRSTEN: Have you ever seen pictures of a Catholic church?

MACK: No.

DOC: Have you ever seen pictures of saints or God in books?

PEGEEN: *Did they look anything like what you saw?*

MACK: Not at all.

PRODUCER: *Can you explain why?*

KIRSTEN: Compare what you saw to what we can see in a book.

MACK: In a book they use colors that look very pretty and these colors around her aren't really colors, they're light and I can't really see her face so clearly and she's not wearing clothes and she's not particularly any size or body shape and she's not holding a rosary or a cross or anything like that and she's not floating on a cloud and there aren't angels around or flowers and she's not always looking up into the sky.

DOC: Does she wear shoes?

MACK: I told you she wasn't wearing anything.

PEGEEN: *Do you ever look at magazines like* Playboy?

PRODUCER: *Does she look like anything in those magazines?*

MACK: No.

KIRSTEN: If she's not wearing any clothes there must be some resemblance.

DOC: Or similarity.

MACK: No similarity.

PEGEEN: *How do you know she's a woman?*

MACK: She sounds like a woman, she has a woman's voice and face.

PRODUCER: *But she doesn't really have any bodily features that show she's a woman?*

MACK: She doesn't really have a body like that I told you.

KIRSTEN: Just tell us what she looks like in simple terms as simply as you can.

DOC: If you can't come up with a clear description how can we believe you?

PEGEEN: *It just sounds like you're making it all up.*

MACK: I'm not.

PRODUCER: *That's why we have to have as clear of a description as we can so that it will be acceptable to the other people, otherwise—*

KIRSTEN: —they'll think you're making it all up.

MACK: You keep asking me all these questions over and over again. Why is the lawyer here?

PEGEEN: *I have to be. We don't want to step on anyone's toes.*

MACK: Have I ever given the wrong answer? Have I ever contradicted myself?

DOC: No, not yet.

PEGEEN: *How many people have been cured?*

MACK: Twenty-five or thirty.

PRODUCER: *And why is this?*

MACK: I don't know why.

KIRSTEN: And why do you think this is?

MACK: I don't know.

DOC: Surely you must know something.

PEGEEN: *Here you saw this woman and told a few people.*

PRODUCER: *And they followed you but didn't see her.*

KIRSTEN: And some people who were sick got it into their heads that this was something supernatural and several were cured.

DOC: And now several have turned into many.

PEGEEN: *Surely you must think there is some connection.*

PRODUCER: *There is a connection isn't there?*

MACK: Yes.

KIRSTEN: Has the woman admitted curing all these people?

MACK: Not really.

DOC: What does she think about all of this?

MACK: She doesn't talk about it.

PEGEEN: *What does she talk about?*

MACK: She just asks me to come back and pray.

PRODUCER: *What kind of prayers?*

KIRSTEN: Any prayers that you know already?

MACK: No.

DOC: Does she give you a certain prayer to say?

MACK: No, she says to pray however I want.

PEGEEN: *Do you pray to her?*

MACK: She says not to pray to her.

PRODUCER: *Do you think she's a god?*

MACK: Not really.

KIRSTEN: Is she working for another god?

MACK: I don't think so.

DOC: Is she from another planet?

MACK: I don't think so.

PEGEEN: *Why won't she tell you who she is?*

MACK: She doesn't think it matters.

PRODUCER: *What do you pray about, who do you pray to, who do you pray for?*

MACK: I just pray for everyone.

KIRSTEN: But when you pray are you just making wishes or asking someone or something in particular to do something?

DOC: Do you think this woman is dead or a ghost?

MACK: I don't really believe in ghosts.

PEGEEN: *Where do you think people go to when they die?*

MACK: Into the ground.

PRODUCER: *And that's it.*

MACK: That's it.

KIRSTEN: No heaven, no hell.

MACK: Right.

DOC: If she told you there was a heaven and hell would you believe her?

MACK: Maybe.

PEGEEN: *So you wouldn't necessarily believe everything she told you?*

MACK: No.

PRODUCER: *Do you think she'd mind or stop coming if you didn't believe what she told you?*

MACK: Well I might believe what she told me and I might not. The one thing I do believe is that she's there.

KIRSTEN: What do the people who are cured and come to pray believe?

MACK: I don't know what they believe or who they believe in.

DOC: Who are they praying to?

MACK: I never ask them but I think they're saying all kinds of Bible prayers.

PEGEEN: *Have any priests come?*

MACK: A lot.

PRODUCER: *And what do they say?*

MACK: They ask me the same questions you do and I tell them the same answers.

KIRSTEN: Do they want certain answers?

MACK: Yes, they want a connection to what they believe in.

DOC: Do they get it?

MACK: They make it up if they can but I tell them there isn't.

PEGEEN: *What do your friends think about this?*

MACK: Some don't talk to me because their parents think I'm crazy. Others come with me and try to see her but they don't and they get mad because they can't see her.

PRODUCER: *What do you tell them?*

MACK: I tell them to keep looking.

KIRSTEN: Do they wonder why they can't see her and you can?

MACK: Yes, but I can't explain it to them.

DOC: Do they think that you're special or a better person because you can see her and they can't?

MACK: Sometimes.

PEGEEN: *Do you still have the same relationship with them that you did before?*

MACK: No, I really don't have any friends now because they think I've changed.

PRODUCER: *Do you think you've changed?*

MACK: Yes.

KIRSTEN: How do you think you've changed?

MACK: Well, I see this person and I'm much calmer now than I used to be and instead of playing and listening to music I pray or go out to the water.

DOC: Do you like the water?

MACK: Sure.

PEGEEN: *Have you always liked the water?*

MACK: Yes.

PRODUCER: *Can you swim?*

MACK: No.

KIRSTEN: Don't you think you should learn?

MACK: I should but I'm afraid of the water.

DOC: Afraid of drowning?

PEGEEN: *Where do you think all this will lead?*

MACK: I don't know, I guess more people will get cured.

PRODUCER: *And what will happen to you?*

MACK: I'll just keep seeing her until she goes away.

KIRSTEN: Do you think she'll go away eventually and people will stop being cured?

MACK: Probably, this can't go on forever.

DOC: Why not?

MACK: It doesn't seem right.

PEGEEN: *Why not?*

MACK: Well, it could get out of hand.

PRODUCER: *If she said she would keep coming back and you would have to pray to her for the rest of your life would you do it?*

MACK: I guess so.

KIRSTEN: If she asked you to make a church and bring people there would you do it?

MACK: I think so.

DOC: Do you think you're an interesting person or a dull person?

PEGEEN: *What do the parents say?*

MACK: They're very upset. They don't want to let me go to the water and pray.

PRODUCER: *And what do you do?*

MACK: I sneak out.

KIRSTEN: You disobey them.

MACK: I have to. She wants me to come and talk to her.

DOC: So you do whatever she tells you.

PEGEEN: *Do all these people and attention make you nervous?*

MACK: A little.

PRODUCER: *You seem very calm.*

KIRSTEN: Are you?

MACK: Yes.

DOC: If you went on TV would you be nervous?

PEGEEN: *Do you want to go on TV?*

MACK: Not really.

PRODUCER: *Why not?*

MACK: I just don't want to. I wouldn't like it.

KIRSTEN: Why not?

MACK: I don't like television.

PEGEEN: *Does it glow the same way she glows?*

MACK: No.

PRODUCER: *What's the difference between the glow?*

MACK: She glows but she's not plugged in.

KIRSTEN: If she asked you to go on TV would you?

MACK: Yes.

DOC: So she isn't a god?

MACK: Probably not.

PEGEEN: *But if she eventually told you she was a god you would believe her.*

MACK: Maybe.

KIRSTEN: Do you want her to be a god?

MACK: No.

DOC: Why?

MACK: I just don't. I'm not interested in that.

PEGEEN: *But if she said she was a god and she was curing all these people wouldn't you accept her as that?*

MACK: I guess I'd have to but I'd rather she not be a god.

PRODUCER: *Why?*

MACK: Who needs it?

KIRSTEN: I don't think your answers are particularly enlightening. They seem honest but they don't shed any great light on the subject.

DOC: You seem to be the tool of someone.

PEGEEN: *He just is too young to really understand all this completely.*

DOC: He has an intuitive understanding.

PRODUCER: *He has an intuitive understanding.*

PEGEEN: *You don't think this is a UFO do you?*

MACK: No.

PRODUCER: *Have you ever heard of stories of people who have been taken up in flying saucers and had experiences?*

MACK: Yes.

KIRSTEN: And so you don't think that's happening here?

MACK: No.

DOC: Why?

MACK: I don't see a spaceship but it might be.

PEGEEN: *Are you worried that people might think you're a fake?*

MACK: But I never said anything to mislead anyone, no one.

PRODUCER: *Yes but—*

MACK: No but.

KIRSTEN: Do you know how your parents died.

MACK: Yes in a car crash.

DOC: The day you were born. Do you think that means anything?

MACK: Do you mean psycho?

PEGEEN: *Yes.*

MACK: No.

PRODUCER: *Are you angry at God for it?*

MACK: No, he didn't do it.

KIRSTEN: But he may have let it happen.

MACK: He didn't let it happen, they were both drunk.

DOC: So that's that.

MACK: They did it to themselves.

PEGEEN: *And then you went to live with your aunt.*

MACK: Yes.

PRODUCER: *Had she seen anything.*

MACK: Anything what?

KIRSTEN: Any visions or ladies.

MACK: No.

DOC: Was she odd?

PEGEEN: *Was she sort of nutty at all?*

MACK: No, not until all this started happening.

PRODUCER: *Who saw things first?*

MACK: I did and then when I told her about all of them she started seeing things pretty soon after.

KIRSTEN: Why?

MACK: I don't know why.

DOC: Is she seeing things?

PEGEEN: *Do you believe her?*

MACK: Sort of.

PRODUCER: *Sort of yes or sort of no?*

MACK: Sort of yes.

KIRSTEN: Do you think she might be lying?

PEGEEN: *Maybe?*

KIRSTEN: Maybe?

PRODUCER: *Does he think you're lying to him?*

MACK: No.

KIRSTEN: He believed you right from the start.

MACK: Yes.

PEGEEN: *And why do you think he started seeing things?*

MACK: I think because his wife died a few years ago.

DOC: I see.

PRODUCER: *And maybe he's flipping out.*

KIRSTEN: Way out.

MACK: Pretty far out.

DOC: What do you think that means?

PEGEEN: *If we know what it means then the information has value to us in understanding this.*

MACK: Understand and incinerate, incarcerate.

DOC: Understand and incinerate?

PRODUCER: *Do you find that symbolic?*

MACK: I hate symbols.

(*Cut*)

*Mack sits on stool, speaks to monitor across diagonal. River scene on ambient monitors.*

DOC: *Well my child, are you feeling sick?*

MACK: Yes sir, doctor.

DOC: *What's the matter?*

MACK: I'm having trouble with my chest.

DOC: *Are we making you tired?*

MACK: Oh, no ma'am I can talk all right today.

DOC: *Don't you drink the water from the spring?*

MACK: Sure.

DOC: *That water cures other sick people, why doesn't it cure you?*

MACK: Maybe the lady wants me to suffer.

DOC: *Why does she want you to suffer?*

MACK: Oh, because I need it.

DOC: *And why do you need it instead of other people?*

MACK: I don't know.

DOC: *Do you still go to the cliff?*

MACK: I go there when the police let me.

DOC: *Why doesn't the police commissioner let you go there whenever—*

MACK: —you want.

DOC: *Because everyone keeps following me.*

MACK: But they say that you've gone there even though you'd been—

DOC: *—forbidden.*

MACK: Yes sir.

DOC: *And why have you stopped going there?*

MACK: Because before I felt a strong urge to go and I couldn't hold myself back.

DOC: *And now you don't feel the urge?*

MACK: No.

DOC: *Suppose you got the urge like before, would you go back?*

MACK: Yes I would.

DOC: *Did the lady tell you what you had to do to get to heaven?*

MACK: No, everyone knows what they have to do.

DOC: *Did she talk to you often?*

MACK: Yes.

DOC: *Every time?*

MACK: No, not every time.

DOC: *What are you doing?*

MACK: I have to wash my eyes.

DOC: *Why?*

MACK: I can't see very well with them, I can't read so well with them.

DOC: *Why is that?*

MACK: I don't know.

DOC: *Have you had trouble with your eyes before?*
MACK: No.
DOC: *What is wrong with them exactly?*
MACK: I can't read so well, it's hard to read the letters so well.
DOC: *Have you gone to the doctor?*
MACK: Yes.
DOC: *And what does he say to do?*
MACK: He can't really explain it. He just says that I'm gradually seeing less well. I think my eyes are somehow getting smaller and letting less light into them.
DOC: *Do you think you're going blind?*
MACK: Yes.
DOC: *Why can't you get cured?*
MACK: I don't know.
DOC: *Have you asked her to help you?*
MACK: Yes.
DOC: *And what does she say?*
MACK: She says I must continue on and that if I go blind it must—
DOC: *—be the way it must be.*
MACK: And if that must be the way it must be—don't you think?
DOC: *That's cruel of her not to help you.*
MACK: No.
DOC: *But she can help you. Why doesn't she?*
MACK: She doesn't because it just has to be that way. That is the way the groove is cut for my life.
DOC: *Did she tell you that?*
MACK: She said that.
DOC: *And you believe that.*
MACK: I believe that.
DOC: *Are people praying for you?*
MACK: Yes.
DOC: *And why won't it help?*
MACK: Some things just won't. That's what she told me and I must accept it.
DOC: *Are you lying to me?*
MACK: No.
DOC: *Are you lying to me?*
MACK: No.
DOC: *If you were lying to me would you tell me?*
MACK: I would tell you if I was lying.
DOC: *Can you see the horizon from here?*
MACK: Yes.
DOC: *What does it look like?*
MACK: It looks like a black line.
DOC: *That's what you see. Do you want to know what I see?*

MACK: Yes.

DOC: *Do you want to know what I see? I'll tell what I see. On the horizon is a row of hills and rocks and the sun behind it. Why do you think your uncle brought you here?*

MACK: He wants me to stop seeing all these things.

DOC: *Do you think you'll ever stop seeing these things?*

MACK: Eventually.

DOC: *Did she tell you that?*

MACK: Yes.

DOC: *Do you think that Mrs. X is seeing things at the spring too?*

MACK: Near a tree.

DOC: *Oh yes that's right. Do you think she sees them?*

MACK: Sure.

DOC: *So she sees them and you see them.*

MACK: We both see them.

DOC: *Are they the same things?*

MACK: I don't know.

DOC: *You don't know.*

MACK: How would I know?

DOC: *I don't know why wouldn't you know?*

MACK: Because she has her eyes and I have my eyes.

DOC: *We'll stop now you're tired.*

(Cut)

*Mack in chair, Pegeen at large table, Cortez pacing. On monitors, closeups of hands writing.*

KIRSTEN: *And who are you?*

CORTEZ: A lawyer and a priest.

KIRSTEN: *In that order?*

CORTEZ: No order particularly.

PRODUCER: *What religion?*

CORTEZ: No particular religion.

PRODUCER: *Let me see if I understand this. This young man was your altar boy and now you are testifying against him to prevent him from being interviewed on this television show.*

CORTEZ: And who are you?

PRODUCER: *The executive producer.*

CORTEZ: Yes. I'm trying to get him to understand that he seems to have hallucinated something and that in itself isn't wrong but it's not something that should be spoken about on television.

PEGEEN: And why is that?

CORTEZ: Because I don't think it's true. As a matter of fact it'll all pass.

KIRSTEN: *Do you think the boy is a hysteric?*

CORTEZ: This could push him into it.

PRODUCER: *And what qualifies you to say that?*

CORTEZ: I've known him for a while.

KIRSTEN: *And has he shown evidence of hysteria-poisoning in or outside of the church? Tell the truth.*

CORTEZ: Not particularly but he has a healthy imagination.

PEGEEN: Is it healthier than yours?

CORTEZ: I don't think that's at issue here.

PRODUCER: *Then what is?*

CORTEZ: His connection with the cures is not altogether convincing.

KIRSTEN: *Why?*

CORTEZ: It just hasn't happened like that historically.

PEGEEN: But he hasn't said the apparitions are affiliated with your church.

CORTEZ: Exactly.

PRODUCER: *Would you like them to be?*

CORTEZ: Obviously not.

KIRSTEN: *Why is it so important that he not be interviewed?*

CORTEZ: Because we do not want any associations whatsoever.

PEGEEN: But you can disclaim, disown.

CORTEZ: We can but we don't want to go so far as to create a disturbance in our community.

PRODUCER: *How far do you want to go?*

CORTEZ: Not very far.

KIRSTEN: *Would you also like to be on the show?*

CORTEZ: No I wouldn't.

PEGEEN: Why?

CORTEZ: I told you I don't want to make a big stink about it all right?

PRODUCER: *But you're doing that right now.*

CORTEZ: I'm making a big stink now so that we won't have to make a bigger one later.

KIRSTEN: *If we go on with this show will your parish be upset?*

CORTEZ: Extremely.

PEGEEN: Why do you wear that thing?

MACK: What thing?

PRODUCER: *That black thing.*

MACK: I always wear it, she told me to wear it.

KIRSTEN: *She, who?*

CORTEZ: She, the lady of the lake or who?

MACK: The lady I saw by the water.

PEGEEN: Do you wear it to the beach?

MACK: Yes.

PEGEEN: Isn't it hot?

MACK: Yes.

CORTEZ: He took it from the sacristy and I'd appreciate it if he'd return it.

MACK: I did return it. This is mine I bought it.

PRODUCER: *Did you like serving mass?*

MACK: Yes.

KIRSTEN: *How many times did you serve mass?*

MACK: Exactly once.

PEGEEN: Why?

MACK: I dropped the Bible and they threw me out.

PRODUCER: *Is that true?*

CORTEZ: Not exactly.

KIRSTEN: *Well what happened, did he drop the book?*

CORTEZ: Yes.

PEGEEN: And what happened?

CORTEZ: He was asked to leave.

MACK: Same thing.

PRODUCER: *And so you think because he's a disaffected altar boy he's now running out and seeing his own thing so to speak and competing with you.*

CORTEZ: Partially.

KIRSTEN: *But how does that explain the cures?*

CORTEZ: It doesn't.

PEGEEN: Do you have an explanation?

CORTEZ: No.

PRODUCER: *Are you sure you don't have one up your sleeve?*

KIRSTEN: *Someone hiding somewhere with a great story about them?*

CORTEZ: No, we do not. We're just trying to be as cautious and fair about this as possible.

PEGEEN: Why don't you believe him?

CORTEZ: He's young and imaginative.

PRODUCER: *But everyone does.*

CORTEZ: That's just it. It's too easy.

KIRSTEN: *And you don't think this is connected with your church or any doctrines in your church?*

MACK: But we missed something.

PEGEEN: What?

MACK: I was never really an altar boy. I never went to church. My cousin Jimmy Riley was sick and so he told me what to do and I went in for him because he said he'd catch hellfire if he didn't go in so I went in for him and it wasn't till I dropped the book that he noticed I wasn't Jimmy Riley.

KIRSTEN: *So that was the only time you were in a church.*

MACK: Right.

PRODUCER: *But Jimmy Riley must have told you things about the church so that you must know more than a little.*

MACK: I know a little more than a little but not much else.

KIRSTEN: *Do you want to have your own church someday?*

MACK: No, I don't want to have anything, I just saw this person, she started talking to me and then the spring started and then people followed me and started getting cured and everyone started to flip out.

PEGEEN: Do you feel holy?

MACK: Not at all.

PRODUCER: *Where are your parents?*

MACK: In Tibet.

CORTEZ: Tibet?

KIRSTEN: *What are they doing in Tibet?*

MACK: Second honeymoon.

PEGEEN: Can't you call them?

PRODUCER: *They're riding camels somewhere in Mongolia.*

CORTEZ: You pulled this stunt Mack Riley just when they left just to get attention why don't you just admit it.

PRODUCER: *Beat it.*

CORTEZ: How could you do something like this? It's deplorable.

PRODUCER: *Beat it.*

MACK: You're just jealous because I got all these miracles and you've been trying your whole life for one and you still didn't get one.

CORTEZ: Deplorable.

KIRSTEN: *It's never too late.*

PEGEEN: What religion are your parents?

MACK: None I told you.

PRODUCER: *Do you believe in God?*

MACK: No.

KIRSTEN: *So what the hell do you think you're seeing if you're not seeing God or one of his minions?*

MACK: I keep telling you I don't even know what I'm seeing but I saw it and I saw it and those people got cured.

PEGEEN: They did get cured.

CORTEZ: They say they did.

KIRSTEN: *So does everyone else. And then there's the dog. How did that dead dog come to life?*

PEGEEN: How many people have reported cures to the Environmental Protection Agency?

PRODUCER: *Seven hundred and twenty-five as of today.*

KIRSTEN: *And what are the cures?*

PEGEEN: Cancer, broken legs, AIDS, terminal spinal meningitis.

CORTEZ: They're all lunatics and hysterics.

PRODUCER: *What is the name of your church?*

CORTEZ: The South Lawn Invitational Congregation.

KIRSTEN: *And what is that? Forgive me is that Catholic?*

CORTEZ: No it's not.

PEGEEN: Is it affiliated with a larger confraternity of beliefs?

CORTEZ: Not formally.

PRODUCER: *Did you go to divinity school?*

CORTEZ: Yes, Harvard and Yale.

KIRSTEN: *Do you know the Pope at all?*

CORTEZ: Of course not.

PEGEEN: Just checking.

CORTEZ: This is all a perversion of everything.

PRODUCER: *What are the cures if they're not miraculous?*

KIRSTEN: *Explain that.*

CORTEZ: I can't explain it.

PEGEEN: Well there you go.

CORTEZ: And you're going to hell young man.

KIRSTEN: *See you there.*

PEGEEN: Lighten up.

CORTEZ: I will not lighten up.

PRODUCER: *You're getting hysterical.*

KIRSTEN: *Would you come on the show if he goes on?*

CORTEZ: No.

PEGEEN: Why not? You could counteract him, defame him, retaliate, clear the air, make your point.

CORTEZ: I don't want to be immodest.

PEGEEN: Okay.

PRODUCER: *He'll have to go on alone.*

KIRSTEN: *Are you sure?*

CORTEZ: I don't want to make a big stink I said.

PRODUCER: *You're inflating this out of proportion.*

KIRSTEN: *He's just another guest of interest to the audience.*

CORTEZ: This is all typical of the disintegration of life on this planet because of people like you.

(Cut)

*Mack in a different chair, Kirsten at small table.*

PEGEEN: *And so what if it is.*

CORTEZ: I want to ask you one thing, can I?

KIRSTEN: Go ahead.

CORTEZ: *When you were walking, where did you say you were walking?*

MACK: I was walking where I was walking, along the riverbank.

CORTEZ: *Along the riverbank. Was there sand?*

MACK: No.

CORTEZ: *Rocks?*

MACK: Rocks and stones.

CORTEZ: *Rocks and stones, I see. And then in your own words what did you see?*

MACK: Well, I saw a glowing thing.

CORTEZ: *What kind of glowing thing?*

MACK: A ball floating in the sky.

CORTEZ: *What color was it?*

MACK: Red or blue.

CORTEZ: *Red or blue but not either one?*

MACK: Sometimes it was red or blue or yellow.

CORTEZ: *And then what?*

MACK: Then that was it.

CORTEZ: *That was it. That was the first time you saw it.*

MACK: That was the first time I saw it.

CORTEZ: *And when was the second time you saw it?*

MACK: The next day.

CORTEZ: *I thought you said it was the next week.*

MACK: I said it was the next week.

PRODUCER: *The records say the next week.*

CORTEZ: *Why didn't you see it the next day?*

MACK: I don't know.

CORTEZ: *Did you go there the next day?*

MACK: Yes.

CORTEZ: *And why didn't you see it?*

MACK: Because it wasn't there or maybe it was there.

CORTEZ: *Maybe it was there and you just didn't see it.*

MACK: Or it didn't show itself to me.

CORTEZ: *What are you talking about when you mean it?*

MACK: It. I mean the glowing ball.

CORTEZ: *At this point it was just a glowing ball?*

MACK: At this point it was just a glowing ball.

PEGEEN: *Objection. He's putting words in his mouth.*

CORTEZ: *I am putting words in his mouth.*

PRODUCER: *Overruled.*

KIRSTEN: So at this point it was just a glowing ball.

CORTEZ: *And then what?*

MACK: Then it was a glowing ball.

CORTEZ: *Purple and—*

MACK: —red and blue, sometimes yellow.

CORTEZ: *I see. How big was it?*

MACK: About this big.

CORTEZ: *This big?*

MACK: No this big.

CORTEZ: *And then what?*

MACK: I told you.

CORTEZ: *Then.*

MACK: What?

CORTEZ: *Nothing?*

MACK: What?

CORTEZ: *So then you didn't see it the next week.*

MACK: I saw it the next week but not the next day.

CORTEZ: *But it was there?*

MACK: Oh yes, I know it was there.

CORTEZ: *Why didn't it show itself to you when it was there?*

MACK: It didn't want to.

CORTEZ: *Why didn't it want to?*

KIRSTEN: Who the fuck knows or cares.

PRODUCER: *I must ask for some restraint.*

PEGEEN: *Restrain Kirsten.*

CORTEZ: *So this glowing basketball.*

MACK: It wasn't a basketball.

PEGEEN: *Glowing ball.*

CORTEZ: *Glowing ball. Was it a meatball, a butterball, a football, a baseball?*

MACK: Fireball.

CORTEZ: *A fireball. And then the next day.*

MACK: Week.

CORTEZ: *Week.*

MACK: What did you see? I saw something inside it.

CORTEZ: *Something or someone?*

MACK: Someone.

CORTEZ: *A person, a child, a dog, a what?*

MACK: First I thought it was a child.

CORTEZ: *A child inside the ball.*

MACK: How big was it then?

CORTEZ: *The same size but this time it got bigger as it came to me.*

MACK: It came toward you?

CORTEZ: *Yes, from very far away on the horizon. And then what? Did it give you a message?*

MACK: No, it just said hello.

CORTEZ: *You say it. What is it? A child, a man, a woman, a dog, a horse, a robot, a teabag?*

MACK: It was a person.

CORTEZ: *Man woman or child?*

MACK: Child.

CORTEZ: *Man or woman?*

MACK: A woman.

CORTEZ: *What kind of woman?*
MACK: A nice woman.
CORTEZ: *What language did she speak?*
MACK: No language.
CORTEZ: *Well, was it English?*
MACK: No.
CORTEZ: *Latin?*
MACK: No, she didn't speak any language I knew but I understand her.
CORTEZ: *And when she came toward you how big did she get?*
MACK: About as big as you are inside the ball.
CORTEZ: *And what color was the ball?*
MACK: No color.
CORTEZ: *Now it's no color.*
MACK: No color.
CORTEZ: *Did she have a wand or anything?*
MACK: No.
CORTEZ: *Was she wearing wings or anything?*
MACK: No.
CORTEZ: *What was she wearing?*
MACK: Nothing.
CORTEZ: *She was naked?*
MACK: I didn't say that.
CORTEZ: *She was wearing nothing you said. She had to be naked.*
MACK: No she didn't.
CORTEZ: *So here you are seeing naked women in colorless basketballs in the sky.*
MACK: No basketball, no naked women and—
CORTEZ: *Have you ever seen—*
MACK: No.
CORTEZ: *I didn't finish. What was she wearing?*
MACK: Nothing I said.
CORTEZ: *Well, if she wasn't wearing anything, what did her body look like?*
MACK: Just light.
CORTEZ: *Light-colored?*
MACK: No, just light.
CORTEZ: *Well, did you see breasts, did she have breasts?*
MACK: No. I didn't and she didn't.
CORTEZ: *So she was just floating there wearing no clothes.*
MACK: Well I didn't see any clothes but she just had light around her.
CORTEZ: *Well, if she wasn't wearing clothes then you must have seen her body and if you didn't see her body then she must have been wearing clothes.*
MACK: Wrong. She just had light around her.
KIRSTEN: Okay. We'll accept that.
PRODUCER: *Thank you dear.*

CORTEZ: *Have you ever seen* The Wizard of Oz?

MACK: What's that?

CORTEZ: *A movie.*

MACK: What is it about?

CORTEZ: *It's about a little girl who sees a woman in a floating ball.*

MACK: No, I've never seen it.

CORTEZ: *Are you sure?*

MACK: Do you know who Judy Garland is?

CORTEZ: *Yes. How can you know who Judy Garland is and not have seen* The Wizard of Oz? *Everyone sees it.*

MACK: I didn't.

CORTEZ: *Did you read it?*

MACK: No.

CORTEZ: *What did the woman say?*

MACK: Nothing at first.

CORTEZ: *So she said nothing, she wore nothing and when she spoke she spoke in an unintelligible, unrecognizable language that you understood.*

MACK: Right.

CORTEZ: *Could I understand it if she spoke to me?*

MACK: No, because she wouldn't speak to you.

CORTEZ: *Why wouldn't she speak to me?*

MACK: First of all you wouldn't be able to see or hear her.

CORTEZ: *Why?*

MACK: She only comes to me.

CORTEZ: *Why?*

MACK: Because she only likes me.

CORTEZ: *Why?*

MACK: Because I can see her.

CORTEZ: *Why?*

MACK: Because she only shows herself to me.

CORTEZ: *Why, could anyone else see her?*

MACK: Maybe.

CORTEZ: *Maybe but not really.*

MACK: Maybe.

CORTEZ: *So she only comes to you.*

PEGEEN: *And you're the only one that sees her.*

CORTEZ: *If you're the only one that sees her then how do you know she's there?*

MACK: Because I see her.

CORTEZ: *What did she say?*

MACK: She sang first.

CORTEZ: *What did she sing?*

MACK: She sang this strange song.

CORTEZ: *Can you remember it or were you in too much of a psychedelic delirium to remember it.*

MACK: Actually it's hard to remember, it was a very complicated chord change. It sort of goes like this.

*Mack sings a melody from Bizet's* The Pearl Fishers *a cappella, using "la la" in place of the words. He sings out of tune for a minute until Cortez interrupts him.*

CORTEZ: *Was there background music?*

MACK: No.

CORTEZ: *A cappella?*

MACK: A cappella.

CORTEZ: *Were there words to the song?*

MACK: No, she was just singing.

CORTEZ: *Was her voice high or low?*

KIRSTEN: This is ridiculous.

CORTEZ: *It is not.*

KIRSTEN: Can I continue for a while, maybe I can shed some light. So she sang a song and then what happened?

CORTEZ: *He was astonished, beatified, wonderized, at peak altitude. Oh Godzilla he thought, what is this?*

PEGEEN: *Don't start up.*

DOC: What did she say Mack?

MACK: She said hello.

CORTEZ: *Was she white?*

MACK: No color really.

CORTEZ: *Well, did she have white—*


(Cut)


*Cortez paces.*

DOC: *Let's put it this way, could she be related to you? I mean did she have features like yours or mine or his?*

MACK: She looked like anyone.

PEGEEN: Was she beautiful?

MACK: Not in that way.

CORTEZ: Well in what way?

MACK: Not in any way.

DOC: *What color were her eyes?*

MACK: She didn't have any eyes, she said they were burnt out, and that I had to help her get them back.

DOC: *And did you?*

MACK: Yes.

DOC: *And how did you do that?*

CORTEZ: This is where the robbery comes in.

MACK: She said they were washed away.

KIRSTEN: *By what?*

MACK: By the mountain of mud and the sound, the noise of mud curdling in the mountain of mud that came up to here.

CORTEZ: This is where the robbery comes in.

KIRSTEN: *What robbery?*

CORTEZ: The eyes that you stole from the statue in the cathedral.

MACK: I didn't steal them.

CORTEZ: Then where are they? Who took them?

MACK: She said they were her eyes and so I gave them back to her.

CORTEZ: He stole those eyes and they are quite valuable. Do you know what those eyes are made out of?

MACK: Some kind of quartz.

CORTEZ: A very expensive quartz.

KIRSTEN: *Can she see now?*

MACK: She can.

PEGEEN: Did she have any message?

MACK: No.

KIRSTEN: *Can you repeat what it was she said to you in the order that she said it?*

MACK: Yes.

PEGEEN: Repeat the entire conversation. The first conversation you had with her.

MACK: The first time I talked to her.

KIRSTEN: *Yes.*

MACK: Well, she said Hello—first she sang.

CORTEZ: Yes, we know she sang some stupid song.

MACK: It wasn't a stupid song. Then I said Hello, then she said—

PEGEEN: In her own words.

MACK: She said, Come closer don't be afraid.

KIRSTEN: *Were you afraid?*

MACK: No. I said all right and I came closer and then she said What's your name?—I said Mack—Where do you live? I said Here, and then—

PEGEEN: What did she say?

MACK: She said to come back tomorrow at the same time and then the bubble popped and she was gone.

CORTEZ: This has gone far enough. If you don't stop these stories we're going to have to prosecute you for aggravating the public, inciting and deteriorating the public's idea of the hereafter.

KIRSTEN: *And the thereafter.*

CORTEZ: You are a liar and a fool. Are your parents telling you to say these things?

MACK: No.

CORTEZ: So they can make money?

MACK: No.

KIRSTEN: *Where are the parents?*

PEGEEN: Both dead.

PRODUCER: *Interesting.*

KIRSTEN: *Maybe it's your imagination.*

MACK: No it's not. I don't have any imagination in fact I could never think up anything like this. It's impossible.

CORTEZ: This is turning into a carnival, a kinderfest. What church do you go to.

MACK: None.

CORTEZ: Are you Catholic? This sounds like the Catholics.

MACK: Not Catholic.

CORTEZ: What are you then?

MACK: Nothing.

CORTEZ: How can you be unaffiliated with a religion and think up all of this, someone must be feeding you all this.

MACK: No one is feeding.

CORTEZ: What religion are your parents?

MACK: No religion.

PEGEEN: Have you read the Bible?

MACK: No Bible.

CORTEZ: You've been quoting from the Bible. What religion is she?

PEGEEN: Who?

KIRSTEN: *Who?*

CORTEZ: The girl in the ball.

MACK: She didn't say she was anything.

CORTEZ: This is Catholic propaganda, a Jesuit plot. Who is the pope?

MACK: What is the pope?

CORTEZ: Surely you know what the pope is.

MACK: What is the pope?

CORTEZ: Are you Jewish?

MACK: No.

CORTEZ: Have you ever been in a church?

MACK: No.

CORTEZ: Call the bishop.

PRODUCER: *He's fishing in the Bahamas.*

CORTEZ: Then get his secretary.

PEGEEN: She's with him.

CORTEZ: Don't tell me that.

KIRSTEN: *But she is.*

CORTEZ: Then get a priest or an underling, this is a Catholic plot.

DOC: *They can't do anything.*

PRODUCER: *Don't get the Catholics involved.*

CORTEZ: Then call the archbishop of Canterbury or a rabbi.

KIRSTEN: *Call the Buddha why don't ya?*

PRODUCER: *Don't get him involved.*

CORTEZ: Do you know anything about the Bible?

MACK: No sir.

CORTEZ: What was she wearing.

MACK: Nothing.

CORTEZ: Do you take drugs?

MACK: No.

CORTEZ: Why are you telling everyone about this?

MACK: I'm not.

CORTEZ: Then how did they find out? The people from the television and all?

MACK: They followed you.

CORTEZ: This is a cult. Do you think you'll make money from this?

MACK: No.

CORTEZ: How much did the people from the television pay you?

MACK: Nothing.

CORTEZ: How much did they pay you?

MACK: Nothing.

CORTEZ: Did they offer you money?

MACK: Yes.

CORTEZ: Did you take it?

MACK: No.

CORTEZ: Did you take it?

MACK: No.

CORTEZ: You took the money.

MACK: No I didn't.

CORTEZ: How much did they pay you?

MACK: Nothing.

CORTEZ: How much did they offer you?

MACK: A thousand.

CORTEZ: Why didn't you take it?

MACK: I didn't want it.

CORTEZ: Why did they give you the money?

MACK: They didn't give it to me.

CORTEZ: Why did they offer it to you then? Don't get smart with me.

MACK: They wanted me to take them to the place.

CORTEZ: They knew where the place was?

MACK: They wanted me to make her show up on the film, if they paid me. I wouldn't take it.

CORTEZ: And so did she show up on the film?

MACK: They stayed there all day and—

CORTEZ: Then what?

MACK: And they developed the film and it was all orange.

CORTEZ: Kodak?

MACK: No, just orange.

PEGEEN: What kind of orange? A bluish orange? A reddish orange?

MACK: Sort of a reddish orange.

PEGEEN: Sort of like this dress?

KIRSTEN: *It must have been a bad roll.*

CORTEZ: Did they try again?

MACK: Yes. Then they offered me five thousand and I said no and they came anyway and the film came out but she wasn't on it.

CORTEZ: She was there. The camera never lies.

MACK: The camera didn't pick it up.

CORTEZ: But I saw some film with a woman standing there.

MACK: That was a fake, she doesn't look like that.

CORTEZ: She looks exactly like you said she looks.

MACK: But that wasn't her it was an actress. She doesn't look like that. They got it all wrong.

CORTEZ: Who shot the film?

MACK: They did.

CORTEZ: Is it a fake? Is it?

KIRSTEN: *Certainly not. My crew shot it.*

CORTEZ: It's a fake.

KIRSTEN: *Are you accusing me of lying?*

CORTEZ: You are lying. It's a fake.

KIRSTEN: *I was there and shot the film.*

CORTEZ: Did you see her?

KIRSTEN: *No.*

CORTEZ: Then how did you know where to point the camera?

KIRSTEN: *We pointed in the direction that she was talking in and it developed with this woman on it.*

CORTEZ: Who is an actress. So you believe him now. All I'm saying is that I don't believe his story about the woman in the basketball and if I don't believe that then how can I believe you shooting film of her? If I believe you, then I have to believe him. Do you believe him?

PEGEEN: I didn't.

CORTEZ: And now you do?

KIRSTEN: *Yes I do.*

PEGEEN: The woman was there. She's on the film.

CORTEZ: So we have proof now of the woman in the basketball.

KIRSTEN: *I believe that he may have seen someone.*

CORTEZ: I don't believe he saw anyone but I believe that you hired an actress and put her up there in front of the film to make this all sound true.

PRODUCER: *We don't do that.*

CORTEZ: You'll do anything you can get your hands on. I want that film taken into custody.

KIRSTEN: *Take it.*

CORTEZ: I want the original negative.

KIRSTEN: *Go ahead, we can shoot another roll.*

CORTEZ: Oh, you mean the actress isn't out of town? Do you take drugs?

PEGEEN: No.

CORTEZ: Do you take drugs?

MACK: No.

CORTEZ: Do you take drugs?

KIRSTEN: *No.*

CORTEZ: How do you feel about that?

MACK: Nothing.

CORTEZ: You should feel strongly on either side no matter what you feel on whatever side but you must feel strongly.

MACK: But why do you have to feel strongly?

CORTEZ: Don't you have an opinion on anything? How do you feel about this?

MACK: The woman on the film is not the woman I saw.

CORTEZ: So you're saying they're lying.

MACK: I wouldn't put it like that.

CORTEZ: How would you put it?

MACK: There may have been some other woman there when they shot it.

CORTEZ: But you were there and you didn't see her.

MACK: I didn't see that one.

CORTEZ: Maybe they're twins.

MACK: Or they could be lying. But I would never call anyone a liar.

CORTEZ: Why not?

MACK: To call anyone a liar is vanity and a chase after the wind.

CORTEZ: Very good. Who told you that?

MACK: No one.

CORTEZ: Did the woman tell you this?

MACK: No.

CORTEZ: I'm going to get to the bottom of this.

PEGEEN: You are at the bottom of this.

CORTEZ: Shut him up.

MACK: Vanity, vanity of toil without profit.

CORTEZ: What are you saying?

MACK: Therefore I loathed life since for me the work that is done under the sun is evil for all is vanity and a chase after the wind.

PEGEEN: You never said that before.

MACK: Nothing.

PEGEEN: He's beginning to sound like a fortune cookie.

CORTEZ: Are you Catholic?

MACK: No.

CORTEZ: What does that mean?

MACK: What does what mean?

CORTEZ: Chase after the wind.

MACK: You know, futility, like an attempt to corral the winds, an infliction of the spirit.

PEGEEN: Can we stop this now?

CORTEZ: Now we are not going to stop this till we get to the bottom of this.

*Mack resumes singing loudly until Kirsten interrupts.*

KIRSTEN: *But we are at the bottom.*

PEGEEN: I'll stay here as long as you will.

CORTEZ: Are you threatening me? I'll have you arrested and put in a birdbath.

PRODUCER: *Our conversation has deteriorated.*

KIRSTEN: *Oh, yes indeed.*

CORTEZ: Don't speak until you are spoken to. Do you hear me?

MACK: Yes.

CORTEZ: Now, the second vision.

MACK: That was the second vision.

CORTEZ: How many have you had?

MACK: Thirteen.

CORTEZ: And when will the next one be?

(Cut)

*Cortez in chair. Day shot of window on monitors.*

KIRSTEN: *So?*

CORTEZ: I saw something last night.

KIRSTEN: *You saw nothing last night.*

CORTEZ: I saw something last night. Do you hear me?

KIRSTEN: *I don't hear you. You saw nothing last night and that's that. Period.*

CORTEZ: No period. I saw something last night whether it was there or not, it was there. It wasn't there but I saw it.

KIRSTEN: *You saw nothing at all.*

CORTEZ: I saw something.

KIRSTEN: *You will tell no one about this.*

CORTEZ: Until I see it again, I will tell nobody but you.

KIRSTEN: *Don't tell me, I won't be listening.*

CORTEZ: You will listen and I will see it again.

KIRSTEN: *You don't want to see it again because you never saw it.*

CORTEZ: I want to see it again and I will see it. Whatever it is.

KIRSTEN: *Whatever it isn't, you won't see it ever again. That was the last time you will ever see it. You saw it once and forever and never again. Do you understand me?*

CORTEZ: No, I don't understand you.

KIRSTEN: *Please don't see it again.*

CORTEZ: I can't help it. I saw it.

(*Cut*)

*Cortez on diagonally opposite monitors, Kirsten paces from one to the other.*

CORTEZ: *Right.*

KIRSTEN: Wrong.

CORTEZ: *Right. I will see it again.*

KIRSTEN: You're not supposed to see it and you won't.

CORTEZ: *I will see it again then just because of that.*

KIRSTEN: You fool.

CORTEZ: *Agnus dei qui tollis pecata mundi miserere nobis.*

KIRSTEN: Shut up.

CORTEZ: *Agnus dei.*

KIRSTEN: Why are you talking like that?

CORTEZ: *Blaspheming against the Lord. It told me to say that. It taught me and I taught you that and now you're spitting it back to me out of context, out of order, out of the wild blue yonder and you will—*

KIRSTEN: Shut up immediately.

CORTEZ: *Agnus dei.*

KIRSTEN: Not one scintilla of a word out of you now get out. I cannot bear the thought of you.

CORTEZ: *Woe to you my foolish shepherd who forsakes his flock. May the sword fall upon his arm and upon his right eye. Let his arm wither away entirely and his right eye be blind forever. Open your doors O Lebanon that the fire may devour your cedars. Wail you cypress trees for the tears have fallen, the mighty have been despoiled, wail you oaks of Bashan for the impenetrable forest is cut down. Hark, the wailing of the shepherds. Their glory has been ruined. Hark, the roaring of the young lions, the jungle of the Jordan is laid waste.*

KIRSTEN: And I don't have to sit here while you pontificate endlessly to the wind. So don't.

CORTEZ: *I won't.*

KIRSTEN: Windwag. Endless pontification endlessly. An endless sermon on the mount. Beat it.

CORTEZ: *I am the pie in the sky, the center of the lie, the fool on the hill, the pill in the swill, the widows' watch, the eye of the needle, the slide rule, the key, the alpha, the omega, the Betamax, the blind mind, the morning noon and night. Do you understand me?*

KIRSTEN: Yes, I understand you completely.

CORTEZ: *Don't tell me that.*

KIRSTEN: Why not?

CORTEZ: *But above all, the frog prince, the ultra twister, jack the wack, the boogie man, the midnight special.*

KIRSTEN: Goodnight dear.


(*Cut*)


*Mack seated at small table, Cortez standing. Pegeen seated at large table, gets up to read report. On interior monitor, Kirsten holds glass of water up to her face, inspects it. On ambient monitors, wind-blown trees.*

KIRSTEN: *Oh dear, it's rained.*

PEGEEN: All over everything.

PRODUCER: *Now is it true that she appears near water?*

CORTEZ: Maybe near this glass of water.

MACK: Maybe.

CORTEZ: This glass of water is supposedly alleged to be from the stream that gushed forth. What if I spilled it.

PRODUCER: *Spill it.*

KIRSTEN: *What would happen?*

MACK: Nothing. I don't know. Just don't spill it.

CORTEZ: The water in itself doesn't represent anything?

MACK: No.

CORTEZ: So why couldn't I spill it?

MACK: You could.

KIRSTEN: *Okay.*

CORTEZ: It wouldn't hurt anything if I did would it?

MACK: No.

DOC: *What if I drank it?*

MACK: Then it would hurt you.

DOC: *Why?*

MACK: Because it would. You're not supposed to drink it.

PEGEEN: What's in it?

KIRSTEN: *Just water particles.*

PRODUCER: *Let's see the scientific report.*

PEGEEN: Now one pharmacist tested the water and found it disgusting in content as if a sewer pipe had exploded. But then a chemist from the NPN analyzed it and found—let me read—"that it contained some primary elements in superabundance: chlorides, carbonates, silicates, iron oxides, soda sulphates, etc. etc., very easily digested and imparting to the bodily system a disposition favorable to the balance of vital functioning. Its constituent substances lead them to believe it is a mineral spring. But that was contradicted by another scientist who in his analysis says it has led him to regard the water in question as a drinking water containing the same elements as most of the spring water met with in the mountains and more particularly those whose soil is rich in limestone, so that he says it is not a mineral spring but an ordinary spring."

CORTEZ: And so what? So what?

PRODUCER: *And what can you make of all that information?*

KIRSTEN: *Now you say she told you to dig for this well and drink from it?*

MACK: Yes.

PRODUCER: *How far down was it?*

MACK: You know all this.

KIRSTEN: *How far down was it?*

MACK: I dug down a foot or so and it started oozing up.

CORTEZ: Now isn't this where you stuck your face in the mud and the crowd laughed?

MACK: Yes.

CORTEZ: Why would she tell you to stick your face in the mud?

MACK: She didn't.

CORTEZ: But you did.

MACK: I had to drink the water somehow.

DOC: *What did it taste like?*

MACK: When it first came up it was muddy but then it got clear and it was fine.

PRODUCER: *What are the doctor's findings?*

DOC: *After more than a few CAT scans I have found—it reads—"Mack is of a delicate constitution, with a lymphatic and nervous temperament. Thirteen years old though he seems not more than eleven. His face is pleasant, his eyes have a lively expression. His head is regular in shape but narrow and rather on the small side. His health he states is very good. He has never suffered from headaches, has experienced no nervous attacks; he eats, drinks and sleeps wonderfully well. However, young Mack doesn't have the good health one might imagine. He is obviously afflicted with asthma. His breathing is slightly irregular and wheezing and at times becomes perceptibly so."*

CORTEZ: Why does he appear then to throw himself on the ground and bite the earth in his attacks of delirium?

PRODUCER: *I have never seen one of these attacks of delirium.*

PEGEEN: Are you trying to fasten the blame indirectly?

CORTEZ: Doesn't he or does he not bite the dust or sand when he is in a state of hallucination?

PRODUCER: *Exaltation.*

DOC: *There is nothing to prove that Mack has had any intention of imposing upon the public. This child is of an impressionable nature. He has possibly been the victim of an hallucination. No doubt a reflection from the light of the water he so usually frequents caught his attention. His imagination is influenced by a mental predisposition and caused him to imagine—*

CORTEZ: As many children do a figure resembling a statue in a church or book or painting.

KIRSTEN: *He's never been in a church.*

CORTEZ: He relates this vision to his friends and they drag him off to the beach.

KIRSTEN: *They follow him.*

CORTEZ: The rumor spreads around town and everyone starts screaming miracle and apparition. Several religions try to claim or reject him.

PRODUCER: *This is a medical report. Let's stick to medicine.*

DOC: *Surely the child's would-be young mind would naturally be more and more affected by this and his exaltation would work up into a peak, wound up tight like a spring.*

KIRSTEN: *Twister.*

CORTEZ: Tornado.

DOC: *Exactly, so what first was a mere hallucination gains more and more control over his mind, it begins to absorb him and isolate him from the outside real world. And at the moment the hallucination becomes an apparition, at that point it results in a genuine state of ecstasy, a mental lesion—*

CORTEZ: —that places the one affected by it under the domination of the absorbing idea.

DOC: *Consequently, the undersigned consider that the boy Mack may possibly have exhibited a state of ecstasy that has recurred several times. There is here a case of mental disease the effects of which explain the phenomena of the vision.*

CORTEZ: So we admit that it is an hallucination, an ecstasy resulting from a cerebral lesion. That is possible, very possible. It is even very probable. I myself follow this method of reasoning in practice.

DOC: *I merely observe that I believe in the possibility of the supernatural but I await further proofs before seeing it in the present case.*

KIRSTEN: *If they're not from the Bible they must be from somewhere?*

PEGEEN: Oh, who cares?

KIRSTEN: *Would you like a roast-beef sandwich?*

MACK: No.

PRODUCER: *Don't be cruel.*

PEGEEN: Milk and honey?

MACK: I hate milk. I don't drink milk.

KIRSTEN: *Water?*

MACK: Yes.

PEGEEN: You've been drinking water for a month.

MACK: So what.

KIRSTEN: *Don't you, aren't you hungry for anything else?*

MACK: No.

PEGEEN: You're going to starve.

MACK: Do I look like I'm starving?

KIRSTEN: *No.*

MACK: Didn't the doctors test me and tell you that I was healthy?

PEGEEN: Yes.

MACK: Then why do I have to eat roast-beef sandwich or milk or honey or anything else but water? If I don't need anything but water then who needs anything else?

KIRSTEN: *What's in that water?*

MACK: Drink it and find out.

KIRSTEN: *What's in it?*

PEGEEN: Didn't the doctors test it and tell you what was in it?

PRODUCER: *Yes.*

MACK: So that's what I'm living on.

KIRSTEN: *It's just water particles in it. Just water in it.*

MACK: So that's what it is. Why don't you drink it?

PEGEEN: You wouldn't let us.

KIRSTEN: *And everyone's afraid to drink it.*

PRODUCER: *They won't even look at it.*

MACK: Drink it.

KIRSTEN: *No, I don't want to.*

MACK: Go on.

PEGEEN: No, I won't.

MACK: Drink it I said.

KIRSTEN: *Mack.*

MACK: I said drink it I said.

PEGEEN: I will not drink it.

MACK: You will drink it.

PEGEEN: No.

MACK: I said drink it I said and I said drink it and you will drink it because I said drink it.

KIRSTEN: *I will not drink it.*

MACK: I'll ask you one more time.

PEGEEN: I'm not going to drink it.

MACK: Don't spill it.

KIRSTEN: *I'm going to spill it.*

MACK: Drink it. Just a sip.

PEGEEN: (*Takes a sip*): It's disgusting. Putrefied.

(*Cut*)


*Mack still at small table, Kirsten standing in front of opposite chair. Cortez standing at one end of large table, facing Mack. Day window on all monitors.*

MACK: Now taste it, the sanctity, the holiness. It's the way of the world.

KIRSTEN: How would you know about the way of the world? All I taste is dirt, mud, ugh.

MACK: Keep chewing, don't spit it out. Don't reject the holy consequence.

KIRSTEN: Forget the consequence, I'm spitting.

MACK: Don't.

KIRSTEN: Sorry.

CORTEZ: How could you do that?

KIRSTEN: I'm sorry it just tastes like dirt to me. What do you taste?

CORTEZ: Nothing really. It sort of tastes like chocolate. Chocolate.

KIRSTEN: It's dirt.

CORTEZ: It tastes like dirt. It is dirt.

MACK: Taste it again.

KIRSTEN: What are you trying to make us do?

MACK: Taste it again.

KIRSTEN: Please.

MACK: Taste it again I said.

KIRSTEN: Forget it. It tastes like dirt.

MACK: It is dirt. It's the dirt of the Lord. From heaven. Heavenly dirt.

KIRSTEN: What's it supposed to do? Cure us? Heavens to betsy.

MACK: Sort of in a way.

CORTEZ: Sort of in a way what?

KIRSTEN: Sort of or not sort of?

CORTEZ: This is not dirt it's chocolate.

KIRSTEN: You're telling us to eat chocolate and telling us it's dirt?

CORTEZ: This is chocolate.

MACK: It's dirt. Just plain dirt from the spring.

KIRSTEN: So why eat it then?

MACK: It doesn't matter how it tastes, it's that it's good for you.

CORTEZ: Like medicine.

MACK: I told you I don't believe in medicine.

CORTEZ: It's holy dirt from the holy spring.

MACK: Do you feel it diffusing through your body?

KIRSTEN: No I don't.

MACK: Strengthening you?

KIRSTEN: I do not feel a thing.

CORTEZ: This is chocolate.

KIRSTEN: What's it supposed to taste like?

MACK: Like dirt because it is dirt and if it's dirt it tastes like dirt and if you taste chocolate then that's what you taste.

CORTEZ: I'm tired of your alchemical, metaphysical tricks. Trickery, blasphemy, heresy, and collusion with the devil and dirt farmers.

KIRSTEN: Dirt from the holy wellspring.

CORTEZ: That's not a holy well.

MACK: Spring.

CORTEZ: That's not a holy well.

MACK: Spring.

CORTEZ: It's not a holy spring.

KIRSTEN: There's nothing holy about it except that it's a hole.

CORTEZ: It's not a holy well.

KIRSTEN: First he gets us to drink that muddy water and now we're eating that holy hell springwellwater.

CORTEZ: Chocolate water.

KIRSTEN: If nothing else it's chocolate I know it.

MACK: It is not chocolate. It's dirt. Holy dirt from the holy spring.

CORTEZ: Dirty well water.

KIRSTEN: What's in that bag?

MACK: Nothing.

KIRSTEN: What's in that bag?

CORTEZ: There's a dead bird in it.

KIRSTEN: What's that doing in there?

MACK: I was going to feed the bird the dirt.

KIRSTEN: And cure it?

MACK: Yes.

CORTEZ: Well go ahead.

MACK: No, no. It's wrecked. You've wrecked the holiness. You know you're making me really mad saying this is chocolate.

KIRSTEN: Get that bird out of here and throw this mud out.

CORTEZ: It's chocolate, chocolate, chocolate!

MACK: Oh, wherefore art thou God? You're trying to make a fool out of me. Turning this all around and making a joke out of it.

KIRSTEN: How do you expect not to be a fool when you make people eat dirt.

MACK: It's not dirt.

CORTEZ: Chocolate! You're turning this all around and making it silly. It's holy. Holy dirt or chocolate, I think it's gone far enough. And they took the body out of the reliquary and plundered it all over the church floor, scattered it, created a sacrilege out of it.

KIRSTEN: Stop it. You're getting hysterical. Stop.

CORTEZ: And when they had created a sacrilege the skies poured down an apocalypse. They threw the toe over here and the teeth over there and paraded the head down the main street of Potsdam for everyone to see that the incorruptible body would in fact be corrupted and could not indeed fight back. How could it fight back when its fists were in separate parts of the world? When its clavicle was in the Philippines and its ear was in Italy and its toe was in Potsdam. How could they expect it to fight back. What could the poor dried-up remnants do?

KIRSTEN: Stop it. Now honey sit down.

CORTEZ: Don't call me honey.

KIRSTEN: Now, now, now, now, now, honey calm down.

CORTEZ: I will not calm down.

KIRSTEN: No, no, no, no, no, no, no, no. Now listen to us.

CORTEZ: Oh, yes, yes, yes, yes, yes, yes, yes, yes.

KIRSTEN: Don't call me honey.

MACK: Now, honey, now.
KIRSTEN: Clam up.


(Cut)


*Pegeen and Mack in chairs, Doc at small table. On monitors, shot of old docks
with pilings sticking up out of the water.*

CORTEZ: *I was cooking one day and I was cooking a vegetable soup from scratch and I
noticed there were little bits of meat floating around in the soup and I knew I hadn't
put meat into the soup because I don't eat meat and there was no meat in the house
anyway.*
PEGEEN: And what did you do?
CORTEZ: *Well, I threw the soup out onto the lawn in back of my house and the lawn caught
fire. So I went to put it out and it wouldn't go out so I threw everything I could on
it and it still wouldn't go out. Then I went and threw holy water on it and it blazed
even higher. By this time the neighbors had started to notice what was happening and
tried to help. Then it caught onto the house and we called the fire department and
they took so long to get there and the house became a flaming disaster. It was just
glowing and it was glowing so big and we couldn't figure out why because there wasn't
much in the house to make it glow up so big and the firemen just couldn't get it out.
The more water they put on the more it would glow and the higher it would get.
There was just nothing to demolish a fire of such magnitude. So we started praying
or I started praying and everyone prayed with me and slowly the fire started to stop
glowing so much and suddenly it went right out just like a light bulb. Just right out.
It was light and bright and suddenly it got dark and was out and there was just a
bit of smoke wiping around. We were all shocked of course and then we noticed that
the residue of the fire was this weird white residue.*
PEGEEN: And then what happened?
CORTEZ: *Not much. I stayed at a friend's house and we swept up the residue into big piles.
There was nothing left of the house, just a big square of residue. I had cut my hand
on something the week before and after I had finished sweeping up the ash I looked
at my hand and there was no cut on it anymore. Now the hand remembered that
there had been a cut on it too. But there was no cut anywhere, not even on the other
hand so it was a miracle.*
PEGEEN: Hardly.
CORTEZ: *Why not?*
PEGEEN: There are all sorts of explanations for things like that.
CORTEZ: *Like what?*
PEGEEN: Who put the meat in the soup?
CORTEZ: *It was the devil.*
PEGEEN: How do you know that?

CORTEZ: *Because I don't eat meat.*

PEGEEN: Let's skip to the next incident.

CORTEZ: *Is it true that the week after you were found—*

PEGEEN: —biting the walls of your parish church?

CORTEZ: *Oh yes.*

PEGEEN: Have you had these fits before?

CORTEZ: *No. The doctors said it was a cerebral malfunction.*

PEGEEN: Who made you bite the walls?

CORTEZ: *It think it was God.*

MACK: I see. And why did you bite the walls?

CORTEZ: *I hated them.*

PEGEEN: You hated the walls so you bit them.

CORTEZ: *Please don't laugh, it's not funny.*

PEGEEN: I think it is.

CORTEZ: *Why?*

PEGEEN: Because it is silly. Were you diabolically possessed?

CORTEZ: *No.*

PEGEEN: Why did you bite the walls?

CORTEZ: *Was this the first time you bit the church wall? Yes.*

PEGEEN: Was this the first time you bit a wall of any kind?

CORTEZ: *Yes.*

PEGEEN: How long after the fire was this?

CORTEZ: *The next week.*

PEGEEN: And you say it was the god that made you do this.

CORTEZ: *Yes.*

PEGEEN: Which god?

CORTEZ: *The only one there is.*

PEGEEN: Which one is that?

CORTEZ: *I'm not here to answer that.*

PEGEEN: How did you say your house blew up.

CORTEZ: *I didn't say it blew up, it burned.*

PEGEEN: You said it blew up. I have it recorded in the interview that you said your house blew up.

CORTEZ: *I never said that.*

PEGEEN: It's here. Shall we play it back? How did you say your house blew up? How did you say your house blew up?

CORTEZ: *Well, it was the fire that caught from the lawn and it caught onto the house.*

PEGEEN: I see. And why did this happen?

CORTEZ: *The pot of stew was possessed by the devil meat and it caught the lawn on fire when I threw it out the window. And it was some kind of miracle and then I saw the lady over by the water. The house just blew up and burned miraculously.*

PEGEEN: It was a gas leak.

CORTEZ: *It was a miracle.*

PEGEEN: It was a gas leak, the authorities have studied it and it was a gas leak, nothing else.

CORTEZ: *How does it explain the meat in the pot? I never have meat in the house.*

PEGEEN: The only thing we can explain is the gas leak and explosion.

MACK: Thank you very much.

DOC: How could you do that to him?

PEGEEN: It's my job. I'm known as a nutcracker. I'm paid to make them unbelieve what they believe. We just can't go around having houses explode for any reason. I'll admit it's an oddity but that's all I'll admit. I don't know who put the meat in the pit.

DOC: Pot.

PEGEEN: Pit, pot, pisspot. He's obviously a nut and I hate hallucinations. On to the next hallucination.

DOC: Exorcism.

PEGEEN: I don't exorcise. I disbelieve, dehallucinate, erase, expose. On to the next one. Can you hear me? Can you hear me? Yes? Good.

(*Cut*)

*Moving rollercoaster images on all video screens. Mack seated at large table, Pegeen and Cortez pacing. Midway through scene, Pegeen helps Mack into toreador jacket.*

PEGEEN: Would you have any reason to, or are you being paid by the church?

CORTEZ: Why would I be paid by the church? Are you being paid by a church?

MACK: Why would I be paid by a church?

PEGEEN: You might be paid to discredit what he's seen.

CORTEZ: And you might be paid to find some meaning in what he's saying.

PEGEEN: They need as many meanings as they can get.

CORTEZ: Maybe we're both being paid by as many churches as can pay us on either side.

PEGEEN: Why would churches want to get involved in all these exploding houses and so on?

CORTEZ: The cures.

PEGEEN: They want as many as they can get.

MACK: Proved.

PEGEEN: Proved or unproved.

CORTEZ: Bully for you.

PEGEEN: Bully for me.

CORTEZ: So if we both agree that we're both being paid.

PEGEEN: But we're not. Neither of us.

CORTEZ: Don't jump down my neck.

PEGEEN: Get your foot off my throat.

CORTEZ: And I won't jump on your neck.

PEGEEN: What do you think about all of this?

CORTEZ: Do you think we're being paid by a church?

PEGEEN: Any church?

MACK: Would they pay you?

CORTEZ: I don't think so.

MACK: Have they offered to?

PEGEEN: No.

MACK: Are you lying?

CORTEZ: No.

MACK: Which one of you is being paid?

PEGEEN: Neither of us.

MACK: What about her?

PEGEEN: I'm not.

MACK: And him?

CORTEZ: No.

PEGEEN: So none of us are being paid by any church any old church from nowhere so let's go on. How did the dog die?

CORTEZ: Which dog?

PEGEEN: The dog that was cured. That was the first cure was it not?

CORTEZ: Yes, that we know of.

PEGEEN: Let him answer.

MACK: Yes.

PEGEEN: It was hit by a car and died and was buried by its owners and they deburied it and unearthed it.

CORTEZ: Exhumed it.

MACK: Thank you and brought it to the spring and stuck its head in it and they left it there soaking for—

CORTEZ: How long?

MACK: Half an hour.

PEGEEN: More or less?

MACK: Less. And then we were sitting there watching it and suddenly it let out this huge groan and started breathing and got up again and started drinking the water and jumping and running around for joy.

PEGEEN: Do you think it was happy that it was alive?

CORTEZ: Of course it was, it didn't want to be dead.

MACK: And then they took it back to the doctor and there was nothing wrong with it.

CORTEZ: What was wrong with it when it died?

MACK: Its body was all smashed up and strangled by the car that hit it. There was no way it could have survived that car.

PEGEEN: And the people that hit it were so happy. The doctor's report says that it was dead on arrival. Suffering multiple contusions and lacerations to all parts of the body and brain as well as internal injuries and broken hipbone, collarbone, arms and legs fractured multiple to the head skull.

MACK: And it was dead and buried.

CORTEZ: How long was it buried before they—

PEGEEN: Unearthed.

CORTEZ: Exhumed it.

MACK: A week.

PEGEEN: Was there any sign of mortality on the body?

MACK: Meaning what?

PEGEEN: Meaning any decomposition of the flesh. Any sign of parasitical insects or organisms invading the corpse.

MACK: None whatsoever.

CORTEZ: Any odor extracting out of it?

PEGEEN: No in fact the owners said that a wonderful flowery odor accompanied the corpse of the body.

CORTEZ: Like what smell.

MACK: Like a flowery smell. Perfumy.

CORTEZ: There wasn't any embalming applied to the animal.

MACK: None whatsoever.

CORTEZ: And what do the owners think what happened?

MACK: They think it's a miracle.

CORTEZ: What religion are they?

MACK: None.

CORTEZ: What religion were they as children?

PEGEEN: They're listed as atheistic.

CORTEZ: Do they attend church now?

MACK: What for?

CORTEZ: In thanks.

MACK: No they don't.

PEGEEN: Have they changed their atheistic lifestyle because of this incident?

MACK: Not at all.

CORTEZ: They must have changed in some way. Your dog doesn't come back to life and you just stay the same.

PEGEEN: Why not?

CORTEZ: It just doesn't happen that way.

PEGEEN: It has happened that way. They're just thankful and accept it and are happy.

CORTEZ: Thankful to who.

PEGEEN: Not to anyone.

MACK: To the dog.

CORTEZ: Why to the dog?

MACK: For coming back.

PEGEEN: Has the dog changed?

CORTEZ: Except for the fact that it came back to life, nothing has changed.

MACK: He eats the same.

PEGEEN: Eats the same, everything the same. Still answers to the same name?

CORTEZ: Does he drink the holy water?

MACK: Won't go near it.

PEGEEN: Why not?

MACK: Will not drink it since that first day. Won't go near it.

PEGEEN: They can lead a dog to water but they can't make him drink it.

MACK: He just turns away.

CORTEZ: Let's just drop it for now it's a dead end.

PEGEEN: Hardly a dead end.

CORTEZ: It doesn't prove anything. They could all be lying.

PEGEEN: Why would you say that?

CORTEZ: You saw the dead dog.

MACK: It looked dead, I don't know if it was dead.

PEGEEN: Was there blood all over it?

CORTEZ: Yes, but it could have been paint and the dog could have been on a drug.

PEGEEN: But there's a doctor's report.

CORTEZ: It could have been faked.

PEGEEN: Everyone has sworn to the facts about the dead dog. Do you believe it came back to life?

MACK: Yes.

PEGEEN: So you don't think it was paint or drugs that made the dog look dead?

MACK: No.

PEGEEN: So dead is dead.

MACK: Dead was dead.

PEGEEN: And nothing was faked. Nothing was faked, dead was dead and live is alive.

CORTEZ: That dog could have been faked.

MACK: It was in smithereens I told you!

PEGEEN: Everyone admits it was in smithereens.

CORTEZ: All right it was in smithereens.

PEGEEN: And came back together.

CORTEZ: And it was not psychically improvised?

PEGEEN: It was not improvised.

CORTEZ: Psychically?

PEGEEN: By the dog or the owners or the boy so we can all agree to that.

CORTEZ: I can't agree on anything yet except the dog might have died and might have survived.

PEGEEN: Where is the dog?

CORTEZ: Now what about the reports that the dog spoke?

MACK: The dog never talked.

CORTEZ: I have reports that it spoke.

PEGEEN: What did it say?

MACK: I was there. It didn't say anything.

CORTEZ: To you it didn't say nothing.

PEGEEN: What did it say?

CORTEZ: Where is the dog?

PEGEEN: There it is.

CORTEZ: Ask it a question.

MACK: That dog never said nothing and you know it. You're just making this up.

CORTEZ: Well, it's among the investigative reports that I have.

PEGEEN: Who made them?

CORTEZ: Several veterinarians.

PEGEEN: Oh and on and on, who cares about the dog?

CORTEZ: Because it was the first instance of the cures.

PEGEEN: Why don't you talk to someone who was cured?

CORTEZ: You know that's impossible and that's just why you're asking me. All right. We all know it's impossible because of the fact that all the cured for some reason cannot speak.

PEGEEN: But they can write and they can . . .

CORTEZ: Now what about the reports that the doll spoke?

MACK: The doll never talked.

CORTEZ: I have reports that it spoke.

PEGEEN: What did it say?

MACK: I was there. It didn't say anything.

CORTEZ: To you it didn't say nothing.

PEGEEN: What did it say?

CORTEZ: Where is the doll?

PEGEEN: There it is.

CORTEZ: Ask it a question.

MACK: That doll never said nothing and you know it. You're just making this up.

CORTEZ: Well, it's among the investigative reports that I have.

PEGEEN: Who made them?

CORTEZ: Several veterinarians.

PEGEEN: Oh and on and on, who cares about the doll?

CORTEZ: Because it was the first instance of the cures.

PEGEEN: Why don't you talk to someone who was cured?

CORTEZ: You know that's impossible and that's just why you're asking me. All right, we all know it's impossible because of the fact that all the cured for some reason cannot speak.

PEGEEN: But they can write and they can—

(Cut)

*Kirsten paces back and forth. On ambient monitors, cars going by on a highway.*

CORTEZ: *I don't even know what I've said.*

KIRSTEN: You haven't said much.

CORTEZ: *Read it back to me.*

KIRSTEN: You wouldn't want to hear it, you're hysterical.

CORTEZ: *Even now?*

KIRSTEN: Even now, you're hysterical, not sparkling, flat and dull. Your head is not a wonderful place to be in.

CORTEZ: *Oh, I know.*

KIRSTEN: Go home.

CORTEZ: *And why aren't you a nut?*

KIRSTEN: Because I'm simply not.

CORTEZ: *Watch out for the car. Why aren't you a nut?*

KIRSTEN: Because I'm simply and clearly not, but why?

CORTEZ: *Because I will vomit the truth. Hear me out.*

KIRSTEN: Not on the rug. Not on the rug I said. Don't vomit the truth on my clean rug again please don't do it.

CORTEZ: *We've had a lot of conversations.*

KIRSTEN: Sweaty conversations.

CORTEZ: *On how to open our heads up from the top and let the truth vomit out.*

KIRSTEN: In.

CORTEZ: *Is it unconnectable? I wanted it to become so clear. It seemed so clear. At critical moments it becomes so clear and now it's just become so unclear. The confusion was so clear in my mind I don't know how it was clear but it was at those few moments. And now that I'm being clearer there is no way to tell you in a clear way. I'm just a nut going on and on. But why isn't he a nut? Why doesn't he sound like a nut. Maybe I look like a nut. Do I look like a nut?*

KIRSTEN: You have such a wonderful sense of desperation but we can't use it for our show it's much too desperate. You understand. You're a fruitcake.

CORTEZ: *Don't be cruel.*

KIRSTEN: You are a stark raving lunatic do you understand? I just cannot interview you on my show it's just going to be impossible. You just aren't making yourself understood properly in a clear way. I would love to but it's going to be impossible.

CORTEZ: *You must interview me. I must get the message out.*

KIRSTEN: It would be ridiculous to interview live or prerecorded. You're just crazy. You're having hallucinations. You should see a doctor.

CORTEZ: *How can you say that about me? I have this message. It must go out to the world. You have to believe me.*

KIRSTEN: Don't you understand? You're hysterical. You're a hysteric. You're disrupting even yourself. You don't even know what you're talking about. You're babbling all kinds of idiotic evidence to the contrary of your own mouth.

CORTEZ: *You've got to believe me.*

KIRSTEN: You're hysterical.

CORTEZ: *But I'm not.*

KIRSTEN: I'm not going to argue this with you.

CORTEZ: *But we must at least argue. I have to get this message across.*

KIRSTEN: Your message is a mess.

CORTEZ: *But we'll all burn.*

KIRSTEN: Then we will burn but you must see a doctor.

CORTEZ: *God will turn his back on you.*

KIRSTEN: Have some water. Now what is it you have to tell us.

CORTEZ: *I have been instructed.*

KIRSTEN: By who?

CORTEZ: *By her.*

KIRSTEN: To tell you—

CORTEZ: *That you have been frequently guilty of misrepresenting the truth and you must not misinterpret the message she gives to me to give to you.*

KIRSTEN: Okay. Now what is the message.

CORTEZ: *Please pray with me.*

PRODUCER: *Shut him up and get him out of here.*

KIRSTEN: We can't just throw him out.

PRODUCER: *Call in the cops.*

KIRSTEN: No, we can't call them. He'll make a scene.

PRODUCER: *I'm tired of hearing about blazing tuna and burned people, somebody gimme a pigfoot.*

CORTEZ: *All of you must fall on your knees and play with me. And pray for us all.*

KIRSTEN: What do you think?

PRODUCER: *Wait till he collapses and then ship him back to where he came from.*

KIRSTEN: He'll come back. I'm going to read to you a transcription of what you told us last night and you tell me if it sounds like it makes sense to you.

(Cut)


*Mack on stool, Kirsten on opposite monitor.*

KIRSTEN: *Tell me the story again about the cure.*

MACK: I didn't have nothing to do with it I was just standing there and I told them I had nothing to do with anything and I couldn't do anything and so not to come near me and they could go to the spring if they wanted to but they couldn't come near me. So I went home but they dragged me to the house and I could taste the poor mother's salt tears, they were all over my arms. Then he fell to the floor and cried a big long cry. Then someone picked him up and his feet stuck out like they were dead. Shall I go to the hospital with you. No, I can go alone, they said. I should go with you. No, I can go alone. I just want to get him right in there. I'll go with Pepito. I'll call Pepito. But I knew all about it. It was happening while I knew it was happening. I was scared, so I walked around the door and he was in there sleeping so I walked outside by the fence and someone was wailing. There was only one star out. Then, I walked by the door and they were in there and he was sleeping sick. I hear crying but I didn't believe it so I looked over by the bed and the mother cried and fell on me and I moved because I didn't want her tears to touch me. I don't want your hot sweaty salty tears to touch me. Then he picked his body up and the legs were stiff so I looked and cried and fell on the floor. My arm was out and my face was wet. Then I stood up and someone else was gone and they tried to push my hand on him and I said, This is unchangeable, he's erased. Then the body fell down and his back was to the floor forever. They pushed my hand on him but I didn't want to touch it. They wanted me to pray. I said, Get up, get up. And he got up. I screamed and ran away. Stop staring at me. What are you looking at?

KIRSTEN: *I'll bet you did.*

MACK: They all ran after me.

(*Cut*)

*Kirsten seated at large table, Mack in chair.*

PEGEEN: *Shall we eat?*

MACK: Of course.

KIRSTEN: What are we going to eat?

DOC: *What time is it?*

MACK: Five o'clock.

KIRSTEN: I thought it was four.

PEGEEN: *It's four o'clock.*

DOC: *It's four isn't it? See my watch?*

MACK: I said it's five and it's five. I said it.

KIRSTEN: Well.

MACK: I said it's five o'clock and let's eat.

DOC: *All right.*

MACK: What are we eating?

PEGEEN: *Sandwiches.*

MACK: I don't want sandwiches.

KIRSTEN: Why not?

MACK: I said I don't want sandwiches.

DOC: *We'll have something else then.*

MACK: We certainly will. Where's the water?

KIRSTEN: What water.

MACK: I said I want the water now.

DOC: *Oh.*

MACK: Get the water I said. I said get the water. I said get the water didn't I?

PEGEEN: *Yes.*

MACK: Then get it and shut up.

PEGEEN: *Shall we eat?*

MACK: Of course.

KIRSTEN: What are we going to eat?

DOC: *What time is it?*

MACK: Five o'clock.

KIRSTEN: I thought it was four.

PEGEEN: *It's four o'clock.*

DOC: *It's four isn't it? See my watch?*

MACK: I said it's five and it's five. I said it.

KIRSTEN: Well.

MACK: I said it's five o'clock and let's eat.

DOC: *All right.*

MACK: What are we eating?

PEGEEN: *Sandwiches.*

MACK: I don't want sandwiches.

KIRSTEN: Why not?

MACK: I said I don't want sandwiches.

DOC: *We'll have something else then.*

MACK: We certainly will. Where's the water?

KIRSTEN: What water.

MACK: I said I want the water now.

DOC: *Oh.*

MACK: Get the water I said. I said get the water. I said get the water didn't I?

PEGEEN: *Yes.*

MACK: Then get it and shut up.

(*Cut*)


*Kirsten and Mack still seated.*

MACK: This vale of tears.

PRODUCER: *That poor withering priest.*

MACK: And when I put my foot down, I put it down and when it stays down it stays down.

KIRSTEN: I don't know what you mean.

MACK: Shall we pray?

KIRSTEN: To who? To what?

PRODUCER: *For what?*

MACK: For you.

KIRSTEN: I never pray for myself.

PRODUCER: *It's so fruitless.*

KIRSTEN: So vain. Vanity, vanity, vanity of vanities. You are vanity. What profit a man from all the labor which he toils at under the sun. One generation passes and another comes but the world forever stays, right?

MACK: The sun rises and the sun goes down then it presses on to the place where it rises, blowing toward the south then toward the north. The wind turns again and again resuming its rounds. All rivers go to the sea yet never does the sea become full to the place where they go. The rivers keep on going. All speech is labored. There is nothing man can say. The eye is not satisfied with seeing nor is the ear filled with hearing. The sun rises and the sun goes down. Then it presses—

PRODUCER: *Oh, so what.*

KIRSTEN: Come on without, come on within.

PRODUCER: *You'll not see nothing like the mighty Quinn.*

MACK: I cannot bear the thought of you.

KIRSTEN: The sun rises and the sun goes down.

MACK: Oh, shut up. Cast your bread on the waters after a long time you may find it again. Vanity, for all is vanity and a chase after the wind.

KIRSTEN: Idiot wind.

MACK: For as the crackling of thorns under a fire pot so is the fool's laughter. This is also vanity. I saw her there floating up to the sky in a blue-green ball of nervousness.

KIRSTEN: And what else did you see?

MACK: A cloud. A purple cloud of miasma.

KIRSTEN: And what else?

MACK: A prison in the sky. She makes lightning flash in the rain and releases storm winds from their chambers, repeat that.

KIRSTEN: Every man is stupid, ignorant. Every artisan is put to shame by his idol. He has molded a fraud without breath of life. Nothingness. They are a ridiculous work. They will perish in their time of punishment. Right.

*(Cut)*

*Doc at small table, Pegeen in chair opposite, Mack in chair. All video screens show Kirsten, Producer, Cortez standing in front of car with headlights on.*

KIRSTEN: *You've spent a month in silence.*

DOC: You haven't said a word for a month.

PEGEEN: Say something.

PRODUCER: *Everyone is asking.*

DOC: Please say something.

KIRSTEN: *If you don't say something we'll have to say something for you.*
PRODUCER: *We're going to say something for you.*
DOC: Speak.
PEGEEN: We're going to make up a statement for you.
KIRSTEN: *They think we've trapped you in here and won't let you speak.*
PRODUCER: *Say something.*
DOC: Have you seen anything?
PEGEEN: Did she come again?
PRODUCER: *Have you seen anything? Anyone?*
KIRSTEN: *Have you seen any lights? Anything moving in the dark?*
DOC: Heard anything?
PEGEEN: Any voices?
PRODUCER: *Anyone say anything to you?*
KIRSTEN: *Had any dreams?*
DOC: Have you decided anything?
PEGEEN: Is there anything we can do for you?
PRODUCER: *Is there anything in the water?*
KIRSTEN: *There haven't been any cures for a month.*
DOC: Is something wrong?
PEGEEN: Is she mad at you?
PRODUCER: *Are you mad at her?*
KIRSTEN: *Does she appear anymore?*
DOC: Is something wrong with the water?
PRODUCER: *Speak.*
PEGEEN: There are people waiting outside every day. Waiting for you.
KIRSTEN: *There's a lot of sick people.*
DOC: Everyone wants to know what's the matter with you.
PEGEEN: Say something.
PRODUCER: *If he doesn't say something soon we're going to have to deny any connection or responsibility.*
KIRSTEN: *Say something.*
DOC: Where is she? What happened to her?
PEGEEN: Is something wrong? How long are you going to sit there?
PRODUCER: *Eat something at least.*
KIRSTEN: *It's been a month since you've eaten.*
DOC: Eat something. Say something.
PEGEEN: Do you want some water?
PRODUCER: *Say something.*
MACK: No.
PEGEEN: What?
PRODUCER: *No.*

(Cut)

*Doc still at small table, Kirsten paces. Mack gets up, picks up glass of water and carries it around with him.*

KIRSTEN: Well then you have to locate her face find me her face.

DOC: Why does this have to be so hard for you?

MACK: There's a fly in here. Kill it.

DOC: Why?

MACK: Kill it. Kill it.

DOC: Why?

MACK: I'm so scared of it. Kill it. What arrangements do you have for killing in-sects? They all must be removed from every room I enter. I cannot have insects around. This is a plot against me. Pick them out like sheep I said. I said it. Set them apart for the day of carnage. How long must the earth mourn and the green of the countryside wither. For even your own brothers, the members of your father's house betray you. They have recruited a force against you.

ALL: Do not believe them even if they are friendly to you in their words. Yet I like a trusting lamb led to the slaughter had not realized that they were hatching a plot against me.

MACK: Let us destroy the tree in its vigor. Let us cut him off from the land of the living so that his name will be spoken no more.

KIRSTEN: Enough.

DOC: Kinderfest.

KIRSTEN: But why?

MACK: They confuse me.

DOC: But how?

MACK: They're ugly. They confuse me and throw me off. They're tiny dead angels. Tiny Lucifers, flies on fire and so they must get out.

KIRSTEN: What are you digging for out there?

MACK: The spring, the water. It's under there.

DOC: How do you know?

KIRSTEN: Did she say something to you?

DOC: Did she come back?

MACK: No.

KIRSTEN: Why are you digging?

MACK: Because I know the spring is there. Get rid of these flies I said.

DOC: We're trying.

KIRSTEN: Why do they bother you so much?

MACK: Get rid of them I said.

DOC: All right.

MACK: I said get rid of them, didn't I?

KIRSTEN: Then get rid of them.

DOC: Okay.

MACK: I might breathe one in. Do you hear a breathing?

KIRSTEN: No.

DOC: It's nothing. A bird, a fly, a buzzard.

MACK: There is only one chair in this room. One room, one chair. We're going to burn in this house. A firefly will drift into the thatch and burn us right up. I'm a hootchie-cootchie man, I'll get you one by one.

KIRSTEN: There's a fly out there. A bull ghost.

MACK: In the field out there. A bullfighter on a horn. They're stuck, they can't get off. What's in that glass there?

DOC: Scotch and ice.

MACK: Look in there. The whiskey is destroying the ice. Melting it away. Tearing it all away from itself. Is there a fly in here? I told you to get them out.

KIRSTEN: There aren't any flies in here, they're gone.

MACK: Then it's a mosquito.

KIRSTEN: What about all the people waiting outside. Don't you want to say something to them?

MACK: Let them eat rock underwater. I see a star up there and it's coming right down on all of us.

KIRSTEN: When?

MACK: Tonight.

KIRSTEN: Enough. You're either going to get up and say something to those people or we're calling an ambulance for intravenous feeding and I don't care what the hell anyone says.

MACK: Go ahead.

DOC: I will.

MACK: One house, one room, one chair, one ambulance, one doctor, one needle, one lady, one ball of fire, one cure, one fool, one fly, get it out.

KIRSTEN: This is your last chance, take it or leave it, because we're leaving it right now.

DOC: Are you going to perform a miracle?

MACK: No.

KIRSTEN: Are you going to see the lady again?

MACK: No.

DOC: Are you going to dig for water?

MACK: No.

KIRSTEN: Are you going to see the lady again?

MACK: No.

DOC: So no more miracle, no more water and no more lady.

MACK: In that order.

KIRSTEN: The ambulance is here, shall we go?

DOC: Sure.

KIRSTEN: What happened to the lady?

MACK: Nothing.

DOC: Where is she?

MACK: I said I don't want any flies in that car.

KIRSTEN: There won't be.

DOC: Intravenous.

MACK: Yes.

KIRSTEN: It's intravenous.

DOC: It'll be your anchor, it'll keep you from coming apart, it'll keep you docked in the harbor.

KIRSTEN: We're a pentangle, a triangle, invisible and indivisible, one nation under a groove. Get back into bed and shut up.

MACK: Hey, fuck you baby, don't order me around. This is my gig.

KIRSTEN: It was your gig and it's over.

MACK: You're trying to trip me up.

DOC: You've already tripped and fallen.

MACK: Then pick me up.

KIRSTEN: Pick yourself up and get into bed and shut up.

MACK: What do we do?

KIRSTEN: Lift your bundle and leave the land.

MACK: I will sling away the inhabitants of the land. I will hem them in that they may be undone, taken. Woe is me. I am undone. My wound is incurable yet I had thought if I make light of my wound, I can bear it. My tent is ruined. All its cords are severed. My sons have left me. They are no more. No one to pitch my tent. No one to raise its curtains.

KIRSTEN: Yes. The shepherds were stupid as cattle. The Lord they sought not. Therefore they had no success. And all their flocks are scattered. Listen, a noise. It comes closer. A great uproar from the northern land to turn the cities of Judah into a desert haunt of jackals.

DOC: Jackasses.

KIRSTEN: Jackrabbits.

DOC: Jack shit.

ALL: Yeah all right!

MACK: Oh dear, dear me.

(Cut)

*Doc still at small table, Kirsten at large table, Producer in chair.*

MACK: *Get this goon food out of here. Get it out I said. Silence!*

KIRSTEN: Silence.

DOC: But—

MACK: *Silence I said.*

KIRSTEN: Listen to the music.

MACK: *Shall we pray?*

DOC: All right.

MACK: *Pray, sing.*

KIRSTEN: And haven't you pretended to become some kind of religious fanatic?

DOC: Oh and look at you poor thing. No one's said a thing about you. Never will.

KIRSTEN: Isn't it a fact that you were drunk on the beach the night you say you saw this vision? Some water.

MACK: *No.*

KIRSTEN: Some water.

MACK: *No.*

DOC: And haven't you pretended all this time to be some kind of religious fanatic?

MACK: *No.*

KIRSTEN: And haven't you lied to everyone including your own lawyer and everyone else you've come into contact with? Isn't it true that you haven't told the truth since you said you saw this thing?

MACK: *She's not a thing.*

PRODUCER: And isn't it true that there isn't a thing or woman in a ball?

MACK: *No.*

KIRSTEN: Isn't it true that there isn't a woman in a ball of light? There isn't a ball of light and that you've masterminded this whole thing. Manufactured this entire Ping-Pong game to attract attention to yourself? And how much money have you made from all of this?

MACK: *A dime.*

KIRSTEN: You've made me pray to walls, to water. To anything you asked me to in search for an answer. You've made me learn prayers in Latin, Hebrew and anything else. Songs, hymns, I don't know how many glasses of this holy water you've made me drink and all for nothing.

MACK: *I didn't make you do anything.*

DOC: Why are you so calm?

MACK: *I'm calm because I'm right.*

KIRSTEN: Wrong.

(*Cut*)

*Mack stands facing a video monitor, on which is a river scene. He clutches the sides of the monitor. Kirsten is on the monitor behind him.*

KIRSTEN: *I want you to tell me everything calmly. I want you to repeat everything you've said to me. I want you to calmly tell me everything. I want you to tell me everything calmly.*

MACK: I stole those eyes from the statue. I didn't give them to any lady in a ball, I threw them into the river. Go and look for them. They're there. Do you think I gave jack shit if anyone was cured? No I didn't. I just talked and talked. I never said there would be a cure but you thought there would be so there was. I didn't do anything and so they all got cured. I had nothing to do with it. Maybe there was a woman in a ball but I never saw her. She was never there when I was there. Maybe everyone else saw her but I sure didn't. But then I didn't like it anymore and there was no way to get out of it so I kept on telling it and then all these things started happening and happening and I couldn't stop them. I even prayed to somebody to make them stop happening. I even prayed to the lady in the ball to make them stop happening but she couldn't because she wasn't there. I even tried to see her. I tried and tried until my eyes got bloody. I prayed every night for it all to stop and then it just kept happening. That's all I know, that's all there is to tell. Nothing ever happened to me. It just happened by itself. All I said was that I saw a woman in a ball and all these things started happening so fast. That's all I know. That's all there is to tell. It was not a miracle. I don't even know why. What are you looking at?

KIRSTEN: *Then what was it?*

MACK: It was luck. Pure fucking luck. I'm lucky. For worse or for better for better or for worse it was luck.

(Cut)

*Cortez at small table. On the monitors, Kirsten, Mack, Doc simultaneously descend, ascend on a lift.*

CORTEZ: There's one in here. I can feel it. Get it out.

KIRSTEN: *There it is.*

CORTEZ: Get out. Get out.

KIRSTEN: *There it goes. It's gone.*

CORTEZ: You diabolical little wretch.

MACK: *I am aren't I?*

CORTEZ: So.

KIRSTEN: *What's the matter with you?*

CORTEZ: I'm suffering from a diabolism. A lesion of the mind, just like the doctor said.

KIRSTEN: *All this stuff is just regurgitating out of you.*

CORTEZ: You are regurgitating out of me.

KIRSTEN: *Where is it all coming from?*

CORTEZ: My heart.

KIRSTEN: *What heart?*

CORTEZ: The black hole in my chest. Right here. See it? That's where it's all coming out of.

MACK: *And that's where the flies are coming out of.*

CORTEZ: Those flies are not coming out of me.

KIRSTEN: *Yes, they are.*

MACK: *We chased them away and they went right back into you.*

CORTEZ: Those flies are not coming out of me.

KIRSTEN: *Yes they are.*

(Cut)

*Doc at small table, Kirsten and Mack standing. Some monitors black, others with night shot of glowing window. After "Atlantis," switch to shot of brick wall.*

KIRSTEN: A thousand people are looking for you.

MACK: It's an oil well.

DOC: It looks like buckwheat.

MACK: It looks like buckwheat I said.

KIRSTEN: Now when this plane lands I want you to be polite to the reporters.

MACK: I hate them.

DOC: They're trying to help you. They're supporting your story.

MACK: I hate them and I want to kill them all.

KIRSTEN: But they're your friends.

MACK: No, they're not. They're trying to trip me up. Trip me up and make me fall over and I don't mean maybe.

KIRSTEN: Just stay cool and answer the questions.

MACK: You answer the questions. *(He lies on his back on large table)*

KIRSTEN: I wrote the questions, you have to answer them and don't answer any questions I didn't write. What's the answer to number four?

MACK: Separation of church and state.

KIRSTEN: Correct.

MACK: My eyes are burning. I want you to tell me everything calmly. I want you to repeat everything you've said to me. I want you to calmly tell me everything. I want you to tell me everything calmly.

KIRSTEN *(Washes Mack's eyes during the following)*: Try this one on for size. There was an island which lay before the great flood in the area we now call the Atlantic Ocean. So great an area of land that from her western shores those beautiful sailors journeyed to the South and the North Americas with ease in their ships with painted sails. To the east, Africa was her neighbor across a short strait of sea miles. Go and look for them. They're there. Do you think I gave a shit if anyone was cured? No, I didn't. I just talked and talked. I never said there would be a cure but you thought there would be so there was. I didn't do anything and so they all got cured. I had nothing to do with it. *(Blindfolds Mack)* The great Egyptian age is but a remnant of the Atlantean culture. The antediluvian kings colonized the world. All the gods who play in the mythological dramas in all legends from all lands were from fair Atlantis. Knowing her fate, Atlantis sent out ships to all corners of the world. On board were the twelve. The poet, the physician, the farmer, the scientist, the magician and the other so-called gods of our legends, though gods they were. And as the elders of our time choose to remain blind, let us rejoice and let us sing and dance and ring in the new. That's what it is.

MACK: So that's what it is.

PEGEEN: Yes.

MACK: Are we going to burn?

PEGEEN: *Oh yes we are.*
KIRSTEN: But we can't.
PEGEEN: *Oh we will and it'll be okay.*
DOC: *Let's get out while we can.*
PEGEEN: *Stay where you are.*
CORTEZ: Don't move.
DOC: *But I don't want to burn.*
PRODUCER: *You want to burn.*
KIRSTEN: We have to stay in the house and don't be afraid.
CORTEZ: Be brave now.
PEGEEN: *Stay still.*
PRODUCER: *Lead us not into temptation.*

(Cut)

*Cortez sits at small table, smoking and taking notes. Kirsten sits opposite, Mack remains on table. During scene, Kirsten gets glass of water and drinks all of it.*

DOC: *Now you've learned.*
KIRSTEN: Get me out of here I want to go to Pittsburgh.
CORTEZ: And from the bottom of my heart I deeply resent your miscalculated implication.
PRODUCER: *Direct hit.*
CORTEZ: It's eroding everything. Corroding it.
MACK: A flaming hysteric.
DOC: *I am not a flaming hysteric.*
PRODUCER: *Flaming.*
KIRSTEN: A long time ago, someone told me this would happen and it has happened and you'll accept it.
PEGEEN: *I can see bright burning days ahead of you. Bright glowing days all around you. Do you need something?*
PRODUCER: *Yes.*
KIRSTEN: Look in my eyes. Do you see it? Look.
PEGEEN: *Look harder.*
KIRSTEN: I see a dark lonely corner inside your eye.
PRODUCER: *That's it.*
CORTEZ: And a body rotting in a dark deep hole at the bottom of your eye.
MACK: A broken body down at the end of it.
KIRSTEN: Keep looking. Do you see anything beyond it?
PEGEEN: *Keep looking, don't look away.*
KIRSTEN: Keep looking.
PEGEEN: *Keep looking. Don't be afraid, don't be afraid.*

MACK: I don't even know what you're talking about.

KIRSTEN: I'm not talking.

CORTEZ: I see a heavy trail of broken heads and they're all ours. Burned charred heads and they're all ours.

PRODUCER: *They're all ours.*

KIRSTEN: Stop shuddering.

PEGEEN: *Stay calm.*

DOC: *Intervene.*

MACK: Intercede.

PEGEEN: *You will find your endless and impenetrable love in my eye at the bottom of my eye and it will serve you forever and no one can deny the love within my eye.*

KIRSTEN: I see bright burning days ahead of you but the fire won't hurt you. You won't feel the flames. You'll feel the flames but there will be no pain. Keep your eye on the sparrow.

PEGEEN: *The fire is getting brighter and hotter but you won't feel it. Keep listening to my voice. The fire will burn for three days but you won't feel it because you'll be ash.*

KIRSTEN: And you will finally blow out through the top of my head in a blinding light.

PEGEEN: *You belong to me and I belong to you and we all belong to each other.*

DOC: *And the cowboys will be slaughtered with their cattle and the Indians will chain their bodies into the hot sun and dry them into dust.*

KIRSTEN: This house will burn but the lion will sleep.

PEGEEN: *Hush my darling, don't fear my darling, the lion sleeps tonight.*

MACK: Where are we?

KIRSTEN: I told you.

CORTEZ: The spring is spewing forth into us. The sky is falling in on us.

MACK: So what.

PRODUCER: *The clouds are on fire and the sky is falling, so big deal.*

MACK: Are they going to burn us?

PEGEEN: *Oh, yes. They're going to burn us and there's no coincidence.*

DOC: *Who is burning us?*

KIRSTEN: Oh everyone is burning us. The left and the right. The top and the bottom. East and west and north and south.

PEGEEN: *Old and young and middle age.*

MACK: But why?

KIRSTEN: When you have a fire in your hand you have to keep it burning and you keep it burning something.

DOC: *Anything.*

MACK: It's a lie.

CORTEZ: The rain will put it out.

DOC: *No it won't.*

CORTEZ: The rain is on fire.

MACK: The water is on fire and so it won't put it out.

DOC: *You didn't tell me that water was flammable.*

MACK: So.

PRODUCER: *You never drank it.*

CORTEZ: It's not water. It's gasoline. Clean clear and pure octane.

DOC: *Sweet petroleum extract.*

MACK: But the spring.

PEGEEN: *It isn't a spring. It's an oil well, a gusher.*

MACK: So.

PRODUCER: *But it was so clear.*

CORTEZ: It was as black as night. A tar pit full of dead bog people rotting in their own tarry simulacra after twenty decades.

MACK: Where's the lady now?

PEGEEN: *I'm here. She'd never leave us.*

MACK: Tell her to get out.

CORTEZ: She can't. What can she do? The water's turned to gasoline. It'll only make it hotter. But she's smiling. Pray.

PEGEEN: *I guess you could say that we have been lucky or we have not been lucky.*

CORTEZ: Bullshit.

DOC: *That stupid glittering critical moment of supreme crucifixion will vanish away from you.*

MACK: You know you never will.

CORTEZ: How do I believe all this?

PRODUCER: *You know you never will.*

MACK: I am absent, a conduit, a funnel and I hate symbols. A lightning rod, an android, a figment, a robot, a misconception, a fucking asshole.

PRODUCER: *A dumb machine. A universe constructed already. Constructible, indestructible.*

KIRSTEN: Not a good question.

CORTEZ: It'll kill me.

PEGEEN: *You will depend on me.*

DOC: *Does it have anything to do with love?*

KIRSTEN: Oh, I would hope so.

MACK: How so?

PEGEEN: *There, do you see it? There's a tiny little flame in the sky over there.*

MACK: I don't see it.

PEGEEN: *Yes you do.*

(Cut)

*Actors remain in place in darkness. On ambient monitors, night shot of glowing window.*

KIRSTEN: *And are you aware that you murdered the two from the talk show?*

CORTEZ: *Well, they burned in the house. It was the fire.*

KIRSTEN: *Why couldn't they get out?*

CORTEZ: *Well, they could have gotten out but the fire caught them.*

KIRSTEN: *The fire caught them because they couldn't get out.*

CORTEZ: *Correct.*

KIRSTEN: *And why couldn't they get out.*

CORTEZ: *I locked the doors.*

KIRSTEN: *What about the windows?*

CORTEZ: *There were no windows.*

KIRSTEN: *So they burned.*

CORTEZ: *Yes they did. They seemed like they didn't mind it. But the water should have put it out. I kept pouring more and more.*

KIRSTEN: *That was gasoline.*

CORTEZ: *I thought it was water.*

KIRSTEN: *I decided a long time ago when I was a little child that I would see something like this. That I would take it upon myself to see it, that I would conjure an event and that I would enlist you into my services. My little army. And that from there we would continue on into our own and that it wouldn't be a heresy that would insult people.*

CORTEZ: *How can you say this? You're only a child.*

MACK: *And does it have anything to do with love?*

KIRSTEN: *Oh yes I would hope so. Yes indeed.*

MACK: *And that I wouldn't be diabolical about it like as if I was a murderer or something and that you could see into my mind. That I would let you see into my mind, into my pain into my happiness into my love for all of you and that because of that you would believe me because you could see all of my pain and stigmata constantly bleeding with love and pain.*

CORTEZ: *And that all this would go around you in a circle and keep you safe from the things you believe and that it would not interrupt your thinking or feeling of anything or any other kind of reality which you might be or might want to be a part of. That it would be an odorless, smokeless, harmless, invisible and indivisible.*

KIRSTEN: *And that you would take me and have me and love me into your heart of hearts with your mind standing by waiting and watching and thinking.*

CORTEZ: *Does it have anything to do with love?*

KIRSTEN: *That's a good question.*

MACK: *But I think I've answered it. That you wouldn't think of me as some kind of mystical idiot. And that we would risk everything. The home, the car, the boat. Everything but the kids.*

CORTEZ: *A sacrifice, a sacrilege.*

KIRSTEN: *But what do you really think about it?*

MACK: *I don't think anything I made it up. It's not to be thought about.*

KIRSTEN: *Oh yes it is. If I could force myself to force the thought like a broken glass through my forehead and out of my hands. I am only a simulacra, an ideology, a dialectic, the water table, poisoned water wells, a hippie dream.*

CORTEZ: *Let's go to Philadelphia.*

KIRSTEN: *Don't mind him. I told you he was a hysteric.*

MACK: *Well, do something about him. You're a priest. Can't you do anything?*

CORTEZ: *What do you want me to do? Hear his confession? Put a spell on him? Give him extreme unction?*

(Cut)

*Mack and Doc remain in place.*

CORTEZ: *No.*

MACK: Sit on that bench and shut up. Sit on that bench and shut up, I said.

KIRSTEN: *What's that on there?*

DOC: What?

KIRSTEN: *That faint stain.*

MACK: Blood.

DOC: From what?

MACK: I don't know.

KIRSTEN: *Shall we wash it?*

MACK: No, I like it. If it's there it belongs there permanently. Forever.

KIRSTEN: *Was it real what you saw?*

MACK: I don't mean it wasn't real. It was real.

CORTEZ: *What was real?*

MACK: The lady in the ball.

CORTEZ: *And why is she doing this?*

MACK: I don't know.

KIRSTEN: *Didn't she tell you?*

MACK: No.

CORTEZ: *Didn't she say she wanted a church?*

MACK: I never saw anything.

KIRSTEN: *Didn't she say to call a priest?*

MACK: I never saw anything.

CORTEZ: *Didn't she tell you to pray?*

KIRSTEN: *Drink the water.*

MACK: These thorns are killing me.

KIRSTEN: *Drink the water.*

MACK: That's not water. You're trying to tempt me with alcohol.

CORTEZ: *Do you have anything to confess?*

MACK: I have nothing to confess.

KIRSTEN: *Everything you've seen is true.*

CORTEZ: *Everything I've seen is true.*

MACK: Except that it's not really true. I never saw it. That's all I have to say. Or I thought I saw it and the more I was asked the more I saw it but now I don't see anything. I never saw anything.

KIRSTEN: *Drink the water.*

MACK: What's in this? You're poisoning me. I know it. Get it out of here. No one leaves this room. Who was it who's trying to poison me?

CORTEZ: *Put the knife down. Put it down.*

MACK: There's something in here I know it. You're poisoning me. Shall we pray?

(*Cut*)

*Kirsten, Doc, Mack remain in place. Day window on all monitors.*

KIRSTEN: We only want to see what you see. Like you see. That's all.

MACK: Why?

DOC: Does it matter to you if I see what you see or if I believe you?

MACK: No. Maybe it's only for my eyes, for my eyes only, only for us to see.

KIRSTEN: Us?

MACK: Me and I.

DOC: Are you sad at all about this?

MACK: No.

KIRSTEN: Are you pretending any of this?

MACK: No. Sometimes when I see something.

KIRSTEN: You will see what I see and how I see it. And I will see what you see and if my world falls apart before my eyes, your world will fall apart before your eyes and we will both see the same and whatever is there we will both or all three see together. Our six eyes will be one eye. We'll all be one eye, see out of one eye. Whether it is deliberately or not, it is just one eye and we will all see out of it. You're only part of a machine, our machine and because you are part of it, we'll all work together whether you want to or not. We will all see the same things together.

MACK: Everything that comes out of my mouth is a lie.

KIRSTEN: Everything that goes into my eye is exactly what is there. Left or right, right or wrong.

DOC: What about the lady?

KIRSTEN: She's the center of the machine. We know the answer is yes. And we can see every moment exactly. Every obscurity. Its dissolving qualities and reflection on the ceiling. The whole shooting match.

(*Cut*)

*Actors remain in darkness. Day window on ambient monitors.*

CORTEZ: *As I was saying to the sky the other day. My love is unspeakable, undeniable, indelible, inalienable, indivisible, shimmering. But though I love you with a love true, who can cling to a rambling rose?*

MACK: *Do you think you were made by anything? Initiated, created, put together, thought up, instigated, appropriated, pieced together, conceived.*

CORTEZ: *These thorns are killing me.*

KIRSTEN: *Though I love you with a love true, who can cling to a rambling rose? So I will not cling anymore.*

MACK: *These thorns are killing me.*

KIRSTEN: *Look in here. What are you seeing?*

MACK: *Watery.*

KIRSTEN: *You're looking at the inside of your own eye. What do you see?*

MACK: *Just something watery.*

KIRSTEN: *Do you see anything else? Anything floating in it?*

MACK: *A desert made out of water.*

CORTEZ: *That's what I saw. Now you see what I saw in my eye.*

KIRSTEN: *Are you happy with what you see or not so happy with what you see?*

CORTEZ: *I'm afraid.*

KIRSTEN: *They will hand your head to you on a plate surrounded by rambling roses burning.*

CORTEZ: *Why?*

KIRSTEN: *Why do you want to know everything? Why do you have to know everything? Why do you have to want to know everything? Everything on earth for God's sake. Does it satisfy you if I said I am the walrus? I don't care if you really saw it or not or if it was really there or not. I just want to know if you were telling the truth about whatever it was. That's the most important thing here, right now in this minute before it passes. I'm going to give you till the morning comes.*

MACK: *Too late.*

KIRSTEN: *And you will believe me and be convinced not because of what I say but because of how I say it.*

CORTEZ: *How many people are in this room?*

MACK: *Six.*

KIRSTEN: *Watch closely now. Six divided by two is three. Divided by two is one and a half. If six was nine divided by two is four and a half divided by two or any other number is two and a quarter so you see any other way you look at it there is only one person in this room. I tried so hard to tell you last night. You wouldn't talk to me. Sooner or later one of us must know that all you see around yourself is yourself. Everything you see around you is yourself and you're not your brother's keeper because there's no brother to keep but yourself and so if that is true, is it true that you saw that lady?*

MACK: *I told you. What does it matter if those people got cured, right or wrong?*

KIRSTEN: *Because if you're right then I'm right and if you're wrong then I'm wrong. One chair, one table, one TV, one each of everything.*

MACK: *But they are cured aren't they?*

KIRSTEN: *Yes. Doctors have testified they are.*

MACK: *Why?*

KIRSTEN: *I don't know why.*

MACK: *You mean to tell me they're cured and you don't know why?*

KIRSTEN: *I'm not a doctor.*

MACK: *My eyes hurt.*

KIRSTEN: *I am not a doctor. Watch closely now.*

CORTEZ: *How many people are there in this room?*

MACK: *Six.*

KIRSTEN: *How many?*

MACK: *Three.*

KIRSTEN: *How many people are there in this room?*

MACK: *Two.*

KIRSTEN: *Who?*

MACK: *You and me.*

KIRSTEN: *How many people are in this room?*

MACK: *One.*

KIRSTEN: *Who is it?*

MACK: *Me.*

KIRSTEN: *There, do you see it? There's a tiny little flame lighting in the sky over there, do you see it?*

MACK: *Yes.*

KIRSTEN: *Who is it?*

MACK: *Me.*

*All video monitors go out.*

# END OF PLAY

# Broken Eggs

Eduardo Machado

# Eduardo
Machado

I was born in Havana in 1953, and lived in Cojimar, a nearby beach town. I went to a Catholic boys school—in Guanabacoa, about six miles away—that my father and his brothers had attended. I was taken there every day. The school had a waiter in the lunchroom, which I always thought was odd. There was a museum and a church, which had in it a woman's body that hadn't decomposed, in a glass coffin. I was terrified of having to sit next to it at mass. When Fidel came it was said that ghosts appeared there, telling us that he was an idol.

I grew up in a big house (it's a school now). All my uncles lived there, and my aunt, and a lot of cousins—around seventeen people. My father was a rich man's son. That was his occupation. Here he's an accountant. My grandfather owned a bus company, and my other grandfather was second in command of the docks, which means he cheated the government on taxation.

The day I was born was the day Fidel landed in Cuba. I grew up in the shadow of the revolution; my grandmother was a big Castro supporter. When I was eight, my parents panicked and sent me and my four-year-old brother out of Cuba, telling us we were coming to Miami for the weekend. I arrived on Halloween, which is what *Once Removed* is about. We lived with my aunt and uncle. They were very young, in their twenties, and were suddenly faced with all these kids. They had two of their own, and then I and my brother and two cousins arrived. They didn't have any money, so they went through some rough times. We had to move out of places in the middle of the night.

My parents came a year later. My father couldn't find work in Florida, so we went to California—the Catholic church had a house in Canoga Park for us. My mother was pregnant when she came here; she had that kid and got pregnant again about five months later, so we quickly became a lot of people.

In Florida I was thrown into a public school instantly. It was a weird, unsettling time; I didn't speak any English at all. There were a lot of Cuban kids, though, people to talk to. In California I still didn't speak English, and there wasn't *anybody*—Chicanos refused to speak to us. Plus everyone in Canoga Park thought we were Communists. But I loved living there, because we were in complete seclusion. I feel the same happiness when I'm in a tech rehearsal. I could spend time with my parents, it was the first and only year there weren't a lot of other people around.

I went to Van Nuys High School. I was a terrible student, except in Shakespeare. When I was in elementary school I read all the books in the library on English kings, including the works of Shakespeare. I must have read every play there was to read. I was always making up stories and acting them out. The first play I ever saw was *Hallelujah, Baby!*, when I was fourteen. I thought it was wonderful. Then when I was sixteen I lived with my aunt in New York for a year, and went to the theatre every day.

I attended college about four months, then later went to acting school. I had no interest in anything except theatre. At twenty I was a stage manager for the Bilingual Foundation of the Arts at the Inner City Cultural Center in Los Angeles. It was a great place; anybody could do anything they wanted. I stage-managed a wonderful production of *House of Bernarda Alba*. In that job you really learn how a play works.

I knew some actors who were at Padua Hills Playwrights' Festival its first summer, 1978. They said, "There's this woman, this Cuban woman, who's a writer. You should meet her." So I went to Padua and met Irene Fornes. I spent the whole next summer with her, working as her assistant on *Fefu and Her Friends*. She taught me more about playwriting than anyone had ever taught me about anything. The following summer I was acting at Padua. During a rehearsal break I went in a room where Irene was giving a workshop. She said, "If you're going to sit you have to write something." So I did. Being around all those writers made me realize it was something I could do.

Once I started writing I couldn't

stop. I had never fulfilled myself acting; I could never really identify with the people I had to play. I came to New York, got an NEA fellowship and gave up everything else to write. I was part of the INTAR workshop its first year. But Irene and I also met every day— I lived across the street from her—and wrote for hours, just the two of us, at little tables. I wrote *Modern Ladies* that year, and *Rosario and the Gypsies*, and half of *Broken Eggs*. I rewrote *Fabiola*. I wrote three more plays I just found last night. It was incredible. It was total addiction. In the middle of it I remember going to the supermarket and not being able to figure out what milk was. From then on there was no turning back.

What disappointed me was that I wanted so much to be avant-garde—the acting I had done was in avant-garde theatre—and I was writing plays that Ensemble Studio Theatre was interested in doing. I would go to the EST playwrights' meetings and just go crazy. They were talking about the "well-made play" while Irene was going right over the wall. None of the EST people could figure out why they were blocked up, and I wasn't. They were trapped within all these rules, while those of us in Irene's workshop had lost the sense of censorship. If I hadn't met Irene I would never have been a writer. No one would have given me that security.

The other really important thing that happened to me was marrying somebody who is Jewish and not right-wing like my parents. Harriett has taught me a thought process that has nothing to do with being Catholic or Spanish. That's one of the reasons I can write plays about Cuba that question the society. The problem of most Hispanic-American theatre, until recently, was that it embraced stereotypes.

The first scene I wrote for *Broken Eggs*, I wrote in Irene's class. One of my sisters was married the day before I left for New York, several years earlier. My parents had divorced when I was twenty-one—the only people in the family who have ever gotten a divorce—and my father had remarried. I was awful, at that wedding. We were all awful. All of a sudden we had to be together, pretending nothing was wrong. I had this thought about all us kids in the family marrying Jewish people—it's as close as we can get to WASPs. That struck me as really funny. But the wedding was also an emotional occasion for me—I hadn't seen my grandfather or my aunt in a long time. In the workshop one day I started writing a scene between my mother and my aunt. My aunt was saying, "Sometimes I think I lived at the same time there as here, and I left the dual spirit there," which was something I always felt. When my grandfather died, on the way to the cemetery I actually did hallucinate that I was in Cuba. So I knew from the start how the play would end. I didn't want it to be about me, so I turned myself into a minor character.

I had always believed the myth that family is family and they care about you more than anybody else, until I came to live in New York. I was broke and called every person in my family, and no one would send me money. They didn't approve of what I was doing. I wound up wondering how we deteriorated to that point. Because the obligations were so intense in a place like Cuba, family really was family there. But time does make a difference, people drift apart. My sister's wedding was the perfect setting for what I wanted to explore.

# Biographical Information

In addition to the Floating Islands trilogy, Eduardo Machado's plays include *Rosario and the Gypsies*, *Why to Refuse*, *Once Removed*, *Related Retreats* and two works written with Geraldine Sherman, *When It's Over* and *The Perfect Light*. In 1987 *Sweet Powder* was commissioned by South Coast Repertory and *Finding Your Way* by Theatre for a New Audience. Theatre Communications Group's Hispanic Translation Project and the Mark Taper Forum have commissioned his translation of Cabrujas' *El dia que me quieras*.

Machado has received three National Endowment for the Arts fellowships and a Rockefeller grant. He is a member of New Dramatists.

# About the Play

*Broken Eggs* is the third play of the Floating Islands trilogy, which begins with *The Modern Ladies of Guanabacoa*, set in Cuba in the 1920s and '30s, and continues with *Fabiola*, which takes place during the 1950s and '60s, also in Cuba. First produced by New York's Ensemble Studio Theatre in 1984, under the direction of James Hammerstein, *Broken Eggs* has also been seen at Stage One in Dallas. The Spanish version, entitled *Revoltillo*, will begin performances at New York's Repertorio Español this fall. *Broken Eggs* was part of TCG's *Plays in Process* series in 1984.

# Characters

SONIA MARQUEZ HERNANDEZ, a Cuban woman
LIZETTE, Sonia's daughter, 19 years old
MIMI, Sonia's daughter
OSCAR, Sonia's son
MANUELA RIPOL, Sonia's mother
OSVALDO MARQUEZ, Sonia's ex-husband
MIRIAM MARQUEZ, Osvaldo's sister
ALFREDO MARQUEZ, Osvaldo's and Miriam's father

# Time and Place

A hot January day, 1979. A country club in Woodland Hills, California, a suburb of Los Angeles.

# The Play

# Broken Eggs

*For Jamie and Dena.*
*And to Harriett, Gilda*
*and their daughters.*

### ACT ONE

*A waiting room off the main ballroom of a country club in Woodland Hills,*
*California, a suburb of Los Angeles. The room is decorated for a wedding. Up*
*center, sliding glass doors leading to the outside; stage right, a hallway leading*
*to the dressing room; stage left, an archway containing the main entrance to the*
*room and a hallway leading to the ballroom. A telephone booth in one corner.*
*Two round tables, one set with coffee service and the other for the cake.*
*In the dark, we hear Mimi whistling the wedding march. As the lights come*
*up, Lizette is practicing walking down the aisle. Mimi is drinking a Tab and*
*watching Lizette. They are both dressed in casual clothes.*

MIMI: I never thought that any of us would get married, after all—
LIZETTE: Pretend you come from a happy home.
MIMI: We were the audience to one of the worst in the history of the arrangement.
LIZETTE: Well, I'm going to pretend that Mom and Dad are together for today . . .
MIMI: That's going to be hard to do if that mustached bitch, whore, cunt, Argenti-
nian Nazi shows up to your wedding.
LIZETTE: Daddy promised me that his new wife had no wish to be here. She's not
going to interfere. *(Mimi starts to gag)* Mimi, why are you doing this.
MIMI: The whole family is going to be here.

LIZETTE: They're our family. Don't vomit again, Mimi, my wedding.

MANUELA (*Offstage*): Why didn't the bakery deliver it?

MIMI: Oh, no!

LIZETTE: Oh my God.

*Mimi and Lizette run to the offstage dressing room.*

MANUELA (*Offstage*): Who ever heard of getting up at 6 A.M.?

SONIA (*Offstage*): Mama, please—

*Manuela and Sonia enter. Sonia is carrying two large cake boxes. Manuela carries a third cake box.*

MANUELA: Well, why didn't they?

SONIA: Because the Cuban bakery only delivers in downtown L.A. They don't come out this far.

*Manuela and Sonia start to assemble the cake.*

MANUELA: Then Osvaldo should have picked it up.

SONIA: It was my idea.

MANUELA: He should still pick it up, he's the man.

SONIA: He wanted to get a cake from this place, with frosting on it. But I wanted a cake to be covered with meringue, like mine.

MANUELA: You let your husband get away with everything.

SONIA: I didn't let him have a mistress.

MANUELA: Silly girl, she ended up being his wife!

SONIA: That won't last forever.

MANUELA: You were better off with a mistress. Now you're the mistress.

SONIA: Please, help me set up the cake. . . . Osvaldo thought we should serve the cake on paper plates. I said no. There's nothing worse than paper plates. They only charge a dime a plate for the real ones and twenty dollars for the person who cuts it. I never saw a paper plate till I came to the USA.

MANUELA: She used witchcraft to take your husband away, and you did nothing.

SONIA: I will.

MANUELA: Then put powder in his drinks, like the lady told you to do.

SONIA: I won't need magic to get him back, Mama, don't put powders in his drink. It'll give him indigestion.

MANUELA: Don't worry.

SONIA: Swear to me. On my father's grave.

*The cake is now assembled.*

MANUELA: I swear by the Virgin Mary, Saint Teresa my patron saint and all the Saints, that I will not put anything into your husband's food . . . as long as his slut does not show up. Here. (*She hands Sonia a little bottle*)

SONIA: No.

MANUELA: In case you need it.

SONIA: I won't.

MANUELA: You might want it later. It also gives you diarrhea for at least three months. For love, you kiss the bottle, and thank the Virgin Mary. For diarrhea, you do the sign of the cross twice.

SONIA: All right.

MANUELA: If your father was alive, he'd shoot him for you.

SONIA: That's true.

MANUELA: Help me roll the cake out.

SONIA: No. They'll do it. They're getting the room ready now. They don't want us in there. We wait here—the groom's family across the way.

MANUELA: The Jews.

SONIA: The Rifkins. Then we make our entrance—

MANUELA: I see—

SONIA (*Looks at cake*): Perfect. Sugary and white . . . pure.

MANUELA: Beautiful.

SONIA: I'm getting nervous.

MANUELA: It's your daughter's wedding. A very big day in a mother's life, believe me.

SONIA: Yes, a wedding is a big day.

MANUELA: The day you got married your father told me, "We are too far away from our little girl." I said to him, "But, Oscar, we live only a mile away." He said, "You know that empty acre on the street where she lives now?" I said "Yes." He said, "I bought it and we are building another house there, then we can still be near our little girl."

SONIA: He loved me.

MANUELA: Worshipped you.

SONIA: I worshipped him. He'll be proud.

MANUELA: Where's your ex-husband, he's late.

*Lizette enters and makes herself a cup of coffee. Sonia helps her.*

SONIA: So how do you feel, Lizette, my big girl?

LIZETTE: I'm shaking.

MANUELA: That's good. You should be scared.

LIZETTE: Why, Grandma?

MANUELA: You look dark, did you sit out in the sun again?

LIZETTE: Yes, I wanted to get a tan.

MANUELA: Men don't like that, Lizette.

LIZETTE: How do you know?

SONIA: Mama, people like tans in America.

MANUELA: Men like women with white skin.

LIZETTE: That's a lie. They don't.

MANUELA: Don't talk back to me like that.

SONIA: No fights today, please, no fights. Lizette, tell her you're sorry. I'm nervous. I don't want to get a migraine, I want to enjoy today.

LIZETTE: Give me a kiss, Grandma. *(They kiss)* Everything looks so good.

SONIA: It should—eight thousand dollars.

MANUELA: We spent more on your wedding and that was twenty-nine years ago. He should spend money on his daughter.

SONIA: He tries. He's just weak.

MANUELA: Don't defend him.

SONIA: I'm not.

MANUELA: Hate him. Curse him.

SONIA: I love him.

MANUELA: Sonia! Control yourself.

LIZETTE: He's probably scared to see everybody.

MANUELA: Good, the bastard.

*Lizette exits to dressing room.*

SONIA: Did I do a good job? Are you pleased by how it looks? *(She looks at the corsages and boutonnieres on a table)* Purples, pinks and white ribbons . . . tulle. Mama, Alfredo, Pedro. . . . No, not Pedro's . . . Oscar's. . . . He just looks like Pedro. Pedro! He got lost. He lost himself and then we lost him.

MANUELA: Sonia!

SONIA: I'll pin yours on, Mama.

MANUELA: Later, it'll wilt if you pin it now.

*Miriam enters. She is wearing a beige suit and a string of pearls.*

SONIA: Miriam, you're here on time. Thank you, Miriam.

MIRIAM: Sonia, look. *(Points at pearls)* They don't match. That means expensive. I bought them for the wedding.

MANUELA: Miriam, how pretty you look!

MIRIAM: Do you think the Jews will approve?

MANUELA: They're very nice, the Rifkins. They don't act Jewish. Lizette told me they put up a Christmas tree but what for I said to her?

MIRIAM: To fit in?

MANUELA: Why? Have you seen your brother?

MIRIAM: He picked us up last night from the airport . . .

MANUELA: Did he say anything to you?

MIRIAM: Yes, how old he's getting. . . . That's all he talks about.

MANUELA: Where's your husband?

MIRIAM: He couldn't come: business.

MANUELA: That's a mistake.

MIRIAM: I'm glad I got away.

MANUELA: But is he glad to be rid of you?

SONIA: Mama, go and see if Lizette needs help, please.

MANUELA: All right. Keep your husband happy, that's the lesson to learn from all this. Keep them happy. Let them have whatever they want. . . . Look at Sonia. *(She exits to dressing room)*

SONIA: Thank God for a moment of silence. Osvaldo this, Osvaldo that. Powder Curse him. Poisons, shit . . .

MIRIAM: Are you all right? That faggot brother of mine is not worth one more tear: coward, mongoloid, retarded creep.

SONIA: Does he look happy to you?

MIRIAM: No.

SONIA: He looks sad?

MIRIAM: He always looked sad. Now he looks old and sad.

SONIA: Fear?

MIRIAM: Doesn't the Argentinian make him feel brave?

SONIA: He'll be mine again. He'll remember what it was like before the revolution. Alfredo and you being here will remind him of that. He'll remember our wedding—how perfect it was; how everything was right . . . the party, the limo, walking through the rose garden late at night, sleeping in the terrace room. I'm so hot I feel like I have a fever.

MIRIAM: "My darling children, do not go near the water, the sharks will eat you up." That's the lesson we were taught.

SONIA: Today I am going to show Osvaldo who's in control. Be nice to him today.

MIRIAM: He left you three months after your father died. He went because he knew you had no defense. He went off with that twenty-nine-year-old wetback. You know, we *had* to come here, but they *want* to come here. And you still want him back?

SONIA: If he apologizes, yes.

MIRIAM: Don't hold your breath. He lets everyone go. Pedro needed him—

SONIA: Don't accuse him of that, he just forgot—

MIRIAM: What? How could he forget. Pedro was our brother.

SONIA: He got so busy here working, that he forgot, he couldn't help him anyway. He was here, Pedro stayed in Cuba, you were in Miami, and I don't think anyone should blame anyone about that. No one was to blame!

MIRIAM: Oh, I'm having an attack . . . *(She shows Sonia her hands)* See how I'm shaking? It's like having a seizure. Where's water? *(Sonia gets her a glass of water. She takes two valium)* You take one, too.

SONIA: No. Thank you.

*Mimi enters, goes to the pay phone, dials.*

MIRIAM: A valium makes you feel like you are floating in a warm beach.

SONIA: Varadero?

MIRIAM: Varadero, the Gulf of Mexico, Santa María del Mar. It's because of these little pieces of magic that I escaped from the path. I did not follow the steps of my brothers and end up an alcoholic.

SONIA: Osvaldo never drank a lot.

MIRIAM: You forget.

SONIA: Well, drinking was not the problem.

MANUELA (Entering): I made Mimi call the brothel to see why your husband's late.

MIRIAM: Where's Lizette?

MANUELA: Down the hall. It says "Dressing Room."

MIRIAM: I got five hundred dollars, brand-new bills. (She exits)

SONIA: The world I grew up in is out of style; will we see it again, Mama?

MIMI (Comes out of phone booth): She answered. She said "Yes?" I said "Where's my father?" She said "Gone." I said "Already!" She said "I'm getting ready for. . . ." I said "For what? Your funeral?" She hung up on me. She sounded stoned . . .

MANUELA: Sonia, someday it will be reality again, I promise.

MIMI: What?

SONIA: Cuba. Cuba will be a reality.

MIMI: It was and is a myth. Your life there is mythical.

MANUELA: That's not true. Her life was perfect. In the mornings, after she was married, Oscar would get up at six-thirty and send one of his bus drivers ten miles to Guanabacoa to buy bread from her favorite bakery, to buy bread for his little married girl.

SONIA: At around nine, I would wake up and walk out the door through the yard to the edge of the rose garden and call, "Papa, my bread."

MANUELA: The maid would run over, cross the street and hand her two pieces of hot buttered bread . . .

SONIA: I'd stick my hand through the gate and she'd hand me the bread. I'd walk back—into Alfredo's kitchen, and my coffee and milk would be waiting for me.

MIMI: Did you read the paper?

SONIA: The papers? I don't think so.

MIMI: Did you think about the world?

SONIA: No. I'd just watch your father sleep and eat my breakfast.

MANUELA: Every morning, "Papa, my bread." (She goes to the outside doors and stays there, staring out)

MIMI: You will never see it again. Even if you do go back, you will seem out of place; it will never be the same.

SONIA: No? You never saw it.

MIMI: And I will never see it.

SONIA: Never say never—

MIMI: What do you mean "Never say never"?!

SONIA: Never say never. Never is not real. It is a meaningless word. Always is a word that means something. Everything will happen always. The things that you feared and made your hands shake with horror, and you thought "not to me," will happen always.

MIMI: Stop it!

SONIA: I have thoughts, ideas. Just because I don't speak English well doesn't mean that I don't have feelings. A voice—a voice that thinks, a mind that talks.

MIMI: I didn't say that.

SONIA: So never say never, dear. Be ready for anything. Don't die being afraid. Don't, my darling.

MIMI: So simple.

*Miriam enters.*

SONIA: Yes, very simple, darling.

MIRIAM: What was simple?

SONIA: Life, when we were young.

MIRIAM: A little embarrassing, a little dishonest, but without real care; that's true. A few weeks ago I read an ad. It said "Liberate Cuba through the power of Voodoo." There was a picture of Fidel's head with three pins stuck through his temples.

MANUELA: They should stick pins in his penis.

SONIA: Mama! *(She laughs)*

MANUELA: Bastard.

MIRIAM: The idea was that if thousands of people bought the product, there would be a great curse that would surely kill him—all that for only $11.99. Twelve dollars would be all that was needed to overthrow the curse of our past.

*Lizette enters wearing a robe.*

MANUELA: We should try everything, anything.

LIZETTE: Today is my wedding, it is really happening in an hour, here, in Woodland Hills, California, Los Angeles. The United States of America, 1979. No Cuba today please, no Cuba today.

SONIA: Sorry.

MIMI: You want all the attention.

SONIA: Your wedding is going to be perfect. We are going to win this time.

LIZETTE: Win what?

MANUELA: The battle.

MIRIAM: "Honest woman" versus the "whore."

MIMI: But who's the "honest woman" and who's the "whore"?

MANUELA: Whores can be easily identified—they steal husbands.

MIRIAM: They're from Argentina.

SONIA: They say "yes" to everything. The good ones say "no."

LIZETTE: And we're the good ones.

SONIA: Yes. I am happy today. You are the bride, the wedding decorations came out perfect and we are having a party. Oo, oo, oo, oo, oo . . . *uh.*

*The women all start doing the conga in a circle. They sing. Osvaldo enters.*

Join the line.

LIZETTE: In back of me, Daddy.

MIRIAM: In front of me, Osvaldo.

*They dance. Miriam gooses Osvaldo.*

OSVALDO: First I kiss my daughter— *(He kisses Lizette)* then my other little girl— *(He kisses Mimi)* then my sister— *(He and Miriam blow each other a kiss)* —then my wife. *(He kisses Sonia)*

SONIA: Your old wife.

OSVALDO: My daughter's mother.

SONIA: That's right.

*Miriam lights a cigarette and goes outside.*

MIMI: We were together once, family: my mom, my dad, my big sister, my big brother. We ate breakfast and dinner together and drove down to Florida on our vacations, looked at pictures of Cuba together.

SONIA: And laughed, right?

MIMI: And then Papa gave us up.

OSVALDO: I never gave you up.

MIMI: To satisfy his urge.

MANUELA: Stop right now.

OSVALDO: Don't ever talk like that again.

SONIA: Isn't it true?

OSVALDO: It's more complex than that.

SONIA: More complex—how? No, stop.

LIZETTE: Please stop.

MANUELA: Don't fight.

MIMI: You see, Daddy, I understand you.

OSVALDO: You don't.

MIMI: I try.

OSVALDO: So do I.

MIMI: You don't.

OSVALDO: I'm going outside.

LIZETTE: Come, sit with me.

SONIA: You have to start getting dressed.

LIZETTE: Thank you for making *me* happy.

OSVALDO: I try.

*Lizette and Osvaldo exit to dressing room.*

SONIA: Mimi, no more today. Please, no more.

MIMI: When you're born the third child, the marriage is already half apart, and being born into a family that's half over, half apart, is a disturbing thing to live with.

SONIA: Where did you read that?

MIMI: I didn't read it. It's my opinion. Based on my experience, of my life.

SONIA: We were never half apart.

MIMI: No, but that's what it felt like.

MANUELA: It's unheard of. It's unbelievable—

MIMI: What is she talking about now?

MANUELA: A Catholic does not get a divorce. They have a mistress and a wife but no divorce, a man does not leave everything.

SONIA (*To Mimi*): As difficult as it might be for you to understand, we were together, and a family when you were born. I wanted, we wanted, to have you. We had just gotten to the U.S., Lizette was ten months old. Your father had gotten his job as an accountant. We lived behind a hamburger stand between two furniture stores, away from everything we knew, afraid of everything around us. We were alone, no one spoke Spanish. Half of the people thought we were Communist, the other half traitors to a great cause; three thousand miles away from our real lives. But I wanted you and we believed in each other more than ever before. We were all we had.

MIMI: I wish it would have always stayed like that.

SONIA: So do I.

MANUELA: In Cuba, not in California, we want our Cuba back.

MIMI: It's too late for that, Grandma.

MANUELA: No.

MIMI: They like their government.

MANUELA: Who?

MIMI: The people who live there like socialism.

MANUELA: No. Who told you that?

MIMI: He's still in power, isn't he?

MANUELA: Because he oppresses them. He has the guns, Fidel has the bullets. Not the people. He runs the concentration camps. He has Russia behind him. China. We have nothing behind us. My cousins are starving there.

MIMI: At least they know who they are.

MANUELA: You don't? Well, I'll tell you. You're Manuela Sonia Marquez Hernández. A Cuban girl. Don't forget what I just told you.

MIMI: No, Grandma. I'm Manuela Sonia Marquez, better known as Mimi Mar-kwez. I was born in Canoga Park. I'm a first-generation white Hispanic American.

MANUELA: No you're not. You're a Cuban girl. Memorize what I just told you.

*Lizette and Osvaldo enter. Lizette is in her bra and slip.*

LIZETTE: My dress, Mama, help me, time to dress.

SONIA: The bride is finally ready, Mama, help me dress her in her wedding dress. Miriam, Mimi, she's going to put on her wedding dress.

*Miriam enters.*

MANUELA: You're going to look beautiful.

SONIA: And happy, right, dear?

LIZETTE: I'm happy. This is a happy day, like they tell you in church, your baptism, your first communion and your wedding. Come on, Mimi.

*All the women except Sonia exit to dressing room.*

SONIA: That's how I felt. I felt just like her.

OSVALDO: When, Sonia?

SONIA: Twenty-nine years ago.

*Sonia exits to dressing room. Osvaldo goes to the bar and pours himself a double of J&B. Alfredo enters.*

ALFREDO: You the guard?

OSVALDO: No.

ALFREDO: Drinking so early in the morning.

OSVALDO: My nerves, Daddy.

ALFREDO: Nervous, you made your bed, lie in it.

OSVALDO: I do. I do lie in it.

ALFREDO: So don't complain.

OSVALDO: I'm just nervous, little Lizette is a woman now.

ALFREDO: You're lucky.

OSVALDO: Why?

ALFREDO: She turned out to be decent.

OSVALDO: Why wouldn't she?

ALFREDO: In America it's hard to keep girls decent, especially after what you did.

OSVALDO: I never deserted them.

ALFREDO: But divorce, you're an idiot. Why get married twice, once is enough. You can always have one on the side and keep your wife. But to marry your mistress is stupid, crazy and foolish. It's not done, son. It's not decent.

OSVALDO: And you know a lot about decency?!

ALFREDO: I stayed married.

OSVALDO: Daddy, she loved me. I loved her. We couldn't be away from each other. She left her husband.

ALFREDO: She wanted your money.

OSVALDO: What money?

ALFREDO: To a little immigrant you're Rockefeller.

OSVALDO: Women only wanted you for your money.

ALFREDO: I know. And I knew how to use my position.

OSVALDO: She loves me.

ALFREDO: Good, she loves you—you should have taken her out dancing. Not married her.

OSVALDO: I did what I wanted to do, that's all.

ALFREDO: You did what your mistress wanted you to do. That is all.

OSVALDO: I wanted to marry her. That's why I did it. I just didn't do what my family thought I was supposed to do.

ALFREDO: You're still a silly boy. *(Looking at wedding decorations and cake)* Well, very nice. Sonia still has taste.

OSVALDO: Yes, she does.

ALFREDO: When she was young I was always impressed by the way she dressed, by the way she looked, how she spoke. The way she treated my servants, my guests.

OSVALDO: She was very well brought up.

ALFREDO: Now your new one is common, right?

OSVALDO: She loves me. Respect her, please.

ALFREDO: So did Sonia. The only thing the new one had to offer is that she groans a little louder and played with your thing a little longer, right?

OSVALDO: That's not true.

ALFREDO: Boring you after five years?

OSVALDO: . . . A little.

ALFREDO: Then why?

*Lizette enters. She is dressed in her bride's dress.*

LIZETTE: I'm ready for my photographs, Bride and Father.

OSVALDO: You look better than Elizabeth Taylor in *Father of the Bride.*

ALFREDO: Sweetheart, you look beautiful.

LIZETTE: Thank you. He took pictures of Mama dressing me, putting on my veil. Now he wants pictures of you and me—than Mama, you and me—then Grandpa, you and me and Miriam—then Mama and me and Grandma—then with Mimi, et cetera, et cetera, et cetera, et cetera; all the combinations that make up my family.

OSVALDO: Are you excited?

LIZETTE: Yes, I am. And nervous, Daddy, I'm so excited and nervous.

SONIA *(Enters)*: Time for the pictures, Mimi will call me when he needs me again.

OSVALDO: Do I look handsome?

ALFREDO: Look at this place, beautiful, Sonia, a beautiful job. *(He gives Sonia a little kiss)*

SONIA: Thank you.

ALFREDO: She knows how to throw parties. Hmmm, Osvaldo, with taste. With class.

OSVALDO: With class.

SONIA: Osvaldo, come here a moment. Pin my corsage. *(Osvaldo goes over to the table with the corsages on it)* I bought myself a purple orchid. It goes with the dress. I bought your wife the one with the two white gardenias. I figured she'd be wearing white, trying to compete with the bride. She's so young and pure, hmmm . . . *(She laughs)*

OSVALDO: She's not coming.

SONIA: It was a joke; I was making a little joke. I can joke about it now. Laugh. Did you dream about me again last night?

OSVALDO: Shh. Not in front of Lizette.

SONIA: I want to.

OSVALDO: We spent too much money on this, don't you think?

SONIA: No, I don't. I could have used more. Mama said they spent twice as much on our wedding.

OSVALDO: Did you tell them the exact number of people that RSVP'd so that we don't have to pay money for extra food?

SONIA: Lizette did, I can't communicate with them, my English—

OSVALDO: Your English is fine. I don't want to spend extra money.

SONIA: How much did you spend on your last wedding?

OSVALDO: She paid for it, she saved her money. She works, you know. She wanted a fancy wedding. I already had one. A sixteen-thousand-dollar one, according to your mother.

SONIA: Didn't *she*? Or was she not married to the guy she left for you?

OSVALDO: She was married. She doesn't live with people.

SONIA: Fool. When you got near fifty you turned into a fool; a silly, stupid, idiotic fool.

LIZETTE: No fights today.

*Osvaldo and Lizette start to exit.*

SONIA: I'm sorry. I swear, no fights . . . Osvaldo . . .

OSVALDO: Yes?

SONIA: You look debonair.

OSVALDO: Thank you, Sonia.

ALFREDO: Don't let it go to your head.

OSVALDO: You look magnifique.

SONIA: Thank you, Osvaldo.

*Lizette and Osvaldo exit to ballroom.*

ALFREDO: Don't let it go to your head.

SONIA: He's insecure, about his looks.

ALFREDO: I tried to talk some sense into my son.

SONIA: Today we'll be dancing every dance together, in front of everybody. And I'll be the wife again. Divorces don't really count for Catholics. We're family, him and me.

ALFREDO: When you married him and moved in with us, I always thought you were like brother and sister.

SONIA: No, lovers. Stop teasing me. He's my only friend.

ALFREDO: Even now?

SONIA: Always, Alfredo, forever.

MIRIAM (*Enters from ballroom*): Sonia, your turn for more snapshots—Father, Mother and Bride.

SONIA: She's happy, don't you think?

MIRIAM: The bride is in heaven.

SONIA: Excuse me, Alfredo, if you want breakfast, ask the waiter.

*Sonia exits. Miriam sits down. Alfredo looks at the coffee and sits down.*

ALFREDO: Go get me a cup of coffee.

MIRIAM: No. Call the waiter, he'll get it for you.

ALFREDO: You do it for me.

MIRIAM: No.

ALFREDO: When did you stop talking to waiters?

MIRIAM: When I started talking to the gardener.

ALFREDO: What a sense of humor! What wit! What a girl, my daughter.

MIRIAM: Ruthless, like her dad.

ALFREDO: Exactly like me; you need to conquer. Go! Make sure it's hot! (*Miriam pours the coffee*) If I were your husband I'd punish you every night: no money for you, no vacations, no cars, no credit cards, no pills, no maid. The way you exhibit yourself in your "see-through blouses" with no bras, and your skimpy bikinis.

MIRIAM (*Teasing Alfredo*): Ooooh!

ALFREDO: How many horns did you put on his head?

MIRIAM: It excites him.

ALFREDO: That's not true.

MIRIAM: He feels lucky when he gets me, that I did not wither like all the other girls from my class, from our country, with their backward ways. Sugar, Daddy?

ALFREDO: Two lumps. No, three, and plenty of milk.

MIRIAM: There's only cream.

ALFREDO: Yes, cream is fine.

MIRIAM: Here, Daddy.

ALFREDO (*Takes one sip and puts coffee down*): What a vile taste American coffee has.

MIRIAM: I'm used to it, less caffeine.

ALFREDO: You did keep in shape.

*Mimi enters from ballroom in her bridesmaid's gown.*

MIRIAM: So did you. Greed and lust keep us in shape.

MIMI: Grandpa, your turn. Both sets of grandparents, the Cubans and the Jews, the bride and the groom.

ALFREDO: How do I look, sweetheart?

MIMI: Dandy, Grandpa, dandy.

*Alfredo exits.*

Who do you lust after?

MIRIAM: Your father.

MIMI: Your own brother?!

MIRIAM: I was joking—your father's too old now. Your brother, maybe.

MIMI: You are wild.

MIRIAM: If I would have been born in this country, to be a young girl in this country, without eyes staring at you all the time. To have freedom. I would never have gotten married. I wanted to be a tightrope walker in the circus . . . that's what I would have wanted.

MIMI: I never feel free.

Eduardo Machado

MIRIAM: Do you get to go to a dance alone?

MIMI: Naturally.

MIRIAM: Then you have more freedom than I ever did.

MIMI: How awful for you.

MIRIAM: It made you choke, you felt strangled.

MIMI: What did you do?

MIRIAM: I found revenge.

MIMI: How?

MIRIAM: I'll tell you about it, one day, when there's more time.

MIMI: Can I ask you a question? Something that I wonder about? Did Uncle Pedro kill himself, was it suicide? Did Grandpa have mistresses?

MIRIAM: How do you know?

MIMI: Information slips out in the middle of a fight.

MIRIAM: He drank himself to death.

MIMI: Oh, I thought he did it violently.

MIRIAM: And your grandpa had a whole whorehouse full of wives.

*Mimi and Miriam laugh.*

MIMI: I'm like Grandpa. I'm pregnant . . .

MIRIAM: Don't kid me.

MIMI: Aunt Miriam, I am.

MIRIAM: Oh God.

MIMI: What are you doing?

MIRIAM: I need this. *(She takes a valium)* Don't you use a pill?

MIMI: With my mother.

MIRIAM: I don't understand.

MIMI: She'd kill me.

MIRIAM: True. Why did you do it?

MIMI: Freedom.

MIRIAM: Stupidity.

MIMI: Will you help me?

*Oscar enters.*

MIRIAM: My God, a movie star.

OSCAR: No, just your nephew, Oscar.

MIRIAM: Your hair is combed. You cut your fingernails?

OSCAR: Better than that, a manicure. You two look sexy today.

MIRIAM: Thank you. She's not a virgin . . .

OSCAR: So?

MIMI: I'm pregnant—

MIRIAM: Don't tell him.

OSCAR: Oh, Mimi.

MIRIAM: What are you going to do?

OSCAR: Pretend she didn't say it. Poor Mimi.

MIMI: You're no saint.

OSCAR: I'm not pregnant.

MIMI: Not because you haven't tried.

OSCAR: Oh, I love *you.*

*Manuela enters.*

MIRIAM: You better not talk.

MANUELA: You're here. Good.

MIMI: If you tell her, I'll tell her you're a fruit.

OSCAR: I don't care.

MIMI: Swear.

OSCAR: I swear.

MANUELA: You look beautiful. Here, sit on my lap.

*Oscar sits on Manuela's lap.*

MIRIAM: He'll get wrinkled.

MIMI: This is revolting.

MANUELA: I promised your mother that we will be polite.

MIMI: The slut is not coming.

OSCAR: Good. A curse on Argentina.

MANUELA: Oscar, if you ever see her, it is your duty to kick her in the ass. But be good to your father today. It's not his fault. We all know that your father is a decent man. We all know that she got control of him with as they say "powders."

MIMI: I think they call it "blowing."

MANUELA: Blowing? She blowed-up his ego, is that what you think?

MIMI: Right.

MANUELA: No. You are wrong. She did it with drugs. But your mother wants you not to fight with your father. She wants him back.

OSCAR: I'll have to react however I feel.

MANUELA: Your mother is weak and she cannot take another emotional scene. And these Jewish people that Lizette is marrying would never understand about witchcraft, after all they don't even believe in Christ.

OSCAR: I can't promise anything.

MANUELA: Today will be a happy day. Lizette is marrying a nice boy, he's buying her a house. And your mother has a plan.

OSCAR: Right . . .

MANUELA: Right, Miriam?

MIRIAM: You're right. But if I ever see that Argentinian.

MANUELA: You're going to be a good girl, right Mimi?

MIMI: I'll do whatever the team decides.

OSCAR: Spoken like a true American.

SONIA (*Enters*): You made it in time for the pictures, thank God.

OSCAR: Do I have to pose with Dad?

SONIA: No fights.

OSCAR: All right. But I'm standing next to you.

SONIA: Thank you. Miriam, Mama, they want more pictures with you. And in ten minutes "The Family Portrait."

MIMI: That'll be a sight.

MANUELA: Is my hair all right?

SONIA: Yes. Here, put on your corsage.

MANUELA: Thank you.

MIRIAM: And for me?

SONIA: The gardenias.

*Miriam and Manuela exit.*

You look neat, Oscar. Thank God. The photographer suggested a family portrait, the entire family. He said it will be something we will cherish forever.

OSCAR: Why?

*Osvaldo enters.*

SONIA: Well, the family portrait will be a record, proof that we were really a family. That we really existed, Oscar. Oscar, my father's name.

OSCAR: I'm glad you named me after him and not Osvaldo.

SONIA: At first I thought of naming you after your father, but then I thought, "That's so old-fashioned, it's 1951, time for something new."

OSCAR: Good for you.

MIMI: What a sign of liberation.

OSVALDO: Oh?!

OSCAR: So . . . continue, Mama.

SONIA: You like the story?

OSCAR: Yes.

SONIA: You, Mimi?

MIMI: Fascinating.

SONIA: Well, and since your grandpa has no son, I named you after him.

OSCAR: I bet he liked that.

SONIA: It made him very happy. I keep thinking he'll show up today. He'll walk in soon, my father. "Papa do you like it?" And he would say . . .

MIMI: "We have to get back to Cuba."

OSCAR: "We have to fight!"

MIMI: "Where papayas grow as large as watermelons and guayabas and mangoes grow on trees. How could anyone starve in a place like that?"

OSVALDO: Then someone took it all away.

OSCAR: He had everything. He had pride, honor—

OSVALDO: True but someone took it away.

OSCAR: That doesn't matter.

OSVALDO: Well it does, he lost.

SONIA: You loved him, I know you did, everyone did.

OSVALDO: Yes, right, I did.

OSCAR: He fought and he knew what he believed in. He knew what his life was about.

OSVALDO: Maybe that's why he wanted to die.

SONIA: No, just a stroke.

*Pause.*

OSCAR: Daddy, do you like my suit?

OSVALDO: Well, it's really a sports coat and pants.

OSCAR: It's linen.

OSVALDO: It'll wrinkle.

OSCAR: I wanted to look nice.

SONIA: It does.

OSVALDO: It doesn't matter.

OSCAR: No, I don't suppose it really does.

OSVALDO: It means nothing.

OSCAR: What means something, Daddy?

OSVALDO: Columns that add up, neatly. Formulas where the answer is always guaranteed!

OSCAR: Guarantees mean something?!

OSVALDO: The answer. That's what means something.

OSCAR: Then I have a meaningless life.

OSVALDO: Stop it.

OSCAR: I never found any answers.

OSVALDO: Stop your melodrama.

OSCAR: I'm going to pretend you didn't say that. I'm twenty-eight years old and I refuse to get involved with you in the emotional ways that you used to abuse our relationship.

MIMI: Time for a Cuba Libre. *(She exits)*

OSVALDO: How much did that piece of dialogue cost me?

OSCAR: Let's stop.

OSVALDO: From which quack did you get that from?

OSCAR: From the one that told me you were in the closet.

OSVALDO: What closet?

*Sonia goes to check if anyone's listening.*

OSCAR: It's an expression they have in America for men who are afraid, no, they question, no, who fears that he wants to suck cock.

*Osvaldo slaps Oscar.*

OSVALDO: Control yourself, learn to control your tongue!

OSCAR: Did that one hit home?

OSVALDO: Spoiled brat.

OSCAR: Takes one to know one. God, I despise you.

OSVALDO: I'm ashamed of you, you're such a nervous wreck, all those doctors, all the money I spend.

OSCAR: Thanks, Daddy, I had such a fine example of Manhood from you.

OSVALDO: Bum!

OSCAR: Fool.

SONIA: You're both the same, you're both so selfish, think of Lizette, her fiancé's family, what if they hear this. Quiet!

OSCAR: Leave us alone.

SONIA: No. I belong in this argument too, I'm the mother and the wife.

OSCAR: The ex-wife, Mama.

SONIA: No, in this particular triangle, the wife.

OSCAR *(To Sonia)*: Your life is a failure.

OSVALDO: Because of you.

SONIA: Don't say that, Osvaldo. He's our son.

OSVALDO: He's just like you.

SONIA: What do you mean by that?!

OSVALDO: An emotional wreck.

OSCAR: That's better than being emotionally dead.

OSVALDO: I hate him.

SONIA: No. Osvaldo, how dare you! *(She cries)*

OSCAR: See what you've made, turned her into?!

OSVALDO: It's because of you.

SONIA: I refuse to be the cause of this fight, today we're having a wedding, so both of you smile.

OSVALDO: You're right, Sonia, I'm sorry.

OSCAR: God.

SONIA: I'm going to be with Lizette. You two control yourselves.

OSCAR *(Whispers)*: Faggot.

*Sonia exits.*

Sissy.

OSVALDO: I bet you know all about that?!

OSCAR: Yes, want to hear about it?

*Alfredo enters.*

OSVALDO: Not in front of your grandfather.

OSCAR: There's no way to talk to you, you petty bastard. *(He starts to cry)*

OSVALDO: Exactly like her, crying.

OSCAR *(Stops crying)*: Because we were both unfortunate enough to have to know you in an intimate way.

OSVALDO: Other people don't feel that way.

OSCAR: That's because they're made of ice. A lot of Nazis in Argentina.

OSVALDO: Your sister needs me today. I'm going to make sure she's happy. Men don't cry. Now stop it. (*He exits*)

OSCAR: Right.

ALFREDO: Be careful.

OSCAR: About what?

ALFREDO: You show too much. Be on your guard.

OSCAR: So what?

ALFREDO: You let him see too much of you.

OSCAR: He's my father.

ALFREDO: He's a man first, my son second, your father third.

OSCAR: That's how he feels? He told you that? Did he?!

ALFREDO: Be a little more like me. And a little less like your other grandfather. He's dead. I'm still alive.

OSCAR: He was ill. It wasn't his fault.

ALFREDO: He was a fool.

OSCAR: No. That's not true.

ALFREDO: He was foolish. He trusted mankind. Money made him flabby. He thought if you gave a starving man a plate of food, he thanks you. He didn't know that he also resents you, he also waits. No one wants to beg for food, it's humiliating.

OSCAR: Of course no one wants to.

ALFREDO: So they wait. And when they regain their strength, they stab you in the back.

OSCAR: How can you think that's true?!

ALFREDO: We are the proof of my theory—Cubans. He did it to us—Fidel, our neighbors, everybody. So never feed a hungry man.

OSCAR: You don't really believe that.

MIMI (*Enters*): The picture, Grandpa. Oscar, the family portrait!

ALFREDO: I'm on my way. Comb your hair. Fix your tie. Your suit is already wrinkled.

OSCAR: Real linen does that.

*Alfredo exits with Mimi. Oscar takes out a bottle of cocaine—the kind that premeasures a hit. He goes outside but leaves the entrance door open. He snorts.*

Ah, breakfast.

*Oscar snorts again. Osvaldo enters but does not see Oscar. He goes straight to the bar, comes back with a drink—a J&B double—and gulps it down. He looks at the corsages. We hear Oscar sniffing coke.*

OSVALDO (*To himself*): White, compete with the bride . . . very funny, Sonia.

SONIA (*Enters*): Osvaldo, we are waiting for you. The family portrait, come.

OSVALDO: No, I can't face them.

SONIA: Don't be silly.

OSVALDO: They love you. They hate me, my sister, my father, my children, they all hate me.

SONIA: They don't. No one hates their own family. It's a sin to hate people in your immediate family.

OSVALDO: They always hated me. Till I was seventeen I thought—

SONIA: That they had found you in a trash can, I know, Osvaldo. We need a record, a family portrait. The last one was taken at Oscar's seventh birthday. It's time for a new one.

OSVALDO: You don't need me.

SONIA: It wouldn't be one without you.

OSVALDO: For who?

SONIA: For everybody. Be brave. Take my hand. I won't bite. (Osvaldo holds her hand) After all, I'm the mother and you are the father of the bride.

OSCAR (Sticks his head in): The Argentinian just drove up.

OSVALDO: Liar.

OSCAR: She looks drunk.

OSVALDO: Liar.

OSCAR: What do they drink in Argentina?

SONIA: Behave!

*A car starts honking.*

OSCAR: Sounds like your car.

OSVALDO: How dare she. How can she humiliate me. How can she disobey me.

SONIA: Oscar go out and say your father is posing with his past family. Tell her that after the portrait is taken, she can come in.

OSCAR: But she has to sit in the back.

SONIA: No, I'm going to be polite. That's what I was taught.

OSVALDO: Go and tell her.

OSCAR: Remember Mama, I did it for you. (He exits)

OSVALDO: Thank you. Hold my hand.

SONIA: Kiss me.

OSVALDO: Here?

SONIA: Yes, today I'm the mother and the wife.

*Osvaldo and Sonia kiss.*

OSVALDO: You did a good job.

SONIA: You do like it?

OSVALDO: I mean with our daughters. They're good girls . . . like their mother.

SONIA: They have a good father.

OSVALDO: That's true.

*Osvaldo and Sonia exit, Oscar reenters.*

OSCAR: The family portrait? This family. . . . My family. The Father, Jesus Christ his only son and the Holy Ghost (*Crossing himself*) . . . why the *fuck* did you send me to this family.

*Blackout.*

END OF ACT ONE

# ACT TWO

*Afternoon. Offstage, the band is playing "Snow," an Argentinian folksong, and a woman is singing. Miriam is in the phone booth. Mimi is looking at the bridal bouquet and pulling it apart. Sonia enters eating cake.*

WOMAN'S VOICE *(Singing offstage)*:
Don't sing brother, don't sing,
I hear Moscow is covered with snow.
And the wolves run away out of hunger.
Don't sing 'cause Olga's not coming.

Even if the sun shines again.
Even if the snow falls again.
Even if the sun shines again.
Even if the snow falls again.

Walking to Siberia tomorrow, oh,
Out goes the caravan,
Who knows if the sun
Will light our march of horror.

While in Moscow, my Olga, perhaps,
To another, her love she surrenders.
Don't sing brothers, don't sing.
For God's sake, oh God, no.

United by chains to the steppes
A thousand leagues we'll go walking.
Walking to Siberia, no.
Don't sing, I am filled with pain.
And Moscow is covered with snow.
And the snow has entered my soul.
Moscow now covered with snow.
And the snow has entered my soul.

SONIA: It's insult to injury an Argentinian song about going to Siberia, Russia. Moscow is covered with snow . . . what do Argentinians know about Moscow? I wish she'd go to Siberia tomorrow. *(To Mimi)* They are walking a thousand leagues to their exile . . . I took a plane ride ninety-nine miles, a forty-five minute excursion to my doom.

MIRIAM *(To phone)*: No, shit no! Liars.

SONIA: Don't sing, Sonia . . . *(She sings)* 'cause Moscow is covered with snow, right Mimi?

MIMI: Right.

SONIA: When I first got here this place looked to me like a farm town. Are you happy, dear?

MIMI: I don't think so.

SONIA: No, say yes!

MIMI: Yes.

SONIA: That's good.

MIMI: Ciao!

*Mimi runs to the bathroom to puke. Osvaldo enters.*

SONIA: So, you had to play a song for her?

OSVALDO: She told the band she wanted to sing it. But it's the only Argentinian song they know.

SONIA: Good for the band! Remember when we thought Fidel was going to send us to Russia, to Moscow? Siberia, Siberia, this place is like Siberia!

OSVALDO: It's too warm to be Siberia. *(He kisses Sonia passionately)* It was a beautiful ceremony. *(He kisses her again)*

SONIA: Dance with me. Tell them to play a danzón.

OSVALDO: Let's dance in here.

SONIA: She'll get angry? It's our daughter's wedding.

OSVALDO: She's my wife.

SONIA: I was first.

OSVALDO: You're both my wife.

*Osvaldo and Sonia dance.*

SONIA: Before my sixteenth birthday your family moved to Cojimar . . . your cousin brought you to the club.

OSVALDO: You were singing a Rita Hayworth song called "Put the Blame on . . . Me"?

SONIA: No, "Mame". . . . I was imitating her . . . did I look ridiculous?

OSVALDO: No!

SONIA *(Starts to do Rita's number, substituting "Cuban" for "Frisco")*:
    Put the blame on Mame, boys
    Put the blame on Mame
    One night she started to shim and shake
    That began the Cuban quake
    So-o-o, put the blame on Mame, boys
    Put the blame on Mame . . .

OSVALDO: You look sexy.

SONIA: I let you kiss me, then you became part of the club.

OSVALDO: On your seventeenth birthday I married you.

SONIA: Well, I kissed you.

OSVALDO: Was I the only one?

SONIA: Yes.

OSVALDO: And by your eighteenth birthday we had Oscar. I should go back to the party. She'll start looking for me.

SONIA: Tell her to relax. Tell the band to stop playing that stupid song. I want to dance. I want more Cuban music.

OSVALDO: All right! What song?

SONIA: "Guantanamera."

OSVALDO: They might know "Babalú."

SONIA: That's an American song.

*Manuela and Alfredo enter, in the middle of a conversation. Osvaldo exits to the ballroom. Sonia goes outside.*

MANUELA: The trouble is Americans are weak . . . they don't know how to make decisions.

ALFREDO: At least they are happy—

MANUELA: Why?

ALFREDO: Money!

MANUELA: You had that in Cuba, Alfredo, but—

ALFREDO: Look at my son—he has an accounting firm—

MANUELA: He's only a partner.

ALFREDO: He has a Lincoln Continental, a classy car, two beautiful houses, with pools and—

MANUELA: Don't talk about the prostitute's house in front of me, Alfredo, please.

ALFREDO: Forgive me.

MANUELA: We knew how to make decisions, we—

ALFREDO: Of course.

MANUELA: Fight who you don't agree with, do not doubt that you are right, and if they use force, you use force, bullets if you have to. Only right and wrong, no middle, not like Americans always asking questions, always in the middle, always maybe. Sometimes I think those Democrats are Communists—

ALFREDO: No, Manuela, you see in demo—

MANUELA: Democracy, Communism, the two don't go together, at least the Russians know that much. They don't let people complain in Russia, but here, anybody can do anything. *(The band is playing "Guantanamera")* At last some good music, no more of that Argentinian shit. *(She hums some of the song)*

ALFREDO: That's one of my favorite songs.

MANUELA: Yes, beautiful.

ALFREDO: May I have this dance?

MANUELA: Yes . . . but do I remember how?

MIMI *(Who has reentered)*: It'll come back to you, Grandma.

*Manuela, Alfredo and Mimi exit to the dance floor. Miriam is still sitting in the phone booth, smoking. Sonia enters. Miriam opens the phone-booth doors.*

MIRIAM: I just made a phone call to Cuba, and you can.

SONIA: They got you through?

MIRIAM: Yes. The overseas operator said, "Sometimes they answer, but only if they feel like it."

SONIA: Who did you call?

MIRIAM: My . . . our house. . . . I sometimes think that I live at the same time there as here. That I left a dual spirit there. When I go to a funeral I look through the windows as I drive and the landscapes I see are the streets outside the cemetery in Guanabacoa, not Miami. A while ago I looked out at the dance floor and I thought I was in the ballroom back home. That's why I had to call. I miss the floor, the windows, the air, the roof.

SONIA: The house is still standing, though, it is still there.

MIRIAM: But we are not.

SONIA: I saw a picture of it. It hasn't been painted in twenty years, we painted it last.

MIRIAM: Sonia, she said upstairs he's crying again.

SONIA: You're sending chills up my spine.

MIRIAM: Is it Pedro crying?

SONIA: No, she was trying to scare you. We have to hold on to it, to the way we remember it, painted.

MIRIAM: I think I heard Pedro screaming in the garden before she hung up.

SONIA: No, he's dead, he went to heaven.

MIRIAM: No, he's in hell. If there's a heaven he's in hell. Suicides go to hell. He was the only one that managed to remain, death keeps him there. Maybe the house filled with strangers is his hell.

SONIA: Why he did it I'll never understand. Maybe he had to die for us?

MIRIAM: No, he didn't do it for *me*.

SONIA: Maybe that's the way things are, maybe one of us had to die. Maybe there's an order to all these things.

MIRIAM: There's no order to things, don't you know that by now? It's chaos, only chaos.

*Mimi enters.*

SONIA: No, there's a more important reason, that's why he did it.

MIMI: What?

SONIA: This conversation is not for your ears.

MIMI: Why not?

*Lizette enters.*

SONIA: Because it isn't, that's all.

LIZETTE: Mama! Daddy started dancing with her and Oscar's whistling at them, whispering "Puta, putica."

MIRIAM: The Americans won't understand what they are saying.

LIZETTE: Americans know what "puta" means. My husband is embarrassed. Other people get divorces and don't act like this. Tell him he must stop. No name-calling in Spanish or in English. This is a bilingual state.

MIMI: No, Mama, don't do it.

MIRIAM: Mimi's right, let them do whatever they want.

SONIA: Right, why should I protect her?

LIZETTE: How about me? Who's going to protect me?

SONIA: Your husband.

MIMI: Tell him to tell them to stop, you've got your husband now, your own little family unit.

LIZETTE: Fuck off, Mimi. I'm begging you Mama, please. Just take him to the side and tell him to leave her alone, to let her have a good time.

SONIA: To let her have a good time?!

MIMI: I'll take care of it. *(She yells out to the ballroom)* Hey you slut, Miss Argentina. Don't use my sister's wedding for your crap. Come in here and fight it out with us!

MIRIAM: Mimi, she's flipping the bird at you. She's gesturing fuck you.

MIMI: Fuck yourself!

LIZETTE: Mama! Stop her! Oh God—

MIRIAM *(Yells to ballroom)*: You're just a bitch, lady.

LIZETTE *(Starts to cry)*: Oh, God, oh, God—

SONIA: In a little while everybody will forget about it—

LIZETTE: Oh God, Mama. Everybody's looking at us. They are so embarrassed. You let them ruin my wedding. You promised. I hate you. It's a fiasco. I hate you, Mimi.

SONIA: Sorry, promises are something nobody keeps, including me.

LIZETTE: You're such assholes.

SONIA: Everybody's got their faults, learn to live with it!

LIZETTE: You failed me.

MIMI: That was great, Aunt Miriam.

SONIA: I'm sorry.

MIRIAM: Thanks Mimi, it was fun.

OSVALDO *(Enters)*: How could you . . .

MIRIAM: Careful!

OSVALDO: Help me, Sonia.

SONIA: Osvaldo, I've put up with a lot.

OSVALDO: How about me? I want you and your children to apologize to her.

SONIA: No.

MIMI: Never.

MIRIAM: She should leave the party and let the rest of us have a good time. What the hell is she doing here?

OSVALDO: For my sake, Sonia.

SONIA: I'm sorry, I can't.

OSVALDO: What am I going to do?

SONIA: Who do you love, me?

OSVALDO: Yes.

SONIA: Who do you love, her?

OSVALDO: Yes.

SONIA: So full of contradictions, so confused. I'll go tell her that. He loves both of us, Cuba and Argentina!

OSVALDO: This is not the time to kid me, look at Lizette, she's upset.

LIZETTE: I'll never be able to talk to my mother-in-law again.

MIRIAM: It's your fault, Osvaldo. He never moved from the garden.

OSVALDO: Miriam?! Who never moved from the garden?

MIRIAM: Pedro. He never left the garden.

OSVALDO: None of us have.

MIRIAM: He stayed. He took a razor blade but remained locked forever in our family's garden.

OSVALDO: He was a coward.

MIRIAM: Maybe you are the coward, you keep running away.

OSVALDO: From what?

OSCAR (Enters, trying not to laugh): I'm sorry. I behaved badly.

OSVALDO: Tell me, Miriam, from what? (He exits)

OSCAR: Don't cry Lizette, forgive me? Hmm?

LIZETTE: Oscar, now they're starting to fight about Cuba. I just want to cry. They're going to tell my husband, "Your wife is from a crazy family. Are you sure she's not mentally disturbed?"

MIMI: Are you sure you're not mentally disturbed?

*Mimi and Oscar laugh. Osvaldo reenters.*

OSVALDO: What do I run away from that he faced?

MIRIAM: That we lost everything.

SONIA: Everything, no.

OSVALDO: You think I don't know that?

MIRIAM: Pedro knew. He became invisible but remains in silence, as proof.

OSVALDO: As proof of what?

SONIA: That we are not a very nice family? Is that what you are saying?

OSVALDO: He had nothing to do with us, he was an alcoholic.

SONIA: He killed himself because of our sins.

OSVALDO: No, Sonia, that was Christ, Pedro was a drunk, not a Christ figure.

MIRIAM: Because of our lies, Sonia.

OSVALDO: What lies?

MIRIAM: Why did you desert him? You, his brother, you were the only one he spoke to, the only one he needed.

OSVALDO: He made me sick.

MIRIAM: You were always together, you always spent your days together.

OSVALDO: He was an alcoholic.

MIRIAM: We were all alcoholics.

SONIA: I was never an alcoholic.

MIRIAM: He needed you.

OSVALDO: He was perverted.

MIRIAM: We were all perverted. That's why the new society got rid of us.

OSVALDO: Our mother is not perverted!

MIRIAM: No, just insane.

SONIA: No, she's an honest woman, now your father—

OSVALDO: My father was just selfish, he had too many mistresses.

SONIA: Fifteen.

OSCAR: Fifteen?

MIMI: All at once?

LIZETTE: Who gives a fuck? Everybody in this family is a—

MIRIAM: I'm the one that suffered from that, not you, Osvaldo. You take after Daddy so don't complain. Why did you let Pedro kill himself?

OSVALDO: He wanted too much from me.

MIRIAM: He needed you.

OSVALDO: He wanted my mind, he wanted my . . ., my . . ., he wanted everything.

MIRIAM: You're glad he did it?

OSVALDO: I was relieved.

MIRIAM: He knew too much, ha!

SONIA: Too much of what?

MIRIAM: The perversions.

SONIA: What perversions?

MIRIAM: Too much about his perversions, darling Sonia, you married a corrupted family, you really deserved better.

OSCAR: Uh-huh.

LIZETTE: I'm closing the door.

*Manuela and Alfredo enter.*

MANUELA: I'll never forget what he said.

ALFREDO: When?

MANUELA: In 1959, after the son-of-a-bitch's first speech, he said, "That boy is going to be trouble . . . he's full of Commie ideals."

ALFREDO: I must say I did not suspect it. I was so bored with Batista's bullshit I thought, a revolution, good. We'll get rid of the bums, the loafers, but instead, they got rid of us.

MANUELA: I hope he rots. Rot, Fidel Castro, die of cancer of the balls.

ALFREDO: Let's hope.

MANUELA: Then they came. And they took our businesses away, one by one. And we had to let them do it. They took over each of them, one after the other. It took the milicianos three days. I looked at Oscar while they did it, for him it was like they . . . for him, that was his life's work, he felt like . . .

OSCAR: Like they were plucking out his heart. Like they were sticking pins into his brain. Like they were having birds peck out his genitals. Like he was being betrayed.

MANUELA: Yes, that's it.

ALFREDO: I hate myself for helping them, bastards.

MANUELA: All he wanted after that was—

SONIA: To fight back.

OSCAR: Right.

MIRIAM: I still do. I still want to fight somebody!

SONIA: But he did fight back. Till the day he died, he never gave up. Right, Mama?

MANUELA: "We are in an emergency," that's how he put it, "an emergency."

MIRIAM: Daddy. Daddy, I am in an emergency now. I have taken six valiums and it's only noon.

ALFREDO: Why?

MIRIAM: Because I want to strangle you every time I look at you.

LIZETTE: Quiet, they're going to want an annulment.

MANUELA: My God, Miriam!

OSCAR: Who?

ALFREDO: Why?

MIRIAM: Why?!

LIZETTE: The Jews, they're a quiet people.

ALFREDO: Yes, Miriam, why?

MIRIAM: Why did you send your mistresses' daughters to my school?!

MANUELA: Miriam, not in front of the children.

ALFREDO: Because it was a good school.

MIRIAM: People in my class wouldn't talk to me because of you!

ALFREDO: Sorry.

OSVALDO: Sorry? That's all you have to say to her?! That's the only answer you give?!

ALFREDO: I don't know, what else should I say?

OSVALDO: Why did you not once congratulate me for finishing the university?! Why did you let me drink? Why did you let Pedro drink?

ALFREDO: I never noticed that you drank.

MIMI: Why did you leave my mother, and leave me . . . and never came to see me play volleyball?

OSVALDO: Leave me alone, I'm talking to my father.

MIMI: And who are you to me?

MANUELA: Good girl, good question.

OSVALDO: You? Why did you make your daughter think that the only person in the world who deserved her love was your husband?!

MANUELA: He was strong.

OSVALDO: He got drunk. He was a coward when he died.

OSCAR: No. That's not true.

MANUELA: He was a real man. What are you?

LIZETTE: You mean old hag, don't you ever talk to my dad again like . . .

SONIA: Don't you ever call your grandmother that. She's my mother!

LIZETTE: I'm going back to the wedding. (*She exits*)

OSCAR: Why did they kick us out?

OSVALDO: We left. We wanted to leave.

OSCAR: No one asked me.

SONIA: We had to protect you from them.

MIRIAM: That's right.

OSVALDO: They wanted to brainwash you, to turn you into a Communist.

OSCAR: No one explained it to me. You told me I was coming here for the weekend.

OSVALDO: It was not up to you.

SONIA: You were just a child, it was up to us.

OSVALDO: That's right.

MIRIAM: And we made the right decision, believe me.

OSCAR: Miriam, why did you let me be locked out? That day in Miami, November, 1962. The day the guy from the Jehovah's Witnesses came to see you. And you took him to your room to discuss the end of the world.

MIRIAM: It was a joke. I was only twenty. I don't believe in God.

OSCAR: Well, you locked me out. And I sat outside and you laughed at me, and I sat there by a tree and I wanted to die. I wanted to kill myself at the age of ten. I wanted to beat my head against the tree, and I thought, "Please stop working, brain, even they locked me out, even my family, not just my country, my family too." Bastards! Fidel was right. If I had a gun, I'd shoot you. I curse you, you shits. Who asked me?

OSVALDO: The revolution had nothing to do with you. You don't *really* remember it, and believe it or not, it did not happen just for you, Oscar.

OSCAR: Yeah, I didn't notice you damaged.

OSVALDO: I had to go to the market at age thirty-two and shop for the first time in my life.

MIMI: So what?

OSCAR: God.

OSVALDO: And I could not tell what fruit was ripe and what fruit was not ripe. I did not know how to figure that out. I cried at the Food King market in Canoga Park. Some people saw me. *(He cries)*

OSCAR: Big deal.

OSVALDO *(Stops crying)*: And Sonia, you refused to come and help me! You made me go do it alone. And shopping is the wife's duty.

SONIA: I couldn't. I felt weak. I was pregnant with Mimi. I'm sorry, Osvaldo. *(To Oscar)* I wanted you to live a noble life.

OSCAR: How?

SONIA: I don't know. I taught you not to put your elbows on the table. You had perfect eating habits . . .

OSCAR: What does that have to do with nobility?

SONIA: It shows you're not common. That's noble.

OSCAR: No, Mama, nobility—

SONIA: Yes.

OSCAR: No, nobility has to do with caring about the ugly things, seeing trash and loving it. It has to do with compassion, not table manners. It has to do with thought, not what people think about you.

SONIA: Stop picking on me.

OSCAR: I'm not picking on you.

SONIA: Everybody is always picking on me. I failed, I know I failed.

OSCAR: No, you just don't try. Why don't you try?

SONIA: Try what?

OSCAR: To do something.

SONIA: No.

OSCAR: Why?

SONIA: I'm not some whore that can go from guy to guy.

OSVALDO: Are you talking about my wife?

OSCAR: Try it.

SONIA: Don't insult me. Stop insulting me.

OSCAR: You need somebody.

SONIA: Stop it!

OSVALDO: Leave her alone.

*Osvaldo grabs Sonia. They walk towards the ballroom, then stop. We hear the band playing "Que Sera, Sera."*

MANUELA: I think they're going to dance.

MIRIAM: I want to see the Argentinian's expression.

*Sonia and Osvaldo are now dancing. The others watch. Mimi and Oscar go into the phone booth to snort coke.*

ALFREDO: Leave all three of them alone. *(He goes outside to smoke a cigar)*

*Miriam and Manuela walk past Sonia and Osvaldo toward the ballroom.*

MIRIAM: Why are you dancing out in the hall . . . afraid of Argentina?

*Miriam and Manuela exit.*

OSVALDO: I'd like to take a big piece of wood and beat some sense into her. . . . No, I want to beat her to death!

SONIA: She went too far . . . she lost control . . . she gets excited.

OSVALDO: They always lose control. Pedro thought there was no limit . . . that you did not have to stop anywhere . . . life was a whim. . . . But I knew that you have to stop yourself . . . that's being civilized, that's what makes us different than dogs . . . you can't have everything you feel you want . . .

SONIA: He was a tortured soul . . . and you loved him . . .

OSVALDO: My big brother. *(He starts to cry)*

SONIA: And you tried to help him . . .

OSVALDO: How?

SONIA: The only way you knew how, with affection.

OSVALDO: Affection?

SONIA: Yes, and that's decent.

OSVALDO: Maybe it is. Maybe I am.

*Sonia and Osvaldo kiss. He takes her out to the dance floor. She smiles. Oscar and Mimi come out of the phone booth. Oscar continues to snort cocaine.*

OSCAR: He did it. Well, at least he had the balls to take her out and dance. She won. You see if you have a plan and follow it . . . *(Sniff, sniff)* ah, hurray for the American dream.

MIMI: It's pathetic. They're still dancing. Oh God help us, she believes anything he tells her.

OSCAR: She had to endure too many things.

MIMI: What, losing her maid?

OSCAR: They never tell her the truth.

MIMI: And you do? You tell her the truth? Well, I'm gonna tell her.

OSCAR: I think you should get an abortion.

MIMI: Why should I?

OSCAR: To protect her.

MIMI: Why should I protect her.

OSCAR: I don't know. Lie to her. Tell Dad.

MIMI: Never mind. Pour me some more champagne.

*Lizette enters.*

I hope one of those horny Cubans just off the boat is ready to rock and roll.

LIZETTE: No more scenes, Mimi. Dad and Mom are enough.

*Mimi toasts Lizette with champagne.*

MIMI: Arrivederci. *(She exits)*

LIZETTE: They're out there dancing like they were in love or something—

OSCAR: Maybe they are.

LIZETTE: Never, he's being polite and she's showing off. And the Argentinian is complaining to me. And I don't want any part of any of you.

OSCAR: You don't! You think your husband is going to take you away from all this. Does he know about the suicides, how they drink till they explode . . . the violence we live with, the razor blades, the guns, the hangings, the one woman in our family who set herself on fire while her three kids watched?

ALFREDO *(Who has reentered)*: We are just hot-blooded and passionate, that's all.

OSCAR: Grandpa told me a week before . . . "Oscar," he told me . . . "they'll tell you soon I'm in the hospital. That means that I'm on my way out . . . this life here is ridiculous."

ALFREDO: Oscar Hernández was a fool. That's a fool's kind of suicide, that's what I told you.

OSCAR: A lot of drinks when your blood pressure is high is not a fool's kind of suicide, it's just suicide. Despair, that's always the story of people that get kicked out, that have to find refuge, you and me . . . us.

LIZETTE: No, you. Everybody dies on the day that they're supposed to. Forget about it.

OSCAR: How can I?

ALFREDO: You better teach yourself to.

OSCAR: How can I? Have you taught yourself? Tell me, why do you want to live? For what?

ALFREDO: Because of me . . . here or over there, I still need me!

OSCAR: You don't have any honor.

ALFREDO: Honor for what?

OSCAR: For our country.

ALFREDO: That little island? . . . Look, Oscar, when Columbus first found it there were Indians there, imagine, Indians. So we eliminated the Indians, burned all of them, cleaned up the place. . . . We needed somebody to do the Indians' work so we bought ourselves slaves . . . and then the Spaniards, that's us, and the slaves started to . . . well, you know.

OSCAR: I can only imagine.

ALFREDO: Well, then we started calling ourselves natives. Cubans.

LIZETTE: That's right, a name they made up!

ALFREDO: Right! And we became a nation . . .

OSCAR: A race.

ALFREDO: Yes. And then the U.S. came and liked it, and bought and cheated their way into this little place. They told us (*He imitates a Texan accent*) "Such a pretty place you have, a valuable piece of real estate. We will help you!" So, they bought us.

OSCAR: We should have eliminated them!

ALFREDO: Maybe. But, what we did . . . was sell it to them and fight against each other for decades, trying to have control of what was left of this pretty place, this valuable piece of real estate. And a bearded guy on a hill talked to us about liberty, and justice, and humanity and humility—and we bought his story. And he took everything away from everybody. And we were forced to end up here. So, we bought their real estate. Do you know how Miami was built?

LIZETTE: With sand that they shipped in from Cojimar! Right?

ALFREDO: That's right. And your other grandfather could not accept the fact that it was just real estate. So he got drunk when he knew he had high blood pressure. What a fool.

LIZETTE: He tells the truth, Oscar.

OSCAR: And Mama thinks it was her country. And someday she'd go back. And I hoped it was my country. What a laugh, huh?

LIZETTE: If you ever tell Mama this, it'll kill her.

OSCAR: Maybe it wouldn't.

LIZETTE: She can't deal with real life, believe me. I'm her daughter, I know what she's really like.

OSCAR: And you can deal with everything?

LIZETTE: Sure. I grew up here, I have a Jewish name now . . . Mrs. Rifkin, that's my name.

OSCAR: Well, Mrs. Rifkin, I'm jealous of you.

ALFREDO: Time for a dance. I haven't danced with the mother of the groom. (*He exits*)

LIZETTE: Try to get away, Mrs. Rifkin!

OSCAR: And the new Mrs. Rifkin is running away. You got away.

LIZETTE: Don't be jealous, Oscar. It's still all back here. (*She points to her brain*)

OSVALDO (*Enters*): One o'clock, Lizette.

LIZETTE: One more dance.

OSCAR: Why do you have to leave so soon?

LIZETTE: It's another two thousand for the entire day.

OSCAR: God.

OSVALDO: God what?

OSCAR: You have no class.

SONIA (*Enters*): Osvaldo, I have to talk to you.

OSVALDO: Why?

SONIA: Please, just do me a favor. I have to talk to you.

LIZETTE: Want to dance?

OSCAR: All right.

*Lizette and Oscar exit.*

OSVALDO: What do you want, Sonia? Tell me, sweetheart.

SONIA (*Hysterical*): Don't be angry at me, there's no more wedding cake, we've run out of wedding cake. There's no more, nothing, no more wedding cake.

OSVALDO: That's all right, we should start getting them out. Tell them to start passing out the packages of rice.

SONIA: No, some people are asking for wedding cake. What do we do? What?

OSVALDO: They've had plenty to eat, a great lunch, a salad, chicken cacciatore, a pastry, all they could drink, champagne, coffee. Tell them to pass out the rice, get this over with, and let's go home.

SONIA: At a wedding, wedding cake is something people expect. I can't embarrass the groom's family again. What do we do, what are you going to do?!

OSVALDO: Let's go up to people we know . . .

SONIA: Only Cubans!

OSVALDO: All right, let's go up to all the Cubans we know and ask them not to eat the cake. Then serve it to the Jews. The Cubans won't care.

SONIA: You do it, I can't. I can't face them.

OSVALDO: No, do it, with me, come on.

*Oscar enters. He is about to eat a piece of cake. Sonia grabs it away from him.*

OSCAR: What are you doing?

SONIA: You can't eat it, there's not enough.

OSCAR: Why?

OSVALDO: Just do what your mother says. Please, let's go.

SONIA: You do it.

OSVALDO: You're not coming with me?

SONIA: No, I'm sorry. I can't, I'm too embarrassed.

*Osvaldo exits.*

OSCAR: Okay, give it back to me now.

SONIA: No, take it to that man over there.

OSCAR: Why should I?

SONIA: He didn't get any cake. I think the waiters stole one of the layers. You take it to him. I think his name is Mr. Cohen, the man who's looking at us.

OSCAR: All right. Who?

SONIA *(Points discreetly)*: The bald man.

OSCAR: Great.

*Manuela and Miriam enter.*

MANUELA: Oh my God, Jesus Sonia. Osvaldo just told me that we are out of cake.

OSCAR: We are. *(He exits)*

MANUELA: We were winning.

SONIA: The stupid waiters cut the pieces too big, Mama.

MANUELA: Americans! This is one of the great follies of my life.

SONIA: Of course Mama, this is worse than the revolution.

*Manuela goes outside.*

MIRIAM: No, in the revolution people died.

SONIA: They really did, didn't they?

MIRIAM: Real blood was shed, real Cuban blood.

SONIA: I forget sometimes.

MIRIAM: Only when I'm calm, that's when I remember, when I'm waking up or when I'm half asleep . . . at those moments.

SONIA: Let's go out to the dance floor and dance like we did at the Tropicana.

LIZETTE *(Enters)*: I ripped my wedding dress.

SONIA: Oh well, dear, it's only supposed to last one day. Maybe the next wedding you go to, Lizette, will be mine.

LIZETTE: Who did you find, Mama?

SONIA: Your father.

LIZETTE: Mama, Daddy can't afford another wife.

SONIA: I'm not another wife, Lizette.

LIZETTE: I hope you are right.

MIRIAM: Wait a minute. *(She gives Lizette five hundred dollars)* In case you decide you need something else when you are on your honeymoon.

LIZETTE: Another five hundred. I think we have three thousand dollars in cash.

*Lizette exits to dressing room. Miriam lights two cigarettes. She gives one to Sonia.*

MIRIAM: Let's go. Remember when we thought Fidel looked sexy.
SONIA: Shh.

*Miriam and Sonia sashay off to the ballroom. Osvaldo and Alfredo enter. Osvaldo is eating a big piece of cake.*

ALFREDO: All women are hysterical.
OSVALDO: I got out there, took the cake from the Cubans, who were outraged. A couple of them called me a Jew. I took it to the Jews and they were as happy as can be. I offered them the cake but nobody wanted any. She made me go through all that for nothing.
ALFREDO: They were being polite, Jews don't like to appear greedy.
OSVALDO *(Eats the cake)*: Well it's delicious.
ALFREDO: It's Cuban cake.
OSVALDO: The only thing that I like Cuban is the food.
ALFREDO: Then start acting like a man. You have one crying in the back and the other demanding in the front!
OSVALDO: I do.
ALFREDO: You don't have the energy to play it both ways.
OSVALDO: What are you talking about?
ALFREDO: Your wife . . . Sonia!
OSVALDO: She'll never change.
ALFREDO: Why should she?!
OSVALDO: To be acceptable.

*Alfredo slaps Osvaldo. Mimi enters.*

MIMI: The rice, we have to hit her with the rice.

*Osvaldo and Alfredo, glaring at each other, exit with Mimi. Lizette enters in her honeymoon outfit and goes outside. She sees Manuela. They come back in.*

LIZETTE: Grandma, you've been in the sun!
MANUELA: I was taking a nap. You know when you get old you need rest.
LIZETTE: You were crying, Grandma. Don't.
MANUELA: We didn't have enough cake!
LIZETTE: Nothing turned out right, Grandma, that's the truth.
MANUELA: You're right. Oscar would have made sure that we had a good time. My husband would have spent more money. I would have been proud. Your mother would have been proud. You would have been proud.
LIZETTE: Grandma, aren't you proud of me?
MANUELA: Yes.
LIZETTE: Did you love each other?
MANUELA: Yes dear, we did.
LIZETTE: And you never doubted it?

MANUELA: No dear.

LIZETTE: I hope I can do it. Wish me luck, Grandma. I don't want to fail. I want to be happy.

MANUELA: I hope that you know how to fight. Everything will try to stop and corrupt your life. I hope your husband is successful and that you have enough children.

LIZETTE: And that I never regret my life.

MANUELA: That will be my prayer.

LIZETTE: That if anyone goes, it's me, that I'm the one that walks. That he'll be hooked on me forever.

MANUELA: That's right.

LIZETTE: Thank you.

MANUELA: A beautiful dress. I'll get the rice.

LIZETTE: No, we are sneaking out. I don't want rice all over my clothes. In ten minutes tell them we tricked them, that we got away.

MANUELA: Go. Don't be nervous. Tonight everything will be all right. Don't worry, have a nice vacation.

LIZETTE: It's eighty degrees in Hawaii, it's an island, like Cuba.

MANUELA: Cuba was more beautiful.

*Lizette exits.*

Then politicians got in the way.

LIZETTE (*Offstage*): Honey, we did it. Give me a kiss.

*Manuela goes outside.*

ENTIRE CAST (*Offstage*): Ah! Uh-Uh! Noooooooooo!

LIZETTE (*Offstage*): My God, rice, run!

*Sonia enters, covered with rice, followed by Osvaldo.*

OSVALDO: It was a beautiful wedding.

SONIA: You're coming home with me?

OSVALDO: I can't.

SONIA: Yes, come with me.

OSVALDO: Not tonight.

SONIA: When?

OSVALDO: Never. (*Pause*) Nothing is left between you and me.

SONIA: Nothing?

OSVALDO: Nothing.

SONIA: I'm not even your mistress?

OSVALDO: That's right. Revolutions create hell for all people involved.

SONIA: Don't do this. We belong together, we were thrown out. Discarded. We stayed together, Cubans, we are Cubans. Nothing really came between us.

OSVALDO: Something did for me.

*Mimi enters.*

SONIA: What about our family? What we swore to Christ?

OSVALDO: I don't believe in anything, not even Christ.

SONIA: And me?

OSVALDO: I have another wife, she's my wife now. I have another life.

SONIA: If I was my father, I'd kill you!

MIMI *(To Osvaldo)*: Your wife is waiting in the car. *(To Sonia)* She told me to tell him.

OSVALDO: Sonia, I'm starting fresh. You should too.

SONIA: I should, yes, I should. *(She takes out the bottle that Manuela gave her in Act One and makes the sign of the cross twice)*

OSVALDO: That's right. *(He starts to exit)*

SONIA: Wait. One last toast.

OSVALDO: To the bride?

SONIA: No, to us. *(She goes to the fountain to pour them champagne, and puts the potion into Osvaldo's drink)*

MIMI: Osvaldo?

OSVALDO: How dare you call me that!

MIMI: Okay, Daddy, is that better? This family is the only life I know. It exists for me.

OSVALDO: This is between your mother and me.

MIMI: No, listen Daddy, the family is continuing. I'm going to make sure of that.

OSVALDO: How? Mimi, how?

MIMI: Never mind, Osvaldo.

*Sound of car horn.*

OSVALDO: She's honking the horn, hurry Sonia!

*Sonia hands Osvaldo the drink.*

SONIA: Money, love and the time to enjoy it, for both of us!

OSVALDO: Thanks. *(He gulps down the drink and exits)*

MIMI: Osvaldo you jerk. Bastard!

SONIA: Don't worry Mimi, he's going to have diarrhea till sometime in March.

MIMI: Finally.

SONIA: Put the blame on me. I don't speak the right way. I don't know how to ask the right questions.

MIMI: That's not true, Mama.

SONIA: When I first got here . . . I got lost. I tried to ask an old man for directions. I could not find the right words to ask him the directions. He said to me, "What's wrong with you, lady, somebody give you a lobotomy?" I repeated that word over and over to myself, "lobotomy, lobo-tomy, lo-bo-to-meee!" I looked it up. It said an insertion into the brain, for relief, of tension. I remembered people who had been lobotomized, that their minds could not express anything, they could feel nothing. They looked numb, always resting, then I realized that the old man was right.

MIMI: No. Mama.

SONIA: So I decided never to communicate or deal with this country again. Mimi, I don't know how to go back to my country. He made me realize that to him, I looked like a freak. Then I thought, but I'm still me to Osvaldo, he's trapped too. He must feel the same way too. Put the blame on me.

*Miriam and Oscar enter.*

MIMI: Aunt Miriam, tell me, how did you find revenge?

MIRIAM: Against what?

MIMI: Your father.

MIRIAM: Oh, when my mother and father got to America, I made them live with me. I support them. Now they are old and they are dependent on me for everything.

MIMI: It's not worth it, Aunt Miriam.

MIRIAM: Yes it is.

MIMI: Grandma, I'm in the car.

MIRIAM: It's revenge.

OSCAR *(Shows Miriam the coke bottle)*: My revenge!

MIRIAM: Everyone in this family's got a drug.

MANUELA *(Enters)*: Mimi is taking me home?

SONIA: Yes, Mama, she's waiting in the car—

MANUELA: You didn't do it right.

SONIA: I'm sorry, Mama . . . I did it the way I was taught.

*Manuela kisses Oscar good-bye and then exits.*

Why can't life be like it was? Like my coming-out party. When my father introduced me to our society in my white dress.

MIRIAM: Sonia, they threw the parties to give us away . . . perfect merchandising; Latin women dressed like American movies, doing Viennese waltzes. "Oh, beautiful stream, so clear and bright, a radiant dream we sing to you, by shores that . . . "

SONIA: I wonder what it would have been like if we would have stayed?

MIRIAM: They would have ridiculed us.

SONIA: We would have had a country.

MIRIAM: We didn't have a choice.

*Oscar exits to ballroom.*

SONIA: Miriam, Pedro took his life because of that.

MIRIAM: No. Pedro did it because of days like today—afternoons like this one: when you are around the people you belong with and you feel like you're choking and don't know why. *(She takes out valium)* I'll give you a piece of magic.

SONIA: How many?

MIRIAM: One . . . no, two. A valium—that's the only certain thing. It reassures you. It lets you look at the truth. That's why psychiatrists prescribe them.

SONIA: You guarantee me Varadero? I'll be floating in Varadero Beach?

MIRIAM: If you take three you get to Varadero, Cuba.

*Miriam and Sonia take the valium. From the offstage ballroom we hear Oscar speaking over the microphone.*

OSCAR (*Sniff . . . sniff*): . . . One, two, three, testing, one, three, three, two, testing. Lenin or some Commie like that said that "you cannot make an omelet without breaking a few eggs." Funny guy. Testing. All right, now from somewhere in the armpit of the world, a little tune my mother taught me.
(*He sings "Isla"*)
In an island
Far away from here
I left the life I knew
Island of mine
Country of mine
Mine and only mine
Terraces and houses
Country do you remember
Do you remember
Remember me?

MIRIAM (*Takes cushions from chair and puts them on the floor*): I want to float down Key Biscayne back to Varadero. Varadero, please, please come.

*Miriam lies on the cushions. Sonia looks at her.*

SONIA: Why is he making so much noise?!

MIRIAM: Shhh. I'm already there . . . miles and miles into the beach and the water is up to my knees . . . I float. The little fish nibble at my feet. I kick them. I'm in. I'm inside the place where I'm supposed to be.

OSCAR (*Singing offstage*):
You were once my island
I left you all alone
I live without your houses
Beautiful houses
Houses remembered.

SONIA: Sonia is not coming back. Cojimar, Sonia will never be back.

OSCAR (*Singing offstage*):
Eran mías
You were only mine
Never forget me
Don't forget me
Mi amor.

MIMI (*Enters*): Mama, what's she doing?

SONIA: Relaxing.

MIMI: Want to dance, Mama?

SONIA: Us?

MIMI: Yes.

SONIA: Yes.

OSCAR *(Singing offstage)*:

En una isla

Lejos de aquí

Dejé

La vida mía

Madre mía

Isla mía

MIMI: They're going to kick us out.

SONIA: That's all right, Mimi. I've been kicked out of better places.

OSCAR *(Singing offstage)*: Te dejé.

*Sonia and Mimi begin to dance. Lights fade as we hear the end of the song.*

## END OF PLAY

# The House of
# Ramon Iglesia

José Rivera

# José
# Rivera

I was born in San Juan in 1955. I lived in a small town called Espino, on a little farm, until I was about four. We left Puerto Rico because my father realized he wasn't going to find much work—the economy was very depressed—and all his brothers and sisters had moved up to the States. But Dad didn't move his family to Newark or the Bronx the way his relatives did. We moved to Long Island because he likes woods, likes country life. Back then Holbrook was rural, we lived on a dirt road. We had a quarter-acre and my parents grew things.

I spoke Spanish until English took over. In Holbrook most of the families were Italian. Unfortunately my Spanish now is very weak, although I understand it perfectly. My parents spoke in Spanish, we answered in English. It was an interesting confusion when I had friends over.

My dad worked as a short-order cook making ninety dollars a week. Every year he asked for a raise: "Mickey, just give me a hundred dollars a week, that's all I want." Dad got ninety-five dollars a week for several years, then ninety-seven. Finally after ten years Dad quit and started his own Mom-and-Pop diner. A mall went up across the street and Dad lost his shirt. He was a janitor, drove a cab, worked in a greenhouse. He was always working, days and nights and weekends, usually three jobs. When he was a night watchman at my high school I kept him company on weekends. That was really the only time we spent together.

My mother had nine children—I'm the oldest. Three died young. She had a third-grade education, but she's a bright woman. She taught herself to read and write English.

I've always wanted to write. I wrote a novel about baseball when I was very young. I wrote comic strips. In sixth grade my teacher put pictures from *Life* magazine up on the board for us to write about, and I wrote furiously. That same year I saw a production of *Rumplestiltskin* which made me want to write plays. I wrote several in high school.

I went to Denison University, a small school in Ohio, on full scholarship. College was a liberating experience for me. I went to school with kids who had the money but not the grades to go to Harvard. I saw possibilities I hadn't imagined, I got the feeling that if you worked hard enough, you could do what you wanted. I had to maintain a B+ average so I felt my scholarship wasn't a handout.

I wrote four plays at Denison, all of which were produced. One, a musical about Sarah Bernhardt, was so bad and so long that we didn't even make it through one performance. I wrote my Ibsen play, and my Tom Stoppard play. I directed them all too, and so came to understand the process.

After graduation I lived at home, worked in a warehouse and saved money. As soon as I could I moved to the Bronx, worked in a bookstore and then at a publishing company. I wrote in a vacuum for a long time, until I joined a group of playwrights who had Monday-night readings. The group, Theatre Matrix, produced a one-act of mine at 78th Street Theatre Lab. I wrote *The House of Ramon Iglesia* during this time.

*Ramon Iglesia* got a fairly good review in the *Times*, just as Norman Lear was trying to find a Hispanic writer for a series he was doing. I met Norman a couple of weeks later and he offered me a job on the spot. I had just left the publishing company, so I figured well, what the hell. I worked for Embassy Television, and wrote several things that have been on the air. Although I learned a lot and felt good about supporting my family— my wife Heather was going to college, I was sending money to my parents—I always felt I was missing something. I didn't write a full-length play in the three years I was out there, and I got homesick for New York. I didn't like the way writers were treated, as if one's as good as another. And of course you don't own what you write; they can do whatever they want with it. So when my contract expired Heather and I decided to come back to New York.

*American Playhouse* did *Ramon Iglesia* while I was in California. Miranda Barry saw the play, liked it and optioned it right away. But when *American Playhouse* went to the Corporation for Public Broadcasting for half the money—a quarter of a million dollars—CPB said, "The play isn't really Hispanic enough." Miranda paid me to go ahead with the one-hour teleplay anyway. I wrote in some music cues, mentioned some foods, threw in a little more Spanglish. That was all I did, anything else would've been silly. Months passed and then we got a call: "We read the teleplay and we're afraid it's just a little too Hispanic for us. We don't think people will be able to have access to this culture." Miranda said to me, "Be patient, they'll come around. If they meet you, they may change their minds." I always believed that a good writer must be critical of his times and of his culture, yet I didn't want people to feel put down by the play, so I took out some things that would seem extreme to a television audience. CPB was reassured by that and finally gave us the grant. The play aired in April '86, the same day Reagan bombed Libya. My East Coast friends who had set their VCRs for 9:00 P.M. came home to the President instead of the play.

I had never thought of writing about my family, until people started saying I should. *Ramon Iglesia* was my first "Hispanic" play. It is based on my life right after I graduated from college. I was living at home but wanted to be on my own. My father was trying to sell his house and was having enormous problems, and we were just not getting along. I was hung up on success, I'd gone to this preppy school. I couldn't accept the world I was in, I yearned for this other world where people were successful. In an adolescent way, in a childish way, I blamed my father for everything.

Now I wince at some of the things Javier says, at the self-hatred evident in him. I just had a production at a small New Haven theatre, the United Theatre of the Americas. High school kids who saw the play were angry that I had portrayed Hispanic characters in such a negative light, that Javier had such hatred for his people. Their reaction made me think again about my own anger at the time and how unresolved it was. I once felt that in order to transcend my culture I had to escape it, to run away from it. In the last several years I've realized that the only transcendence possible is through embracing the culture, learning it, growing up out of it. Javier does learn his lesson in the play, but looking back on it now, I think he doesn't learn enough.

This summer I was part of the Hispanic playwrights' program at South Coast Rep; it was my introduction to other Hispanic writers. We spent a lot of time discussing our problems with the label. I've been sending my plays to major regional theatres for years, so I feel I'm *in* the mainstream. When someone says, "We're trying to mainstream Hispanic writers," I think, "Well, why? I am already." Putting the Hispanic label on me takes me *out* of the mainstream. It's a strange situation, I'm constantly wrestling with it because I have enormous pride in the culture I come from. I've been devouring books by Latin American writers. I'm in love with magic realism, trying to make it work on stage.

Iglesia means church in Spanish. By giving the family that name, I wanted to endow their home with great meaning. But the Catholic church hasn't played much part in my life or writing. I *am* interested in the part Santería plays in Caribbean culture. My grandfather in Puerto Rico had chickens and his neighbor had corn. The chickens went into the neighbor's backyard and destroyed the plants, so he killed all the chickens with a machete. It's family legend that my grandfather put a spell on this man; he was dead six months later. I asked my grandfather about it and he said, "Oh, yeah, I did that." I said, "Grandfather, it's not murder?" and he said, "Oh, no, it's magic, it's not murder, don't worry about it." Whether or not it ever happened is beside the point.

I have a few vivid memories of my childhood in Puerto Rico. I remember digging in the backyard and coming across a huge centipede. I have a memory of running away from home and being stopped by lightning. I remember the day we left Puerto Rico, the airport, the plane ride. I remember the heat and some of the smells. I remember staring at the sun while clouds were passing over it. I remember being in a cradle, staring up at the mosquito net all night because there was a spider up there and I was afraid it was going to fall on my face.

I think of Puerto Rico as a lush place. When things are green they are intensely green and the heat is intense and the soil is intensely red clay and when you get bitten by a bug it hurts a lot. I try to transplant this exaggerated environment into the world of my plays.

# Biographical Information

José Rivera's most recent plays are *The Promise*, scheduled for production by New York's Ensemble Studio Theatre in 1988, and *Each Day Dies with Sleep*, commissioned by Albany's Capital Repertory Company. Earlier plays include *The Dollmaker* and a number of one-acts, among them *Angel of Mercy*, *The Firestorm*, *The Laundry Room* and *Starship Louie*.

Rivera spent three years as a staff writer for Embassy Television. His one-hour teleplay *Dislocations* was optioned by Columbia Pictures Television.

# About the Play

In 1983 *The House of Ramon Iglesia*, selected by Ensemble Studio Theatre as its winner of one of the first FDG/CBS New Plays Awards, was produced under the direction of Jack Gelber. Rivera's teleplay was aired nationally as part of the *American Playhouse* series in 1986. The acting edition is published by Samuel French, and a monologue from the play will be included in *The Actor's Book of Contemporary Stage Monologues*.

# Characters

DOLORES IGLESIA
CAROLINE
JULIO IGLESIA
CHARLIE IGLESIA
RAMON IGLESIA
JAVIER IGLESIA
NICK CALLA

# Time and Place

February, 1980. Holbrook, Long Island, New York.

# The House of Ramon Iglesia

*For Heather*

## ACT ONE

### Scene 1

*The action begins in the living room of the Iglesia house—a small, lower-class home located in Holbrook, New York, about an hour and a half east of New York City. It is a cold evening in February 1980. The living room has a slightly uneven floor, disheveled furniture, windows with towels stuffed around the cracks, scores of photographs on the wall, and a stack of cardboard boxes in one of the upstage corners. The upstage wall has a window facing the street. There are four exits: the front door, an exit to the kitchen, an exit to the upstairs bedrooms, and an exit to the basement.*

*Dolores Iglesia, a Puerto Rican woman of forty-five, sits at a little homemade altar, dedicated to her deceased daughter, Felicia. There are icons everywhere, as well as a photograph of the infant Felicia. Dolores prays to the photograph and kisses it. Note: It should be clear that Dolores is speaking in Spanish throughout the play, though we hear her words in English. Characters who do not speak Spanish cannot understand her.*

DOLORES: Don't worry, Felicia, my angel, we're going home. *(A knock is heard at the front door. She spins around)* Ramon?

CAROLINE *(Off)*: Hey, Mrs. Iglesia? It's me, Caroline.

DOLORES: Oh.

CAROLINE (*Off*): Could you open up? It's *freezing—*!

DOLORES (*Crossing to front door*): It's Javier's girlfriend . . .

*Dolores opens door. Caroline, an attractive, eternal adolescent, wearing lots of makeup and chewing gum, enters. She is twenty-eight and irresistible.*

Come in, hurry. Did you see my husband out there?

CAROLINE: I don't know about this weather. (*Takes off coat and earmuffs*) Oh geez— it's *murder;* you know? I just hate it.

DOLORES: Excuse me?

CAROLINE (*Looking her in the eye*): Murder. I just hate it.

DOLORES (*Speaking slowly*): Caroline, you know I don't speak English . . .

CAROLINE (*Speaking slowly*): Uh . . . the *weather.* It's freezing! (*Pantomimes being cold*) Esta mucho frio!

DOLORES (*Smiles*): You don't have to tell me: it's freezing.

CAROLINE: What?

DOLORES: It's murder. I wish it would stop.

CAROLINE (*Giving up*): Look. I want Javier. Your son. (*She looks around the room*) Is he *here?*

DOLORES: Javier, he's not here.

CAROLINE: Do you have any idea where he is?

DOLORES: Ramon went to Puerto Rico. Every time he's on an airplane, I get so scared. He should have been back by—

CAROLINE: *I don't know what you're saying!* (*She sits on the sofa*)

DOLORES: Would you like some coffee?

CAROLINE: What?

DOLORES: Coffee?

CAROLINE: Did you say coffee?

DOLORES: I can make you a cup of—

CAROLINE (*Overjoyed*): Coffee! Would be great! Yes! Please, get me some. Thank God for coffee.

DOLORES: I think, I think you're a very pretty girl. But you're not very smart, are you?

CAROLINE (*Totally confused*): . . . What?

*Dolores kisses Caroline on the cheek and exits to the kitchen. Caroline starts walking around the room, looking into all the boxes. She calls to Dolores.*

I bet you guys are really nervous, huh? I think I'd be freaking out if it was me moving away. I turn into a real crybaby when it comes to goodbyes and stuff like that. You should see me at weddings. (*Laughs*) I should see me at weddings. (*She comes across a photograph of Javier*) I don't believe it. Javier Iglesia. The stud himself. (*She takes the photograph from the box*) And where the frig are *you* hanging out anyway? You better have a great explanation for the way you've been disappearing you little baby. Selfish, sneaky, rotten . . . cute little baby. Don't give me those eyes!

*The door opens and Charlie and Julio enter. Charlie is tall and thin and sixteen years old. Julio, nineteen, is built like a tank.*

CHARLIE *(Seeing Caroline)*: Oh, hi. Look who's here.
CAROLINE: Hi Charlie.
JULIO: Oh great.
CAROLINE: Hello Julio.
JULIO: Oh wonderful.
CAROLINE: Don't start.
JULIO *(Winking at Charlie)*: Somebody call the ASPCA, break out the pooper-scoopers, blow the dog-in-heat alert.

*Charlie crosses to chair, sits.*

CAROLINE: Listen, fatso . . .
JULIO: . . . Are you going to start spraying the furniture again?
CAROLINE: Are you finished?
JULIO: Fatso? You should talk. There's more area on those thighs of yours than on the *Nimitz* flight deck. Did my father come home?
CAROLINE: I don't know.
JULIO *(Shouting into the kitchen)*: Is Dad home?
CAROLINE: I can't even find *Javier* . . .
JULIO: Javier went to Manhattan to get laid. *Dad, are you here?*
DOLORES *(Entering with coffee)*: No. He didn't come back. I'm scared . . .
JULIO: Great. Unpack the boxes again.
DOLORES: Maybe they gave him trouble . . . *(She crosses to Charlie, kisses him)*
JULIO *(Crosses to Dolores, kisses her)*: Maybe he went to the wrong Caribbean island, Mom.
DOLORES *(Exiting to kitchen)*: Pérez's people always make trouble . . .

*Julio sits on sofa with Caroline.*

CHARLIE *(To Caroline)*: It's colder in here than it is outside.
CAROLINE *(To Charlie)*: What's Javier doing in Manhattan?
CHARLIE *(Crossing to thermostat)*: You're asking me? I'm going to turn up the heat, Julio.
JULIO: Not too far. You'll turn this place into a gas chamber again.
CHARLIE *(To Caroline)*: He didn't come home Friday night, that's all I know.
JULIO *(To Caroline)*: Forget him. He's a floozie. *(To Dolores)* I told you we shouldn't disconnect the phone so soon; Dad could be calling from JFK. *(To Caroline)* Right, Spot?
DOLORES *(Off)*: Don't yell at me, it was Ramon's idea to disconnect it . . . the money . . .

CAROLINE: You don't know how impossible it is to follow a conversation in this house. You speak in English, she answers in Spanish . . . and I don't know where to put my ears half the time.

JULIO (*Hanging up coat*): Well, you should take your ears, and the rest of you, and pack them off to a convent, and stop screwing up my brother's life.

CAROLINE: Thank you.

JULIO (*Crossing to sofa*): Javier is not the baby-buggy, home-for-dinner, Fred-and-Ethel type. Go marry a nice, stable cop or something.

CAROLINE: Why don't you give me a straight answer, Julio?

CHARLIE: Why don't you give her a straight answer, Julio?

JULIO: Why don't you go outside and shovel the steps, Charlie?

CHARLIE: You do it, wimp.

JULIO: How would you like to suck the flowers off the wallpaper?

CHARLIE: Ya big clone.

JULIO: *You're talking to a future marine, lady!* (*He lunges for Charlie, catches him, and puts him in a headlock*) I'm going to use that enormous mouth of yours to shovel the sidewalk. *Who's a wimp?*

CAROLINE: Tell him he is.

CHARLIE: You are.

JULIO (*Tightening*): *Don't listen to her! Who's a wimp?*

CHARLIE (*Struggling*): Me! Me! Me! Me! *Just let go!*

*Julio releases Charlie, who whacks Julio on the arm as hard as he can.*

Colossal wimp! (*He bolts into the kitchen*)

CAROLINE: You're just a plain old thug, Julio.

JULIO (*Flexing*): You want to see a trap bounce? I bet you'd love to see a nice inspiring pec flex, wouldn't you, girl? I'm gonna dazzle the Marine Corps, woman!

CAROLINE: Get away from me you horse. I like intellectuals.

JULIO: I don't know. When I first met you, you could appreciate a good healthy lat spread.

CAROLINE: Julio, if I asked you a serious question would you turn down the gorilla hormones and give me a serious answer, please?

JULIO (*Looking through* Marine Magazine): What is it?

CAROLINE: I want to know what Javier's been telling you about us. What he's been doing the last couple of days.

JULIO: Are you kids fighting?

CAROLINE: Fighting? That'd be a pleasure! All he does these days is act real polite, real quiet, like he's thinking things he doesn't want to tell me. He doesn't get mad at me or anything, he just smiles a lot. I hate it! (*Beat*) Oh man. I don't need this. I'll see ya. (*She gets up and puts on coat*)

JULIO: Hey wait a minute.

CAROLINE: I hate being in the dark and you people feeling sorry for me. I learned to make rice and beans for him, and he got mad.

JULIO *(Intercepting her)*: Whoa . . . wait a minute . . . relax your face, there . . .

CAROLINE: I'm so *pissed* at him!

JULIO: Hey, have dinner with us, hang out, and do not judge the Iglesias by that moody Javier, all right Private? He thinks he's in like, turmoil, you know? His stupid life. Like he doesn't know what or where it is. But hey. If he's messing you up, I'll talk to him myself, okay?

*Caroline smiles "Okay." The front door bursts open and Ramon Iglesia comes in. He is forty-nine years old, Puerto Rican, with a pronounced limp. He looks fifty-nine. He is wearing a coat far too thin for the weather and a bright yellow hat. He is carrying a suitcase.*

RAMON: Hello, hello, hello! *(To Julio)* Is that my soldier?

JULIO *(Crosses to Ramon, kisses him)*: All *right!* La bendición, Sarge!

RAMON: Que Dios te bendiga, soldier. How are you, Caroline?

JULIO *(Crossing to kitchen)*: Dad's home!

DOLORES *(Off)*: I'll be right there!

*Dolores and Charlie enter. Dolores and Ramon embrace.*

Oh God, Ramon! Thank God you're here! *(Kisses him)*

CHARLIE: Hey Pop. We were worried.

DOLORES: Look at you. What a pretty hat.

RAMON: Where's Javier?

DOLORES: In the city.

RAMON: Why he's not here to see me?

DOLORES: He's mad at you.

RAMON *(Giving suitcase to Charlie)*: Let him be mad at me. *(Crosses to chair)* It's cold outside!

DOLORES *(Exiting to kitchen)*: Have you eaten . . .?

CAROLINE *(To Julio)*: What are they saying?

JULIO: Mom just said, "Is that a papaya in your pocket, or are you just glad to see me?" and Dad just said—

CAROLINE: Kiss off, Julio.

JULIO *(Crossing to sofa, sits)*: How did you get here?

RAMON: I took the Long Island Railroad and then I took a taxi to the house. Simple.

JULIO: Taxi? You're a big spender when it comes to Calla's money, aren't you?

CHARLIE *(Taking Ramon's hat)*: Did you do any swimming down there?

RAMON: No time.

JULIO: Did you have any time to . . . uh . . . you know . . . get a little nookie-nookie down there?

DOLORES *(Entering with a bowl of soup)*: Julio!

JULIO: Tell me in English, Dad.

DOLORES *(Smacking Julio)*: Julio! I'll kill you!

*General laughter. Ramon absently begins to rub his foot with his hand.*

RAMON (*Joking*): I had no time for nookie-nookie; I was so worried trying to find Doña Pérez, and . . . ah . . . I . . .

JULIO: You all right? What's the matter?

RAMON: Nothing.

CHARLIE: It's your foot?

RAMON: Let me tell you, when I landed in San Juan—

JULIO: Do you want the bucket?

RAMON: No! I took a bus to—

JULIO: Charlie, get the bucket for Dad.

RAMON: It's okay, there's nothing wrong.

JULIO: Right. Take off that shoe, it smells like death . . .

*Julio begins to untie Ramon's shoe. Charlie goes into the kitchen. Julio looks at the shoe, then up at Ramon suspiciously.*

Did you drink a lot of alcohol down there?

RAMON: No. I didn't have anything.

JULIO: You were drinking, weren't you?

DOLORES: You weren't, Ramon.

JULIO: You're a diabetic and you promised to stop drinking. You want to lose that foot?

RAMON: Who cares? I have *stories* to tell—

DOLORES: Why did you do that? How can you be so stupid, Ramon?

RAMON: I'm trying to tell you . . .

DOLORES: I knew you'd do something like that. Do I have to watch you like one of the children?

RAMON: Don't talk to me that way. I'll go to Tony's Bar and tell him my stories and drink until I faint.

DOLORES: You can take your bed to Tony's Bar too!

JULIO: *All right, kids, knock it off!*

RAMON: These are my feet, Dolores!

DOLORES: Not for long, Ramon!

JULIO: Mom, yell at him later. Hurry up with that bucket, Charlie! (*To Ramon*) Did you get the deed? Can you sell the house?

RAMON (*To Dolores*): Kiss me first.

DOLORES: Never.

JULIO: I'm gonna strangle them . . .

CAROLINE: Did he get it, Julio?

*Charlie enters with the bucket, puts it in front of Ramon.*

DOLORES: Talking to you is like talking to a stone. You'll drink until that foot falls off—

JULIO (*To Dolores*): Shhh! (*To Ramon*) For God's sakes, what happened down there? Did you bring it? Are you moving back or not?

RAMON (*Putting his feet in bucket*): When I landed in San Juan, I took a bus to Adjuntas. No Doña Pérez there. "Where I can find Doña Pérez?" "Utuado," someone told me. I drove to the rain forest of Utuado, there was a storm, a waterfall, I remembered the days I explored—

JULIO: What about Pérez, Dad?

RAMON: I found out she did a bad thing. She had a baptism party—on the day of a local saint. She slaughtered a pig that day, in the baby's honor: a big, red pig that screamed for hours before it died . . .

DOLORES: She shouldn't have done that, Ramon . . .

RAMON: The next day, while she was making sopa de fideo, she heard an animal screaming outside her door. When she went outside to look, there was nothing there. But when she returned to her soup, she discovered the pot had moved from the stove to the table, all by itself . . . and inside the pot . . . all the noodles had turned into long red ugly pig's hair. She screamed. "The devil has come to my kitchen to punish me!"

JULIO: This is the town you want to go back to?

RAMON: Later she found pig's hair in the middle of a coconut she *just opened* with a machete. And every night, outside her door, there was the sound of a pig screaming to death. One night, in a full moon, she got out of bed, and ran toward that terrible noise . . . until it led her, that poor woman, to the place where her husband was put to rest. That screaming was the tormented cry of Lumín Pérez in the grave. *(Beat)* Doña Pérez, they told me, lost her mind and died.

DOLORES: *What?* She's dead?

RAMON: What? She's dead? That's what I said! They said yes: the devil killed Doña Pérez.

JULIO: That's incredible.

CAROLINE: I am completely lost, folks . . .

CHARLIE: Dõna Pérez died.

CAROLINE: The lady who owned this house?

DOLORES: What did you do, Ramon?

RAMON: I felt so sad for her . . . and for us because the proof that this house really belongs to me . . . is gone forever. So I sat under an avocado tree and cried until I fell asleep.

DOLORES: How many others have died while we've been here, Ramon?

RAMON *(Laughing)*: The next morning, I was awakened by an old woman pulling on my sleeve. She was saying "Ramon Iglesia, is that you?" I looked at her and said, "Doña Pérez, is that *you?*" And her withered little face grew thirty years younger and that smile came to her and she said, "Yes Ramoncito, it's me . . ."

CHARLIE: Wait a minute, Pop . . .

RAMON: It was Doña Pérez!

JULIO: Dead or alive?

RAMON: Alive! She was alive! I told her what everyone said and she howled and slapped her knees! They all think she's a witch! They think she can fly and bring the dead come to life! They are always making stories about her!

DOLORES: Why did you scare me like that?

RAMON: I don't know . . .

JULIO: She signed the deed for her old man?

RAMON: Yes sir.

JULIO: Did you bring it? Do you have it?

RAMON (*Standing, pulling out a folded piece of paper*): I sure did! Here it is! It's the deed to the house! Our freedom!

DOLORES (*Taking deed*): Ramon . . .

RAMON: We're going home.

JULIO: I don't believe it.

RAMON: It's signed, it's perfect. She even signed the names of her daughters.

CHARLIE: Really? Why?

RAMON: And now I can slap this deed down on Calla's lawyer's desk and say, "Take me home!"

JULIO: Wow, Dad . . . this is great.

DOLORES (*Hugs and kisses Ramon*): You fixed it, Ramon.

RAMON (*Laughing*): Well . . . I think I want to tell your mother some few bedtime stories. Do you want to hear some few bedtime stories, Mother?

DOLORES (*All smiles*): Yes.

JULIO: Oh brother, what a line.

RAMON (*Soft*): Come on.

JULIO (*To Dolores*): Guess we won't be seeing much of *you* this week . . .

DOLORES: Julio, stop.

*Ramon crosses to the bedroom with Dolores.*

CAROLINE: Do you think it's okay if I sacked out and waited for Javier?

RAMON: You're very welcome.

JULIO (*Standing, saluting*): Hey—Sarge!

RAMON: Hey soldier!

JULIO: You did good. Real good, Papi.

*Julio and Charlie cross to Ramon and give him a kiss.*

RAMON: Tell Javier what I did.

*Ramon and Dolores exit upstairs.*

JULIO (*Crosses to kitchen*): Well, hogs, dinner time. Bring that bucket, Charlie.

CHARLIE: Tote that barge, Charlie, lift that bale, Charlie. (*He lifts the bucket, looks inside, drops it*) I don't believe it . . .

JULIO: What's in there? Pig's hair?

CHARLIE: You got the color right.

JULIO: What is it?

CHARLIE: It's blood. Dad's foot's bleeding again, look.

JULIO (*Looking*): Jesus God, that's ugly. (*Beat*) Don't tell Mom.

*Blackout.*

## *Scene 2*

*Later that night, 1:00 A.M. Caroline is asleep on the sofa, wrapped in several thick blankets. A small night-light burns in the corner. The door opens and Javier enters. He is twenty-two, of medium height and build. He enters as quietly as he can and locks the door behind him. He is carrying several newspapers and magazines. He checks a small table for mail, finds a letter, rips it open, and reads it rapidly.*

JAVIER: This is great. *(He crosses to the sofa and sees Caroline, smiles, takes off his shoes and unbuttons his shirt)* The Sleeping Assassin, take ten. Ambush of Love, starring that hot young couple, Javier and Caroline. *(He bends down over her, kisses her)* Guess who's got a friend in high places . . .

*She slaps him hard across the face.*

CAROLINE: That's for today. *(She swings at him again)* Here's for yesterday!

*Javier grabs her hand. He bites her on the wrist. She cries out. Javier kisses her and pushes her back down. She struggles underneath him.*

JAVIER: Here's for your love, concern, caring, patience . . .

CAROLINE: Bullshit! And don't—do not—look at me like I'm supposed to think you're cute!

JAVIER: You're so cute when you're mad: cute suburban rage. Listen, a friend of mine just got a job at the State Department. Isn't that great?

CAROLINE: Who cares? Do I care? I don't care. I'm mad.

JAVIER: Okay—time to take you home. *(He gets off sofa, crosses to chair)* What? Your old man kick you out of the house again?

CAROLINE: I'm the one asking the questions. I want to know where the frig you've been for three days while I'm having friggin' nightmares and ulcers over you.

JAVIER: Frig's a really beautiful word, Caroline, I wish you'd use it more often.

CAROLINE: Fuck you!

JAVIER: Don't you realize what this letter means? This guy was my *roommate.*

CAROLINE: I don't give a damn, Javier. I want you to talk to *me*, not look at your friggin' mail. I haven't seen you for *days* . . .

JAVIER *(Putting on shoes)*: I'm not up to it. Let me take you home before your old man comes after me with his best shotgun.

CAROLINE: My father happens to think you're nice. He thinks you're honest and thoughtful and all the things *I* used to think. What's happened to you?

JAVIER: Carrie. I'm sorry. I was thoughtless.

CAROLINE: You should see me at home, bored, pissed off, hoping Daddy isn't blitzed out of his mind, watching him treat Mom like shit, and I keep thinking: where's Javier? He used to keep me safe from this.

JAVIER: You're still safe . . .

CAROLINE: I want to be safe.

JAVIER: All you have to do is ask me.

CAROLINE: What do you think I'm doing now?

*Javier holds her and rocks her gently back and forth.*

JAVIER: I didn't disappear. I was visible the whole time.

CAROLINE: And you're a laugh-riot. *(Beat)* Don't I keep you safe?

JAVIER *(Starts kissing her again)*: Of course you do.

CAROLINE *(Pushing him back)*: Tell me where you were, liar.

JAVIER: Okay. It's Friday afternoon at the warehouse and I've just gotten those zom-bies to load five thousand units on the trucks before the second coffee break. I tell the guys to break early—but who should come along but Krinski, the boss, clacking his steel hands . . .

CAROLINE: Oh! The one who had his hands chopped off.

JAVIER: What a memory.

CAROLINE: Ten years ago.

JAVIER: Right. And now he's president of the company. Not bad for a man who can't type, right?

CAROLINE *(Laughs)*: You're a nice guy . . .

JAVIER: Anyway, here he comes: those mean steel hands glistening in the haze of forklift fumes . . . and I'm doing my imitation of Krinski on a date, unhooking a bra, and the guys are rolling on the floor, and Krinski pulls me over. Demands to see my charts. I show him the charts. He grunts. I point to the export col-umn: *five thousand units.* He drools a little. I tell him the guys and I need a break because we're ahead of schedule and he flips out. He pulls out a computer print-out and says my last shipment had sixteen errors because I *rushed* too much! I flip out! I tell him sixteen errors in an order of ten thousand is so unimpor-tant, it's a waste of time talking about it, and no one gets it out as fast as I do, and besides, I only have two hands! Why didn't they tell me he'd take that personally?

CAROLINE: What a stupid thing to say.

JAVIER: He fired me.

CAROLINE: He *what?*

JAVIER: Fired me! The only college grad that toad's ever met and the best shipping clerk that company's ever had—*fired* by a man growing moss in his crotch. I tell you, this guy has a real thing against Puerto Ricans.

CAROLINE: It's probably your big mouth, ace.

JAVIER: But *listen* . . . I realized . . . I was suddenly free. So I ran home, changed clothes, and took the first train to Manhattan.

CAROLINE: You went to Manhattan without me?

JAVIER: It was three o'clock. You were still at the bank.

CAROLINE: I get off at three-thirty Fridays, you know that.

JAVIER: I couldn't wait any longer. I had to see people who could help me get work.

CAROLINE: A lousy half hour?

JAVIER: I'm a year behind schedule. I've spent a year helping Dad stay dry, giving him money for the house, helping him find better work, thinking maybe he'll get it together and do something right.

CAROLINE: He did. He got the deed.

JAVIER: He did? He's back?

CAROLINE: This afternoon. It's all settled. You can't stop him from going—

JAVIER: Great. That's my whole year wasted. He just doesn't care what I think.

CAROLINE: He's not your son. You don't have to fix him up. And maybe he's right. Maybe you're not right . . .?

JAVIER (*Annoyed*): Who knows? (*Beat*) Okay, I'll stop fixing him up. They can go to Puerto Rico and eat green bananas all day. I'm not sticking around to watch. As long as I have friends at the State Department, it's crazy for me to be here— rotting in Holbrook. I have nothing here! I mean . . . barely nothing . . .

CAROLINE: So who'd you end up staying with?

JAVIER: A person from school.

CAROLINE: Oh—do I know this person from school?

JAVIER: No, you don't know this person.

CAROLINE: What's this person's . . . gender?

JAVIER: Her gender is female, Caroline sweetheart.

CAROLINE: Her gender is female! What a surprise! Did you sleep with her?

JAVIER: Of all the things to ask about—

CAROLINE: If you slept with her, I swear, I'm getting my dad's fattest shotgun and I'm blasting your friggin' rocks off!

JAVIER: Do you kiss your old lady with that mouth?

CAROLINE: *Did you sleep with her or not?*

JAVIER: No, I did not sleep with her or any other female during my three terrible days of absence—okay? And if you can't believe that, you can take your monogamous little ass and trot it out of here. (*He stands up, takes off his shoes. Caroline looks at him, puzzled*) If I *were* sleeping with someone else, you better believe I'd tell you. You'd get every inch of every detail. Until then, assume that I am yours . . . assume when I come home and want to take someone to bed . . . I'll knock on your door, come to your room, and make love with you for as long as you can stand it.

*They embrace and kiss as the lights go down.*

## Scene 3

*The next afternoon. There are half-filled boxes all over the living room, piles of clothes, and garbage. The walls are nearly bare and some of the clutter of the room has been relieved. Charlie is playing loud salsa music on a radio. He's packing boxes. Javier enters, putting on a shirt. He lowers the volume on the radio.*

JAVIER: *Charlie . . .*

CHARLIE: Carlos to you, bro.

JAVIER: *Charlie . . .*

CHARLIE: It's Carlos now.

JAVIER *(Noticing the boxes)*: When are you going to learn to *spell?*

CHARLIE: What? I can spell.

JAVIER: Did you mark up all the boxes like this? *(Inspects the other boxes)*

CHARLIE: That's the spelling I got from Mom.

JAVIER: "That's the spelling I got from Mom."

CHARLIE: Hey, you better watch your step, when Julio leaves, *I'm* the beast of the house.

JAVIER: How the hell do you figure that . . . *Charlie?*

CHARLIE: 'Cause I got these. *(Grabs crotch)* I don't know what you got!

JAVIER: Look at this mess. I wish you guys would check with me before doing stuff like this.

CHARLIE: What stuff?

JAVIER: Sending half your clothes to Doña Pérez. Getting rid of half the furniture.

CHARLIE: If we listened to you, we'd never leave.

JAVIER: You guys just go ahead and do these mindless things.

CHARLIE: "You guys."

JAVIER *(Sitting down to write letters)*: I mean, I didn't know Dad quit his job last week. No one told me.

CHARLIE: He was afraid you'd have a hemorrhage.

JAVIER: Wouldn't you? Dad's spent Calla's down payment already. What's he going to do for cash after it's gone?

CHARLIE: After today, Calla can pay Dad the balance on the house.

JAVIER: That's not the point. It's just that you guys never plan properly.

CHARLIE *(Crossing to Javier)*: Why do you call everybody "you guys"? It really sucks. You're part of this family too, you know.

JAVIER: Don't remind me.

CHARLIE: You try to make everybody in the family feel stupid.

JAVIER: I don't try—it just happens. *(Charlie gives him a dirty look)* I'm sorry, Charlie—Carlos—whoever you are this week. I just wish you guys would consult with me sometimes.

CHARLIE: Consult with you! We have trouble eating meals with you.

*Julio enters through the basement door, partially covered in soot, carrying a flashlight and screwdriver.*

JULIO *(To Javier)*: Hey, look who's working!

JAVIER: Pull this one, buddy.

JULIO *(Crossing to kitchen)*: I don't know about you and Caroline. Lots of funny forest noises coming from this side of the house last night.

JAVIER: Nice of you to listen. How's it going down there?

JULIO (*Off*): We might have heat by July.

CHARLIE (*Taking a book from a box; to Javier*): Did you put this in my box?

JULIO (*Off*): What'd you put in Charlie's box?

JAVIER: A book.

JULIO (*Laughs*): A book! He put a book in Charlie's box . . .!

CHARLIE (*Reading*): *Decline of the West*. Spengler. (*Throws book on floor*)

JAVIER (*To Charlie*): You said you'd read it.

CHARLIE: I tried and it's boring.

JULIO (*Entering*): You're just a boring guy, Javier. (*He exits through basement door, eating*)

JAVIER: Where did I go wrong? Where did I fail?

CHARLIE: You went wrong by calling everybody in the family "you guys." (*They continue packing boxes*) Man, I don't know where you get all your hemorrhoids from. This is the best thing that could happen to Mom and Dad.

JAVIER: To Mom, maybe.

CHARLIE: You don't go shopping with Mom—me and Dad got to talk to everybody in the store for her. She don't read English. Dad drives her everywhere. This place is worse than San Quentin to her.

JAVIER: It's her own fault. She could have learned English: she still can.

CHARLIE: I think it's neat she don't know English.

JAVIER: Doesn't know English.

CHARLIE: It's pure of her. And I think it would be great if you got happy for them, encourage them—

JAVIER: I don't like encouraging people to quit—

CHARLIE: I mean, Dad wanted to go back five years ago, but he said, "No, Javier's got to go to college first."

JAVIER: Am I going to be tormented because of my education?

CHARLIE: Because you forgot where it came from!

JAVIER: It came from *me*, buddy boy—*me*, busting my ass, seeking out financial aid. If I hadn't taken the time to ask the right—

CHARLIE: And where'd you get the time? From Dad!

JAVIER: Oh Christ . . .

CHARLIE: *Dad*, who went around ripped-up and filthy dirty working two jobs so you wouldn't have to work *any*. Dad bent down to clean floors so you'd be able to . . . to . . . walk all over his back, wipe your feet, and go . . . (*They work for a few moments longer*) Anyway, I think Puerto Rico will be fun. Jungles and farms—you can't get that in Holbrook. And Mom says we can buy a horse down there—something else you can't get in Holbrook.

JAVIER: You can't get malaria in Holbrook either . . .

CHARLIE: And hang out at the beach all day long . . .

JAVIER: . . . or tarantulas and hurricanes . . .

CHARLIE: . . . And all those pretty girls to fall in love with.

JAVIER: Early marriage, lots of brats, and a fat middle age!

CHARLIE: Racist!

JAVIER (*Laughing*): Mom hates it when she asks, "Why don't you marry a nice Latin girl?" and I always say, "Nice Latin girls are fat and mean by the time they're twenty-nine."

CHARLIE: Mom thinks . . . you really dislike our people.

JAVIER: Charlie, I was *joking*. That was a joke.

CHARLIE: Yeah? That why you don't speak Spanish anymore? Is that why you don't kiss Dad?

JAVIER: I don't speak Spanish because . . . I don't know. Got out of the habit. (*Beat*) But I've been starting to think. About our people, you know? And I don't even know what those words mean, "our people." Chicanos in California? Dominicans? Cubans in Florida? Puerto Ricans in New York who still go back to the island and never made a commitment here? I don't know. I look around. I know what our people feel and need and want—and I want to help them someday—and I know I will someday—but, something pushes me away . . .

CHARLIE: You're mixed up. That school really made you confused.

JAVIER: A lot of it is Dad. Too many things have gotten between me and him. If I could figure him out . . .

CHARLIE: Like what?

JAVIER: Oh Charlie, like . . . I don't know . . . all the times Dad brought a live pig home and slaughtered it in the backyard the way they used to do it in Puerto Rico. And lucky me gets to hold the bucket to catch the blood I'd eat later that night in blood sausages . . .

CHARLIE: I love blood sausages.

JAVIER (*Beat*): There was my Christmas at drunk, crazy Uncle Wilfred's who beat the living shit out of his son, cousin Javier, that day. I'll never forget Javier crying, twisting around on the floor, bleeding and vomiting all over the Christmas nativity thing, a little plastic doodad the Department of Welfare had given to them. (*Beat*) Or my first sexual flight to heaven. Another cousin, I won't tell you which, the shock would kill you. She stalked into my bed one night, I was ten, she was curious, I faked sleeping, she found her way into my pants, I was scared and quiet; she was gentle and warm. Or my second flight. Another cousin who crawled into the bathtub I was innocently bathing in—he pushed me face down into the water—I was eleven—I almost drowned—terrified—I was ripped up the way you rip up paper—then I was blasted from here to God. (*A knock is heard at the door*) Who's that?

CALLA (*Off*): Calla!

CHARLIE (*To Javier*): I hear you.

CALLA (*Off*): Open up!

JAVIER (*To Charlie*): Did Calla get the deed yet—?

CALLA (*Off*): I want to talk to you!

*Javier opens the front door and Nick Calla, a tall, rough Italian in his forties, enters.*

Javier—I want your father! I have to talk to that brilliant businessman!

JAVIER: He and my mother are—

CALLA: *Ramon, are you in this house??*

JAVIER: He and my mother are—

CALLA: Days and days go by. I'm only next door. Why don't you people come to me?

JAVIER: This morning they went—

CALLA: I swear little children are easier to keep track of than you Puerto Ricans!

JAVIER: Mr. Calla—

CALLA: No telephone! No telephone! (*He crosses to the upstairs exit*) Are you upstairs?

JAVIER (*Soft, to Charlie*): I think I need Julio.

CALLA: You need an accountant. A lawyer. An interpreter. A *plan*. I gave your father a down payment, one thousand bucks, and he said he'd give me the deed *right away*.

JAVIER: Dad's showing it to your lawyer—

CALLA: So why doesn't he get in touch with *me*? I've got people waiting for me: repair people, insurance people, my family, creditors. What do I tell them?

JAVIER: I don't know.

CALLA: You don't know! Do you know I could have kept that money in the bank, *earning me interest*?

JAVIER: We've been having trouble—!

CALLA: *I've* been having trouble! I've got a brother-in-law in Brooklyn who thinks he's moving into this house April first! What the hell am I going to tell him?

JAVIER: I don't know, Nick—

CALLA: We're talking *real estate*—people uprooting themselves, promises I gotta keep. Meanwhile, I'm putting out money on trust and my old lady's in the hospital with a spastic colon, a weak bladder, a skin rash, and you people got me in this *limbo*! You realize if I don't buy this dump no one goes back to Puerto Rico? You people would have been up the devil's asshole if it wasn't for me!

JAVIER: You should be canonized.

CALLA: I've given you money every time you needed it!

JAVIER: And we're giving you the best real estate deal since the Italians stole America from the Spanish!

CALLA: *I'll be damned if I give you people one penny more!*

*Pow! A loud explosion rocks the house. Smoke pours into the living room through the basement door.*

What the hell—?

JAVIER: Oh no.

CALLA: What is that smell?

CHARLIE: Julio!

JAVIER (*Realizing*): Julio . . .?

CALLA: What is that . . .?

JAVIER: That's my brother working on the furnace.

CALLA: The furnace? What's wrong with it? What's wrong with the furnace?

JAVIER: I'll catch you later. (*He exits through basement door*)

CALLA: I'm losing my shirt on this deal, and *I'm going to lose my mind!* I swear, I'm going to have a goddamn stroke because of you people!

CHARLIE: Last time the furnace did this, it was thirty below zero with the wind chill.

CALLA: Do you hear that noise? That's my brain revving up for a stroke. *(Charlie crosses to basement door, looks in)* I'm basically a good person. I'm honest. I'm not a yelling person. You people are making me into a yelling person. *(He sits, his head in his hands)*

CHARLIE: I better open the windows. *(He does)* When the oil fumes come up here, it's the most incredible smell of your life. *(He crosses to Mr. Calla)* We had to evacuate the house once. Do you know that if you push against the walls or slam a door, you can feel the house *give?*

*Calla walks away from Charlie.*

CALLA: I love it. Tell me more.

CHARLIE: Just wait till it's summer and you have to deal with the cesspool out back.

CALLA: I'd rather deal with my wife's colon condition, thank you. *(Crosses to Charlie)* Look, Charlie, tell your father to tell your father's *brain* that I came by and to get in touch with me real fast—or next time, I'm bringing my big Italian buddies.

CHARLIE: Javier says there hasn't been a smart Italian since they stabbed Caesar.

*Calla crosses to the front door, stops, turns around, looks at Charlie, smiles.*

CALLA: Everybody in this house has a decent wit, but nobody in this house has a brain. You people have to learn that time is money. I swear, you're so poor only 'cause you're so slow.

*Calla exits. Charlie crosses to the basement door and looks in. No more smoke comes out of it.*

CHARLIE *(Calling into the basement)*: Are you guys alive?

*Julio and Javier emerge from basement. They are both covered in soot.*

JAVIER: Oh God . . .

CHARLIE: What happened down there?

JULIO: Aarggh . . . arrghargarrrrrgh . . .

JAVIER *(To Julio)*: Why don't you go clean up?

JULIO: Aarrgharghargh . . .

JAVIER: Wash your face, you'll feel better.

*Julio exits into the kitchen.*

CHARLIE: What happened?

JAVIER: Where's Calla?

CHARLIE: He went home to do something to his wife.

JAVIER *(Sitting)*: I tell you, that basement's a scene out of Fellini.

JULIO (*Off*): *Shit! Big disgusting shit! Big disgusting runny pukey shit!*
JAVIER: What's wrong . . .?
JULIO (*Off*): *I can't believe this place!!*
JAVIER: What's wrong?
JULIO (*Off*): *Send the beast to boot camp now!*
JAVIER: Julio! What is it?

*Julio enters, wiping his face on a dry towel.*

JULIO: Everybody better enjoy the way they smell right now—Javier, do you enjoy the way you smell right now—?
JAVIER: What happened?
JULIO: I just used the last, final drops of water in our well. There is now . . . no water . . . not a *drop* . . . coming from the faucet.
JAVIER: You're kidding me.
JULIO: *I hate this goddamn place!* Oh God, thank you, thank you, in one week I will be in boot camp and boot camp will be a luxury paradise compared to this! (*He throws the towel to Javier*) Here. I spit on this. You can use it to bathe with. *Goddammit why is it so cold in here?*
CHARLIE: I opened all the windows.
JULIO: *Close* them! It's *winter!! Christ*, Charlie!
CHARLIE: It was smoking and smelling in here.
JULIO: It's not smoking in here any pissing longer! *Is it?*

*Charlie scrambles around, closing windows.*

I'm surrounded by fools, lunkheads, dolts, a natural leader like me.
JAVIER: Well listen to *her*.
JULIO: I'm not a her!
JAVIER: Just sit there and rest yourself awhile, sweetie.
JULIO: A warning, bro.
JAVIER: Don't call me bro. I'm not a bro.

*The front door opens. Dolores enters, crying, and sits.*

Aaaaaand—it's Mamacita . . .
JULIO: Oh boy, have we got good news for you.
DOLORES (*Holding back her tears*): Hello . . .
CHARLIE: Hi beautiful. (*He crosses to her and gives her a kiss*)
JULIO: So what's the news?
JAVIER: Where's Dad?
DOLORES: Out—
CHARLIE: Why are you crying?
DOLORES: I'm not crying—
CHARLIE: What's the matter?
DOLORES: Nothing—

*Ramon enters and slams the front door hard behind him.*

JULIO: What's going on?

DOLORES: Ramon, please—

JULIO: What's up?

DOLORES: —don't slam the door that way!

RAMON *(To Dolores)*: Don't tell me what to do. If I want to slam the door, I'll slam the door! *(He opens the door again and slams it hard)*

JULIO: Dad—

CHARLIE: You'll shatter the *glass*—

RAMON *(To Dolores)*: I'll break anything I want to!

DOLORES: Don't make noise! Just don't make noise!

RAMON: *Noise?*

JULIO: Hey, kids—

RAMON: Noise? Noise? *(He goes to one of the taped-up boxes, rips it open, and turns it upside down. Pots, pans and utensils spill out)*

JULIO: What the hell are you doing?

CHARLIE: You're going to break that stuff!

JULIO: What the hell happened out there?

RAMON: Look at this stuff. This junk. All this is junk that came from my big business, my big diner. You know something? I'm stupid . . .

JULIO *(To Javier)*: Say something to him—

RAMON: —stupid about money, friends, everything.

*Ramon finds a plate among the debris and shatters it on the floor. Dolores screams.*

JULIO: All right, Dad, that's *it*—

JAVIER: Oh God, this family . . .

CHARLIE *(To Ramon)*: *Are you going to keep breaking all this stuff?*

RAMON *(To Charlie)*: *Don't you dare talk to me that way!*

JULIO: EVERYBODY STOP SHOUTING!

CHARLIE *(To Julio)*: Are you going to let him have a tantrum all over the house?

JULIO: *I want everybody—quiet—now!*

DOLORES *(Crying openly)*: None of this is our fault, we never hurt anybody.

JULIO: We know, we know, we know . . . everyone's okay . . . let's all be *calm* right now.

*Ramon pulls a bottle of rum out of his back pocket. He pours himself a shot and drinks.*

CHARLIE *(To Ramon)*: What the hell are you doing now?

RAMON *(To Charlie)*: I want you to go to the liquor store and get me another bottle of this—

DOLORES: What are you doing?

RAMON *(To Charlie)*: Did you hear what I told you?

JULIO: No drinking. Alcohol's gonna—*(to Javier) say something—you're his son!*

DOLORES *(To Ramon)*: If you're going to drink, I'm not going to stay here, that's a promise . . .

RAMON: Your promises are full of shit, old lady.

DOLORES: You're going to squeeze the breath out of me.

RAMON: Don't talk that way to me, or I swear I'll—I'll—

DOLORES: You'll what? What are you going to do to me?

RAMON: I'll show you!

*Ramon goes for Dolores. She screams. Julio intercepts him.*

JULIO: You put one hand on her, and I'm going to make you wish you never had sons—!

RAMON *(Simultaneously)*: I'm going to punish her—nobody should talk to a man the way that bitch talks to me—!

*Dolores falls to the floor.*

JAVIER: Oh no . . .

JULIO *(Rushing to Dolores)*: Mom . . .

JAVIER: Mom, Mom . . .

JULIO: Mom, cut it out . . .

CHARLIE *(To Ramon)*: See what you did?

*Ramon, numb, sits on the stairs, and drinks some more while Julio and Javier attempt to revive Dolores.*

JULIO: Mom, please . . .

JAVIER: Can you hear me . . .?

CHARLIE: Mom, stop this—!

JULIO: Mom . . .

JAVIER: Mom . . .

JULIO: Pick her up.

*Julio and Javier lift Dolores and put her on the sofa. Her breathing is loud and irregular. She thrashes about. Ramon is quietly crying.*

Dammit, old lady, stop.

CHARLIE: Call a doctor!

JAVIER: She'll be okay, don't worry.

CHARLIE *(To Julio)*: Don't you know any Marine lifesaving shit?

JULIO: I'm not a marine yet, moron!

JAVIER: Shut up, Charlie! She'll be okay!

CHARLIE: What if she stops breathing?

JAVIER: She won't.

RAMON: You should have heard me trying to talk your mother into coming to the beautiful United States with me. All the lies I had to tell her!

*Julio crosses to Ramon and quietly tries to take the bottle from him throughout this scene. Ramon resists him.*

JULIO *(To Ramon)*: Sí, Papi, sí, sí . . .

RAMON: We moved to Holbrook when Grundy Avenue was still a dirt road. We pulled up to the house—it looked like a witch's cap—and your mother started laughing when she saw it, she thought I was making a joke.

JAVIER: See? She's coming out of it.

JULIO: There better be a great reason for all this hitting around here.

CHARLIE *(To Ramon)*: Will you stop drinking?

RAMON *(To Charlie)*: Learn what I learned: it's right for a man to drink a drop of rum for every drop of water he has cried. *Two* drops if he can get away with it! *(Drinks shot)* Good! This shot's for success! *(Drinks)* For Ramon Iglesia! Cook! Janitor! Manager of a failed, greasy diner!

JULIO: Shut up, Dad.

RAMON: For welfare! Welfare lines. Welfare meat. Welfare beans. Christmas welfare.

JAVIER: Son of welfare.

JULIO: For Godsakes, Dad, cool out!

RAMON: Find work, they told me. Good janitor work. Slop sinks and oil mops. I cleaned floors in Javier's high school and he never told his friends who I was. And your mother at the window, day after day—the clock in her head counting the slow years until our return to Puerto Rico. Each year I *lied*; I said, "*This* year we go back." But she didn't know how the kids loved me at the school I cleaned. The comic, the funny Ramon!

*Dolores has come out of her fit and is opening her eyes.*

JAVIER: Can you see me?

DOLORES: Yes.

JAVIER: Do you want to sit up?

DOLORES: I'm okay.

*Ramon takes another shot of rum, sits.*

CHARLIE *(To Ramon)*: Will you put that junk away?

RAMON: Leave me alone—show some respect.

CHARLIE: Who can respect you the way you down that stuff, and Mom's all hurt?

JULIO: Mom . . . what *is* it? What happened to you guys?

CHARLIE *(To Ramon)*: Everybody lets you get away with murder.

JULIO: Charlie, will you calm down?

CHARLIE *(Stands)*: Look at him! Look at him! *That's* why we're in one mess after another! That's why his foot's gonna burst right open someday! *(He goes to Ramon and pulls the bottle from his hand)* Will you leave this alone?

RAMON: *Who do you think you are?*

*Ramon stands and slaps Charlie across the face. Charlie cocks his fist as if to strike back. Julio grabs Charlie's wrist and twists it behind his back. He pushes Charlie offstage.*

JULIO: WHY DON'T YOU JUST CALM DOWN?
CHARLIE: LET GO OF ME!
JULIO: ARE YOU GOING TO CALM DOWN?!

*Javier crosses to the exit and pulls Julio back onstage as best he can.*

JAVIER: Come on, Julio, knock it off.
JULIO: He was going to hit Dad!
JAVIER: Come on.
JULIO: He was going to hit your father! *Stop pulling me! All right!*

*Julio pulls free of Javier. No one moves for a few moments. The two of them look at each other.*

Charlie.

*Charlie enters, wiping his eyes.*

CHARLIE: I'm sorry—
JULIO: Go give Dad a kiss and tell him you're sorry, go.

*Charlie crosses to Ramon and kisses him on the cheek.*

Put that stuff away.

*Ramon caps the bottle and puts it away. Julio crosses to Dolores.*

Are you going to live, sweetie?
DOLORES: I think so.
JULIO: Okay, good. I like the way the house sounds right now, nice and *silent*. Okay, I want to know what happened.
DOLORES: They won't let us go. We can't sell the house.
JULIO: Why?
DOLORES: Because the deed to this house was not legally signed and Calla's lawyer won't accept it.
JULIO: What's wrong with it?
DOLORES: Doña Pérez had to get the signatures of her two daughters because the house is in their names too. So she signed for them.
JULIO: It's a forgery. It's a goddamn forgery.
RAMON: That's exactly what the lawyer said . . .
JAVIER (*Crossing to Ramon*): You knew about this?
RAMON: Knew? Of course I knew. It was my idea. I thought it would save time.
JAVIER: You thought you were going to get away with this? (*No answer*) How can you be so stupid?

RAMON: Don't yell at me—I wasn't thinking.

DOLORES: Nobody blames you. The boys don't blame you.

JULIO (Crosses to Ramon): What's the problem? You send the deed to Doña Pérez today, she'll get the girls to sign the stupid thing.

RAMON: This came in the mail today. It's a letter from Mercedez Terrón and Perdita Santoval. They say they won't put their names to any deed that doesn't give them every penny that comes from the sale of the house. They're getting lawyers to make sure they're not cheated. (Beat) It's somebody else's house, children. Again. (He stands up, puts on a coat and crosses to the front door) Charlie, clean up this mess. I'm going to Tony's Bar. If anybody want to stop me, they can try.

*Ramon exits. Charlie begins to pick up the garbage. Lights fade.*

## Scene 4

*A week later. In front of the Marine Corps Recruiting Office in Holtsville, New York. It's 4:00 A.M. It's very cold. Julio and Javier enter, carrying bags.*

JAVIER: God, Julio.

JULIO: This is it.

JAVIER: God, Julio.

JULIO: Stop being a wimp.

JAVIER: God, Julio.

JULIO: Go stay in the car if you're so cold.

JAVIER: You had to pick the coldest night of the millennium, didn't you?

JULIO: Go back to the car if you're cold.

JAVIER: I don't want to sit there by myself—

JULIO: I don't want to miss anybody—

JAVIER: No one's stupid enough to be out here this early, in this freezing weather . . .

JULIO: Well, you wanted to come out with me—

JAVIER: I thought you would have the good sense to stay in the *car.*

JULIO: A marine's got to get used to the cold, wimp!

JAVIER: Mother of God, spare me.

*Julio puts his bags down and looks around. He checks his watch.*

JULIO: Nobody.

JAVIER: Who's supposed to come?

JULIO: Sergeant Overbaby.

JAVIER: Who?

JULIO: Overbaby.

JAVIER: You're giving your future to a man named *Overbaby?*

JULIO (Looking into the office): It's not quite four; I'm early . . .

JAVIER: He's probably in a snowbank doing pushups in the nude . . .

JULIO: I think he said he has to come from Hempstead.

JAVIER: "I sing of Olaf, glad and big." Do you know that poem?

JULIO: Maybe I should give him a call . . .

JAVIER: "I sing of Olaf, glad and big."

JULIO: Who's Olaf, your boyfriend?

JAVIER: He was a Swede, a pacifist, who got the life kicked out of him in a poem because he would not kiss your fucking flag.

JULIO (*Looking at Javier*): Sometimes I think you have the basic mentality of a handball.

JAVIER: I'm going to give your recruiting officer a copy of it . . .

JULIO: Great. They'll have me shot for having a flake for an older brother. Why don't you stop living in the sixties? Be like me! Adjust to the times! Be a beast!

JAVIER: I'd rather be in bed, thank you. (*He walks over to the recruiting office and looks inside the window*) That's interesting. Hmmrummmmmm. That's very, *very* interesting. Wow.

JULIO: What is it?

JAVIER: Well. Up against the wall. In there. Are all these little boxes . . .

JULIO: I sense something profoundly stupid coming on.

JAVIER: . . . *and* above each of the little boxes is a name, rank, and serial number . . . and inside each of the little boxes—let me make sure—(*He looks into the window*) Yep! Inside each of the little boxes is a pair . . . of human testicles . . . little Marine testicles.

JULIO: Har. Har. Har. Yuck. Yuck.

JAVIER: Isn't that part of the Deal? You give Uncle Sam your balls, and what's left of your nervous system, and *zap* they turn you into a grunt!

JULIO: I'm not going to be a grunt—I'm going to be a technician, asshole, a hydraulics *technician.*

JAVIER: Right. Just like the ads. "High school dropout? Can't read English or do long division? Join the Marines and become a neutron physicist!"

JULIO: It's not like that, Bolshevik!

JAVIER: "Learn bio-warfare and global defoliation!"

JULIO: Hey, at least I didn't waste four years in some obscure little college, learning political science, just so I can come home and hang my brain on the loading dock of a warehouse! *That's* good. That's progress.

JAVIER: Leave me alone.

JULIO: I, howsoever, am getting my brain together in a big way, with a future, and a job, out in the world where the real power is.

JAVIER: The real world? You're going from Mommy's bosom to Uncle Sam's. Fed, clothed, and told what to do. *And* you might get killed in the process. Might get mistaken for a Southeast Asian and blown to bits—

JULIO: Javier, for Chrissakes, it's 1980, it's *peacetime.*

JAVIER: Accidents can happen in peacetime!

JULIO: Accidents *don't* happen in peacetime! Not to marines!

JAVIER: And promise me you won't develop a drug habit, or go to Iran.

JULIO: Promise me you'll never run for public office! You're so hopeless! What a mother hen! I can't believe you!

JAVIER: I am not.

JULIO: You are. You're a mother hen.

JAVIER: I am *not*.

JULIO: I know the real Javier. Nonviolent, nonalcoholic, boring, abnormal . . .

JAVIER: Listen, have a great military career. I'll see you later.

JULIO: Javier the Saint. The unhappy Javier.

JAVIER: Leave me alone.

JULIO: Awwwww, I know why he's unhappy. I know why he broods. What does Caroline want from your ass this time? What is the evil woman doing to our hero now?

JAVIER: Nothing. She's . . . been looking for bedroom furniture, that's all. *(Beat)* Do you think Overbaby will let me join the corps?

JULIO: The corps don't take the mentally ill . . . or the castrated, bro . . . *(He walks away from Javier)*

JAVIER *(Lost in thought)*: Don't call me bro. *(Looking at Julio)* Do you remember *Patton? (Takes Julio's arm, imitates George C. Scott)* "When you put your hand into a mess of goo that ten seconds ago was your best friend's face, you'll know what to do!"

JULIO *(Smiling)*: *Apocalypse Now?*

JULIO AND JAVIER *(Imitating Robert Duvall)*: "I love the smell of napalm in the morning. It smells like victory!" *(They laugh)*

JULIO *(Beat)*: So. What are you going to do about Dad?

JAVIER: I don't know. He told me he wants to start a restaurant in Arecibo—but he hasn't even found a place to live yet. He hasn't even sold the house.

JULIO: Don't fuck with his dreams.

JAVIER: His dreams are killing him.

JULIO: *Your* dreams are killing him. He's not the failure you think he is. He bought a house—okay it's got problems; and his son went to college—okay he's a moron; but his *other* two sons were raised healthy and brilliant. That's not successful?

JAVIER: I don't know . . . I don't know . . .

JULIO: And you're supposed to be smart? Hey. When I'm gone you have to keep that house together. It's your *job*.

JAVIER: I don't want that job. I want to solve my problems. I always used you to protect myself— *(A car can be heard pulling up)* Wait; listen— *(Julio looks out into the distance)* Yep. The Marines have landed.

JULIO: Already? Really? *(Getting his stuff together)* This is it, my friend.

JAVIER: Dammit. I had . . . so many things I wanted to tell you. Ideas, advice—all sorts of things.

JULIO: Unless you can say them in ten words or less, you better just say good-bye. I can feel myself turning into government property even as we speak.

JAVIER: I'm going to miss you.

JULIO: I'm going to miss you too. Hey, the truth—doesn't that Overbaby look like a grim guy?

JAVIER: Terrifying. Awesome.

JULIO: You take care of everybody—and make sure they write—and keep Mom from getting too excited—and for Godsakes, make it big already. I expect great shit from you. I mean, doesn't that Overbaby look like a *really grim guy?*

*Julio salutes Javier and exits. Javier waves to Julio. Julio reenters and embraces Javier. Blackout.*

END OF ACT ONE

# ACT TWO

## *Scene 1*

*Later that week. As the lights come up we see Dolores sitting on the sofa, writing a letter. Javier enters, partially dressed.*

JAVIER: Did we run out of water again?

DOLORES: I had to wash some clothes for your father.

JAVIER: I need water. I have to take a bath.

DOLORES: They went out for water. They'll be back soon.

JAVIER: Why hasn't Dad called a repairman? Get some guy to fix the pump, we'll have water like civilized people.

DOLORES: Wash what you can.

JAVIER: I have an interview today with the campaign manager of a guy running for Congress.

DOLORES: I wish you'd speak to me in Spanish sometime!

JAVIER: What for? You're deaf in Spanish too.

DOLORES: Besides, we're moving. The pump is Calla's problem.

JAVIER: You'd rather see Dad go from house to house begging for water?

DOLORES: In Puerto Rico he'd walk from his house in Miraflores to my house in Arecibo with two barrels of water—one on this shoulder, one on this shoulder. In the sun. Barefoot.

JAVIER: That's because Dad would do anything for a date.

DOLORES: Javier! He was a good boy.

JAVIER: I'm sure he was a very good boy. And you were a good girl, right?

DOLORES: Yes. I was. *(Javier laughs)* Javier!

*The door opens. Charlie enters carrying a bucket of water.*

CHARLIE: Man oh man oh man . . .

JAVIER: Little water boy!

CHARLIE *(Crossing to kitchen)*: Thanks for the help. Jesus it is *freezing* out there! I think this bucket froze—put your face in it, Javier, find out for me. *(He exits)*

RAMON *(Entering with bucket of water)*: Jesus, it's freezing out there! There's a wind you can't believe.

DOLORES: I was telling Javier how you used to carry water to my house in Arecibo. So strong!

RAMON: Still strong! Right, Javier?

JAVIER: Strong like mule and just as stubborn.

CHARLIE *(Reentering)*: How would you like to be drowning in this bucket, Javier?

JAVIER: Two buckets of water for bathing, cooking, cleaning, and drinking. Of all the goddamn days. *(He takes a bucket of water and exits upstairs)*

CHARLIE: Julio's gone a week, and everybody falls apart. Hey. I'm going next door to watch some TV, okay?

RAMON: You should read those books Javier gave you, instead.

CHARLIE: Come on, *Wide World of Sports* is on.

RAMON: All right. Don't stay out too long. Your mother needs you here.

CHARLIE: Just save me water to brush my teeth with. I feel like I got a roll of old pennies in my mouth.

*Charlie departs. Dolores continues to write. Ramon sits.*

RAMON (*Suspiciously*): What are you writing?

DOLORES: Nothing, it's nothing.

RAMON: What is it?

DOLORES: I'm writing to Doña Pérez. I'm telling her I'm sad about Julio. How much I miss him.

RAMON: He had to do what he had to do. There was nothing for Julio to do in Holbrook.

DOLORES: He could die where he's going. What if he dies?

RAMON: He's not going to die. Julio is a beast!

DOLORES: If they hurt my little boy, I don't know what I'll do . . .

RAMON (*Crossing to Dolores*): Come on, old lady, stop.

DOLORES (*Crossing to sofa, sits*): He never *relaxed*. He worked after school every day—

RAMON (*Reading her letter*): He loves responsibility. Loves to give orders.

DOLORES (*Packing clothes in a box*): Was he angry with us, Ramon?

RAMON: Mamacita, please . . . (*He crumples her letter and puts it in his pocket*) I don't want you talking about this and writing it in your letters. You have no proof.

DOLORES: Javier is my proof. When he came home from school he was a stranger. The same will happen to Julio: they'll change him.

RAMON: Shhhhhh, Javier will hear.

DOLORES: Javier doesn't kiss you good-night anymore. Up to the day he left, he kissed you. That made me feel so good. It meant the family survived another day.

RAMON: I don't know what's wrong with him but he's still my Javier. Maybe he'll come to Puerto Rico one day.

DOLORES: No he won't. And we won't beg him. Do you hear? I'll never beg for my son's affection and neither will you.

*A knock is heard.*

RAMON: Come in, it's open.

*Calla enters with two huge buckets of water. Ramon stands and crosses to Calla.*

I was going to see you today!

*Calla puts buckets down.*

CALLA: Why didn't you tell me you had no water?

RAMON: I didn't want to bother you.

CALLA: How long has it been like this?

RAMON: A week.

CALLA: Excuse me, Dolores—*that's really stupid, Ramon!*

RAMON: I planned to call a repairman today!

CALLA: Sure you did! Here! From Nick Calla, your local neighborhood Red Cross. Free of charge.

RAMON: That's very kind.

CALLA: Look, if you want more water, hook up a hose to my spigot out there, all right? Do you have a hose?

RAMON: No.

CALLA: No. I'll lend you mine. It's stupid to be without water. *(He crosses downstage away from Dolores, motions to Ramon to follow him. To Ramon)* What's new with the deed, anything?

RAMON: Doña Pérez talks to Santoval and Terrón every day.

CALLA: And?

RAMON: They don't want to change their minds.

CALLA: I don't know how much longer I can wait. I'll level with you: I'm gonna look at another house today. I don't want to, I want *this* one, but you don't leave me much choice, do you?

RAMON *(Taking crumpled letter from pocket)*: My wife is writing her another letter.

CALLA: *Letters!* Christ, sometimes I think your heart's not really in it.

RAMON: How's your wife? Still sick?

CALLA: She's getting there. It's tough for her—I'm an ox, but she's a bird. I know she'd feel better if this was over with.

RAMON: It should be soon.

CALLA *(Crossing to door)*: Let me know *very* soon. Good to see you again, Dolores.

DOLORES *(To Ramon)*: Tell him I hope she feels better soon.

RAMON: She says she hopes your wife feels better soon.

CALLA: Thanks. Be in touch.

*Calla exits. Ramon takes a bucket to the kitchen and returns.*

DOLORES: I heard what he said—

RAMON: You always understand when you want to understand, don't you?

DOLORES: You can't let him buy another house. He has to take this one. This house!

RAMON: This house is Ramon Iglesia's house.

DOLORES: Ramon Iglesia's house is in Puerto Rico.

RAMON *(Crossing to Dolores)*: Do you really think I can start my own business down there? Can you really see us going back there? Back to the little farms and the hills and the people who never left? What I'm going to do down there? *(Dolores crosses away from him)* I thought about this all week, about my house, about the way it's grown with things, for nineteen years, all the bits and pieces of Ramon Iglesia. Even the accidents—

DOLORES: Not accidents, Ramon: mistakes.

RAMON: Mistakes then. *(Beat)* The night I lost the diner and the boys and I filled the station wagon with food and all the things we could save. Brought it here. Boxes of pots and plates and bags of rice. The house was full and fat and beautiful.

DOLORES: I swear on the spirit of my Felicia, if you keep me here another year, it'll be our last year together. Every year you promise me we'll go back and every year you break your promise. No more, Ramon! I let you do what you want to do for nineteen years, now I do what I want. If you don't, I'll leave you. I'll go home by myself.

RAMON: *We don't have any money!*

DOLORES: There's somebody in this house with enough money to help you.

RAMON: I'm not going to him. I can't go to him.

DOLORES *(Pointing offstage)*: He's right there. He knows what we need. When he returned from school what did we hear but big, big talk about helping the poor? Giving to the poor. Well, Ramon, *we* are the poor. You and me.

RAMON: I can't take from him, Dolores, will you listen to what I say!

DOLORES: No! It's only fear talking to me. You're so afraid of him, I turn red with shame thinking about it!

RAMON: I'm not afraid of Javier—

DOLORES: You're afraid of him and he's ashamed of you.

RAMON: Javier is not ashamed of his father! I wouldn't let him live in the house—

DOLORES: You let him live in the house. You let him eat your food and spit it back in your face. You let him keep you in this country because you're afraid of him.

RAMON: Don't use that word with me again!

DOLORES: Coward! Coward!

JAVIER *(Enters dressed in three-piece suit)*: Hi folks. I'm on my way, wish me luck.

*Javier begins to get his things ready. Dolores pokes Ramon.*

DOLORES: Ramon!

RAMON *(Crossing to Javier)*: Javier!

JAVIER *(Crossing to door)*: I've got a train to catch, I'll talk to you later.

RAMON *(Intercepting Javier)*: You look very nice. I've never seen you wearing that.

JAVIER *(Smiling)*: I bought it at school. Cost me a bundle. It's wool.

RAMON: When is your talk?

JAVIER: Talk?

RAMON: Eh—your talking—your *speaking*—

JAVIER: Interview? It's not for a while. If I catch the one-thirty train, I'll be in at three, have lunch with a friend from school whose gender is female, and the interview is at five. Do I look all right?

DOLORES: Maybe you'll be governor of Puerto Rico.

JAVIER: This job's not that good. This guy's running for reelection in Brooklyn; I'd be on the field team.

RAMON: Kissing babies?

JAVIER: That comes a lot later.

DOLORES: Is there any money?

JAVIER: Very little. The man's not rich but he's organized rent strikes and gotten people heat for their apartments.

RAMON: We need him in Holbrook!

*Javier attempts to exit. Dolores grabs him and sits him down.*

DOLORES: I'm going to make you lunch.

JAVIER: I don't have time for that.

*Dolores hurries into the kitchen. Javier looks at Ramon.*

What's up?

RAMON: What's up? Doña Pérez wrote. She can't convince her daughters to sign the deed. I have to go home and talk to them. I need money to go. I'm broke.

JAVIER: Well, can you take out a loan?

RAMON: No bank on Long Island will give me a loan at this point.

JAVIER (*Crossing to Ramon*): Dad, how many times did I urge you to get out of that school and get a better-paying job? Do you see, finally, why I kept pushing you?

RAMON: Javier—

JAVIER: You've spent all of Calla's down payment, haven't you?

RAMON: Yes. I had debts.

JAVIER: If you had listened to me . . .

*Dolores enters from kitchen.*

You know what I think? I think it's good—this whole Doña Pérez thing. It's your chance to change your mind.

DOLORES (*Gives Javier tray of food*): He's not going to change his mind.

JAVIER: Why not? Because you haven't given your permission?

RAMON: Nobody tells me what I can or cannot do.

JAVIER (*Putting tray on floor*): What do you *really* want? All you do is what someone else wants. You moved to the States because everyone else was doing it. Now that everyone's going back, you're going back. It's so accidental, so random—

RAMON: Nobody tells me what to do!

JAVIER: Jump, fetch, and carry your whole life long. And when Calla snaps his fingers, you faint. And if you don't faint (*He points at Dolores*) she does!

DOLORES: *Will you speak to us in Spanish or not?*

JAVIER: Spanish and English have a word in common, Mom, and that word is no. No, I will not give you money to go back. (*Beat*) When I graduated, I had a choice: take a job in D.C., or come home and help you guys. I came because of all your emotional letters for help. The house! The car! Ramon's foot! So I came and took a job I hated and tried to get Dad to take a civil service test, dry out a little, start a savings account—*but I never got through.* (*He turns away from Ramon and Dolores*) Mañana, Javier, mañana!

DOLORES: You did only what you *had* to do—as a son! An Iglesia!

JAVIER: I didn't *have* to do anything!

DOLORES: I thought you came back out of love.

JAVIER: You thought I came back out of obligation—

RAMON *(Crossing to Javier)*: *Are you calling your mother a liar?*

JAVIER: I was twenty-one, I wasn't obliged—!

RAMON: *Did you hear me?*

JAVIER: *I heard you!*

DOLORES: *Don't yell at your father! Respect your father!*

JAVIER: I wouldn't have returned if I didn't respect him. But I don't respect him now. Giving up on everything this place has to offer and going back to Puerto Rico, almost empty-handed, means you failed. I want out. I want my freedom.

DOLORES: Freedom from being Puerto Rican?

JAVIER: Freedom from . . . fatalism . . . superstition . . . docility . . . from thinking like a peasant . . .

RAMON: *What's wrong with being a peasant??* What's wrong to be Puerto Rican? What's wrong with you? We have the same blood . . .

JAVIER: Excuse me, I have a train to catch . . .

*Javier starts to leave. Ramon intercepts him.*

RAMON: Please lend me this money, I'll fix the deed, sell the house, and pay you back.

JAVIER: No you won't. You'll go there and those people will overwhelm you—and you'll mess everything up, the way you always do.

RAMON *(Crossing to front door)*: I'm getting out of here. *(To Dolores)* He's ashamed of me.

DOLORES *(To Javier)*: Apologize to him!

JAVIER *(To Ramon)*: Put on a pair of boots!

RAMON: I don't have a pair of boots!

JAVIER: So buy a pair! Wait, I forgot! You're broke! You have debts! You can't make a janitor's salary stretch between playing the horses, playing the numbers, lotteries, alcohol, alcohol, and more alcohol—!

RAMON *(Exploding)*: ME CAGO EN DIOS, CARAJO! *(He crosses to Javier)* I want you to move out, don't wait until the house is sold. I can't live with you if you don't love me. Don't be here when I'm getting back. *(He leaves the house)*

JAVIER *(Gathering his stuff)*: Fine with me . . .

DOLORES: Where are you going?

JAVIER *(Crossing to front door)*: I've got an interview. I've got to kiss babies!

DOLORES: Stay here and talk to me.

JAVIER: I have no time.

DOLORES: You have time for me—

JAVIER: I have a train to—

DOLORES: *Don't talk to me about trains! (She grabs Javier from behind but can't hold him. She spins around and staggers downstage, her eyes closed)* I can't see, Javier! I can't see! *(Javier looks at her and shakes his head. She staggers around)* You've betrayed him . . .

JAVIER (*Crossing to Dolores*): I haven't betrayed him . . . I'm just trying to do what I think is best . . .

DOLORES (*Eyes closed*): . . . that poor old man, what's he going to do . . .?

*Javier takes Dolores by the shoulders and leads her to the sofa. He sits her down.*

JAVIER (*Holds out his hand*): Let's go, Helen Keller. How many fingers do I have up? Huh?

DOLORES (*Pushing his hand away*): It's a hoof.

JAVIER: Okay, it's a hoof. How many tails do I have? How many horns?

DOLORES: Many, many.

JAVIER: Uh-huh. Many, many. (*Checks watch*) Are you going to be okay, or what?

DOLORES: I'll never be okay until I go home again.

JAVIER (*Crossing to chair*): Oh Mom . . .

DOLORES: What's wrong with you? The first sky you saw was a Puerto Rican sky. Your first drink of water was Puerto Rican water. But you don't remember. You were just a baby! But I remember. Son, I want to see chickens run across my yard, all year round. I want to hear my language spoken by everyone I meet, even little children. Spanish is so beautiful when children speak it. I left everything I cared about when I left Puerto Rico.

JAVIER: Hasn't this ever been home?

DOLORES: Never. This place has never been good to any of us—

JAVIER: It's been good to me. I think I can go far here. (*He crosses to Dolores and takes her hand*)

DOLORES: I don't doubt it for a moment. But Ramon is not you.

JAVIER: Is that why you can't accept this as your home?

DOLORES (*Crosses to her altar*): This "home" took away my little girl . . .

JAVIER: Mom, you've got to let her go. You've got to bury her. You can't blame this house for—

DOLORES: Yes I can!

JAVIER: It would have happened down there. She would have died down there—

DOLORES: For six days she lived here! This cold house killed her!

JAVIER: She was born sickly, Mom; anything could've—

DOLORES: She was strong. I could feel how strong she was. I could feel it in her hands. I could see it in her busy, red face. I heard it when she cried. (*Trying not to cry*) I came to her. I warmed her. I held her against me, keeping her from the cold air in this dying house. For six days Ramon worked on the furnace, trying to start it, but it wouldn't start. One day, as I was making coffee, while Ramon was at work, she died. I . . . stood by that window for a whole day, facing Puerto Rico. And poor Ramon. He almost went crazy. (*She starts to cry openly*)

JAVIER: Oh Mom, don't do that.

DOLORES: Every room in this house is absent with my little girl!

JAVIER: Come on . . .

DOLORES: My little Felicia would have stayed with me after all the boys have gone . . .

*A knock is heard at the door.*

I better go—
JAVIER: Don't go—
DOLORES *(Crossing to upstairs exit)*: I don't want anyone to see—
JAVIER: Mom . . .

*Dolores exits upstairs. Door knock is heard again.*

Come in! It's open!

*Caroline enters.*

CAROLINE: Hi.
JAVIER: You have incredible timing.
CAROLINE *(Exiting)*: Bye.
JAVIER: You knocked. Get over here.
CAROLINE *(Enters, closes door)*: If somebody had a phone, somebody else would have better timing.
JAVIER: All right, okay, I'm sorry, all right, I'm sorry, okay?
CAROLINE *(Noticing his clothes)*: So who's your date with?
JAVIER: Destiny. So what are you *doing* here?
CAROLINE: A: I came to see you, which I know is pretty selfish. After all, I shouldn't presume I can just pop over any old friggin' time I get the itch—
JAVIER: Knock it off.
CAROLINE: B: I came to give your parents a house present for Puerto Rico. *(Takes out a small glass ball, with a house and snow in it)* Isn't it cute? I got it at a boutique. It's a house with snow. They can shake it up and make winter.
JAVIER *(Smiles weakly)*: How clever. How are you?
CAROLINE: Lonely.
JAVIER: Forget I asked . . .
CAROLINE *(Smiles, crosses to Javier)*: Hey, you look kind of nice, bro. Don't dress up for *me*, of course . . .
JAVIER *(Pulling away)*: These are job-hunting clothes, not seduction clothes . . .
CAROLINE *(Putting arms around him)*: Oh, I don't know . . .
JAVIER *(Crossing downstage)*: Look, I've just had a stupid, ugly screaming scene with my mom and dad. My father kicked me out of the house. There's no heat, very little water and I'm late for my interview—
CAROLINE *(Crossing to Javier)*: So talk to me. Come on boy, loosen up! Loosen up that face! You're such a troll!
JAVIER *(Pulling away)*: Just don't *touch* me, okay?
CAROLINE: I bet you let your friend from school touch you, huh? Your little college friend. How's she doing, anyway?

JAVIER: She's fine. She's been a real sweetheart about helping me find a place to live. So much of it is word-of-mouth.

CAROLINE: I bet she's good at word-of-mouth.

JAVIER: And . . . I think we've found a place to live—for me, not for her, she already has her own place.

CAROLINE: Is it nice?

JAVIER: Yes it's nice, and why don't you go home?

CAROLINE: I want to know if your place is nice.

JAVIER: It's everything a man could ask of four tortured walls, four flights of stairs, and waterbugs big as my shoes!

CAROLINE: You're really climbing that ladder. I knew you'd make it big someday. So when are you going to let me break it in?

JAVIER: Do what?

CAROLINE: Break it in. You know, after it's all fixed up, comfy, civilized, you have your Bobby Kennedy poster on the wall . . . and a few tough nights have gone by. I'll come over, bring some beer, and we'll do it: break it in. Do you know what I'm talking about?

JAVIER: I'm afraid you're too subtle for me.

CAROLINE: And I'll break it in for as long as you can stand it . . .

*Caroline attempts an embrace. Javier walks away.*

JAVIER: That's just about the most generous thing I've heard all day, but there's a problem.

CAROLINE: What?

JAVIER: You can't help me break it in.

CAROLINE: What?

JAVIER: The apartment.

CAROLINE: Why?

JAVIER: Because you're not going to know where it is. *(No response)* I'm not giving you my new address. I don't want you to visit me, sleep with me, or even call me up.

CAROLINE: What are you talking about?

JAVIER: I'm talking about it's over. You and me, us; it's *over;* did you hear that?

CAROLINE *(Beat)*: Why? What have I ever done to hurt you?

JAVIER: Nothing. Nothing was ever *done.* Do you remember that concert in Stony Brook? The New Year's Eve Rock-'n'-Roll Blitz?

CAROLINE: Yeah . . .

JAVIER: You had just frosted your hair and you were so excited because you had gotten this great dope. The whole concert came and went and all I could do was stare at you—

CAROLINE: If you didn't have fun, we could have gone home . . .

JAVIER: You were chewing gum, smoking grass, jumping up and down on your seat and I realized, I didn't love this. Not these people. This music. This wasted time—

CAROLINE: Wasted time?

JAVIER: You know what I felt? I felt like your parent and you were my retarded teenage daughter!

CAROLINE: Hey thanks.

JAVIER (*Crossing to Caroline*): Carrie, you've been great to me. Given me everything. But what have I done for you beside push you away? We're too different. I can't live on sex, drugs, and rock-'n'-roll anymore.

CAROLINE: Sex, drugs, *and* rock-'n'-roll? You're giving me a dab too much credit, aren't you? Of course I can't do half the things your college girl can do. I can't fuck and do trig at the same time!

JAVIER: Why don't you go home?

CAROLINE: Yeah, just go home! Forget this whole year! Forget how I fell in love with you, said yes to you, listened to all your ambitions, your high-horse bullshit—

JAVIER: *I am tired, Caroline!* I don't want to see you anymore! This is the end of the conversation!

CAROLINE: This is not the end of the conversation!

JAVIER: Please . . .

CAROLINE: Forget all the serious balling we did! Just so you can move out, find a place, disappear out of my life without wiping your bloody jaws—without saying, "Thanks for the meal, bitch!" Without even wondering, what do *you* think, Caroline? *Do* you think, Caroline? Do you *feel? Sex, drugs, and rock'n'roll?* Who the frig do you think you are anyway? (*Beat*) Ask me the capital of Spain! Huh? Will you? What about square roots? Ask me. I can do those. Ask me how to make babies. How love is made. Ask! Ask me who's been mother, sister, and whorehouse to you for the toughest, loneliest year of your life. (*Beat*) I thought you were full of sympathy and mystery and fun and I gave you everything I could without dropping dead and you don't think you got enough. You think you can do better than me, don't you?

JAVIER: Yeah . . . I guess that's the problem.

*Caroline puts on her coat and crosses to front door. Javier tries to stop her.*

Wait a—

CAROLINE: *Don't touch me, all right?*

*Caroline exits. Javier, upset, gets his stuff together.*

JAVIER: Good afternoon, Congressman. No sir, I didn't read your article in the *Times.* I was too busy breaking up with my . . . with my whorehouse. Who? Oh, just this woman I used for a while, about a year, who I tossed away. Why, sir? I don't know why. I thought I had to. (*Beat*) I don't know why . . . I let my father run out into the snow, either. With his bad foot. (*Beat*) Come on. Where are you, Dad? (*He puts on gloves and scarf. He tears up train schedule*) Here I come Dad—again.

*Javier exits. Blackout.*

## Scene 2

*About six hours later. In front of the Marine Recruiting Office in Holtsville. Ramon enters, limping, disoriented. He stumbles around for a few moments. He has been drinking. He knocks on the window of the office. He walks away from it and falls in the snow. He sits there for a moment or two, dazed. He gets up and walks toward the recruiting office again. He collapses against the brick wall, barely holding himself up. Javier runs up to him.*

JAVIER: *Dad . . . ! Dad . . . !* Oh, Jesus, Dad . . . what did you think you were going to do here? *(He tries to pull Ramon to his feet)*

RAMON: No . . . no . . .

JAVIER: Come on, get away from there . . .

RAMON: Tell my son, tell my Julio, to come get me . . .

JAVIER: Julio's long gone, Dad, the smart one took off and left you . . .

RAMON: Who are you?

JAVIER: Let's just *go* . . .

RAMON: Who are you?

JAVIER: Javier. Your son.

RAMON: Javier Iglesia! That's what you are . . .

JAVIER: Yes. Come *on.* You'll *freeze* . . .

RAMON: Let go of me . . .

JAVIER: You're going to freeze here!

RAMON: I'd rather freeze to death than go anywhere with you.

JAVIER: Oh . . . Dad . . . don't say that . . .

RAMON: I'd rather lie right here, turn over in the snow, right now, right in front of you, and just die.

JAVIER: Why do you say that?

RAMON: You've left me alone . . .

JAVIER: I just want to do for *myself* . . .

RAMON: Turned your back . . .

JAVIER: . . . I don't want the world to leave me behind.

RAMON: You're going to be left behind, like me . . .

JAVIER: No I'm not! No I'm not!

RAMON: When you're not as young as you are now. When you're no longer the angel so easy to forgive.

JAVIER: I don't want to be forgiven. I just want to be allowed to forget the old world, *your* old world. Because that world has forgotten you and the new world doesn't want you. And I won't let that happen to me.

RAMON: It'll happen. Do you think they really love you? It'll happen to you *worse,* worse than me.

JAVIER: No . . .

RAMON: You've made them so important! You eat their food, wear their clothes, love their women, talk their language but you're still their little Puerto Rican.

You're their entertainment, their fun. Something new. Dance for us, Javier! Salsa for us, Javier! Wear the clothes, Javier! Fool yourself, Javier! Keep fooling yourself, Javier! You're a little Puerto Rican, Javier! *Let go of my arm!*

*Javier lets him go. Ramon crosses to the Marine Recruiting Office window. He leans against it, disoriented.*

JAVIER: I can just leave you here. You know that? I'll just leave you here and you can die in the cold. I'll leave you here if I want!

RAMON: Leave me alone . . .

JAVIER: Half of me wants to do that. Lie right down there, Dad! Cover yourself up! Go to sleep! Let them find you tomorrow morning! You'll be doing me a favor! I won't have to point to you, saying, "That's my father, that janitor there!" See the bent old man with the mop? The old slave dragging his feet? That's my proud old man! *(Ramon falls in the snow)* GET UP FOR CHRISSAKES! *Don't you have any pride at all?* Are you going to let this snow kill you while I stand here watching you? If you don't get up, I'll walk, I'll leave, I swear! *(Bending down over his father) Why can't you help yourself! Why? (Low)* Why can't you help . . . yourself? You should never have bent down so I could wipe my feet on your back. I never asked you to do that for me. Why did you do that for me? Why were you that way for me? Why did you suffer so fucking *quietly?*

*Javier runs off. Ramon remains on the ground a few seconds, then struggles to his feet and attempts to exit in the opposite direction. He falls again. Javier runs on, lifts him, and carries him off.*

## Scene 3

*A few hours later, the Iglesia house. As the lights come up, Dolores and Charlie enter through the front door. Charlie crosses to the kitchen while Dolores rushes upstairs.*

CHARLIE: Dad! *(Crosses to the basement door, opens it)* Javier! Dad!

DOLORES *(Coming downstairs)*: Where are they? If they're not here, where are they?

CHARLIE: Calla says we should call the cops.

DOLORES: We have to call Julio.

CHARLIE: Julio's in South Carolina.

DOLORES: We need Julio!

CHARLIE: You can only get him through the Red Cross, for an emergency.

DOLORES: *This* is an emergency! It's supposed to get *colder* tonight!

*The front door opens. Javier enters.*

JAVIER: Well, look who's here.

DOLORES: Where's Ramon?

JAVIER: Dad's fine, don't worry.

CHARLIE: You found him?

JAVIER: Yeah, I finally caught up with him.

DOLORES: Why isn't he with you?

JAVIER: He's at the hospital.

DOLORES: He's dead!

JAVIER: No, he's not dead . . .

DOLORES: He was hit by a car!

JAVIER: He's okay. He went on a long walk. He walked to Tony's Bar, then he started wandering all over Holbrook.

CHARLIE: Calla took us everywhere. Up to Sunrise, to Grundy Avenue.

JAVIER: Did he take you to the Marine Recruiting Office?

CHARLIE: He went all the way out *there?*

JAVIER: That's where I found him, wandering around, drunk. He said he was looking for Julio.

DOLORES: Javier . . . he misses his boy.

JAVIER: I know, I know.

DOLORES *(Almost crying)*: That poor old man, I have to see him.

JAVIER: You can't. Visiting hours are over. They're holding him for observation.

DOLORES: Why?

JAVIER: You can't have diabetes, go around drinking beer all the time, and expect your foot to withstand a lot of cold. They're afraid he might be severely frostbitten, so they're going to hold him awhile.

DOLORES: I told him. Didn't I tell him day after day?

JAVIER: He's okay now. It's all cleaned out and bandaged and he's in a big, clean bed, nice and warm. All right, Mom?

DOLORES: It was your fault you know. You upset him.

JAVIER: I know I did. I talked to him. I said I was sorry.

DOLORES: He wants your blessings in what he does.

JAVIER: I know. I haven't been very good to him, lately. I don't feel good about anything . . .

DOLORES: He needs you.

JAVIER: He's okay now. Everything's all right.

*Dolores turns away from Javier.*

DOLORES: Everything's not all right.

*Dolores crosses to the window and looks out. Javier looks at Charlie.*

CHARLIE: Calla doesn't want to buy the house no more.

JAVIER: You're kidding.

CHARLIE: He's been cheating on Dad! He says he's looking at another house . . .

DOLORES: Maybe if you talked to him.

JAVIER: What do you want me to tell him?

DOLORES: That he has to take this house!

JAVIER: Mom, I told you, I don't know if this move is the best thing for you. I don't know if I can talk to Calla.

CHARLIE: Javier, don't be stupid.

JAVIER: I'm trying to do what's best.

CHARLIE: Best? For who?

DOLORES: Charlie, please . . .

JAVIER: For you. For Mom.

CHARLIE: You're doing it because you don't want to tell your college friends your parents couldn't make it in America!

DOLORES: Charlie, don't talk that way to him.

CHARLIE: Why not? *Somebody's* got to! All he does is complain!

DOLORES: He's your big brother!

JAVIER: Charlie, I'm doing it for you.

CHARLIE: Me?

JAVIER: You.

CHARLIE: *Me?*

JAVIER: *Yeah you!* You have to have a good education! Without that you won't get anywhere.

CHARLIE: How do you know I can't get a good education down there? You think everything down there is bad. The schools, the food, the music—the people. You think Puerto Ricans are stupid, worthless, and that's really sick.

JAVIER: I never—I'm sorry if—

CHARLIE: You learned a lot of stuff in college. Came back looking different. I was proud of you. But I think you learned some bad things, too. You want to be so much like everybody else, you learned how to hate your people. Man, I feel sorry for you. I hope I never learn that.

JAVIER: I don't hate—

CHARLIE: —anybody; that's what you say. Prove it. Do what Julio can't do because he's not here and Mom can't do because Calla don't speak Spanish and I can't do because he won't listen to me. Stand up in Dad's place, man. Talk to Calla.

*Javier walks away from Charlie. He's exhausted and shows it.*

JAVIER: I don't know . . .

DOLORES: Why can't you say yes? *(No answer)* You can't say yes. And you're my Javier, my smart Javier. *(Sarcastic)* Smarter than me. Smarter than Ramon—

JAVIER: Please, just do what—

DOLORES: So I must be wrong to love my island. My dream must be stupid because it separates my sons and hurts my husband. I must be wrong!

CHARLIE: You're not wrong, *he* is.

DOLORES: And if I'm wrong, we'll stay here. Is that good, Javier?

JAVIER: Please, just do what you want . . .

DOLORES: I'll stop dreaming about that stupid island. You can bury us here while you're at it. Bury us here with Felicia. The baby's soul wants to go home . . . *(She crosses to the little altar, takes Felicia's picture and gives it to Javier)* You tell her she can't go home—*you tell her!*

*Javier takes the picture. A brief pause. He places the picture back on the altar.*

JAVIER: Just one thing. One thing, and I'll talk to Calla. Make Charlie work hard, *push* him, push him hard.

CHARLIE: Nothing's free with you, is it?

JAVIER: *Are you going to work hard down there? Are you going to do well?*

CHARLIE: YOU BET I AM! *(Beat; he smiles)* I just kicked your ass in this argument, didn't I?

*Javier laughs, tired.*

JAVIER: Why can't I think straight about this . . .?

DOLORES: What are you going to do?

JAVIER: I'll talk to Calla.

DOLORES: You will?

JAVIER: I'll do my best. And if I have to . . . I'll go to Puerto Rico in Dad's place. I'll make Santoval and Terrón sign the deed.

CHARLIE: With *your* Spanish?

JAVIER: I'll pretend I didn't hear that. *(To Dolores)* Okay?

DOLORES: Yes. Yes Javier.

JAVIER: Okay. Charlie, go get Calla.

CHARLIE: Oh man . . .!

JAVIER: Hurry before I change my mind! *(Charlie crosses to the door)* Charlie. You better come through for me.

CHARLIE: Carlos will come through! *(He goes)*

DOLORES: Thank you, Javier.

JAVIER: This doesn't mean I think you're right, Mom. Don't think I believe in what's going on.

DOLORES: Are you really going to Puerto Rico?

JAVIER: Sí. Christ, I wish my Spanish was better.

DOLORES: You have to go to Miraflores.

JAVIER: What's in Miraflores?

DOLORES: You were born there. And you have to go to Utuado, it's beautiful.

JAVIER: Okay, I will.

DOLORES: And when you meet Santoval and Terrón, yell at them for me.

JAVIER: I'll strangle them for you.

*The door opens. Charlie enters, pulling Calla, who is wearing a T-shirt and holding a shirt.*

CHARLIE: Company!

JAVIER: Oh boy, oh boy . . .

CALLA: Charlie, Christ, what the hell are you doing . . .?

JAVIER: . . . company . . .

CALLA: You people are really pushing me to the edge of my—

CHARLIE: Safe and unsound.

JAVIER *(Putting arm around Calla)*: Hi Nick.

CALLA: —of my brain. *(Pulling away from Javier)* For Chrissakes, let go!

DOLORES: Ask him if he wants a cup of coffee.

JAVIER: My mother would like to know if you want a cup of coffee.

CALLA *(Putting on shirt)*: I want an explanation, thank you, tell her that.

JAVIER *(To Dolores)*: He would love a cup of coffee.

*Dolores exits into kitchen.*

CALLA: Hey, wait, I think I just suffered in the translation—

JAVIER: I'm sorry if this is a little sudden, but I'm afraid I've got some news for you—

CALLA: Wait. Hold it. Whoa. I'm afraid I have a little news for *you*. Are you ready for this?

JAVIER: What is it?

CALLA: I've found another house to buy. At the edge of town, right by the tracks, you might have seen it.

JAVIER: You're lying . . .

CALLA: It's smaller than this, no upstairs, but I won't have to sink a whole lot of extra money into it—the furnace there doesn't explode every ten minutes, I mean.

JAVIER: I don't believe you.

CALLA: And the people don't have this helter-skelter way of stumbling around with other people's time and money . . .

JAVIER: You're lying.

CALLA: I'm telling you the truth! I went there today, talked to the gentleman, *he* didn't produce a piece of paper with forgeries all over it, *he* didn't stumble around without having a plan. I admit—it's going to cost me more initially, true, it hurts, but almost any price is worth it to get you people out of my stomach for good!

JAVIER: Oh Nick . . .

CALLA: I'm sorry, you weren't fast enough. But that, as they say, is life.

JAVIER: Nick, you have to buy this house.

CALLA: No way!

JAVIER: I have a plan. I have a plan to get the house to you.

CALLA: Too late.

JAVIER: Have you paid these people yet?

CALLA: No.

JAVIER: Have you signed anything?

CALLA: No, and I don't care! I just want to be untangled from you people once and for all. I've spent nineteen years bailing you people out, left and right, rain or shine, *no more*. The man at the other house speaks my language.

JAVIER: You're not dealing with my father anymore, you're dealing with me.

CALLA: Excuse me, I'm not impressed.

JAVIER: You're dealing with *me*, Mr. Calla, not with Dad.

CALLA: There's a difference? I don't see a difference. Like father, like son: losers breed losers. It's like some assembly line in Heaven got stuck one day and turned out a whole island of you: these little Spanish people who don't know shit about the world. There's this *smell* coming from you people, Javier, the smell of fear, it's all over you, don't tell me it ain't. You just don't know how things get done in the world.

JAVIER: Get out of our house and don't *ever* talk that way about my family again—

CALLA: Suit yourself.

*Calla starts to leave. Javier stops him.*

JAVIER: Wait. I won't say I'm not afraid, because I am. Just like Dad. I'm afraid for them because I don't know what's going to happen to them in the future. And I'm afraid of people like you who declare that "losers breed losers." But you were afraid once. Like Dad. *(Beat)* I need some help. I need you to be brave for me.

CALLA: That's just words. *(Rubs his fingers together to indicate money)* Words.

JAVIER: Okay. *(Crosses to desk, gets his checkbook)* You gave Dad a one-thousand-dollar down payment on this house. It's gone; he spent it. Here is your down payment back: but in exchange, I want three days in Puerto Rico so I can clear up this mess with the deed. *(He writes check)*

CALLA: Three days? *(Javier gives him check. He examines it)* Okay. But if you fail you may be living in the bottom of the Long Island Sound, and believe me, my family will put you there.

*Calla exits. Dolores enters with coffee.*

CHARLIE: Good-bye Long Island!

*Blackout.*

## Scene 4

*Two weeks later. The Iglesia house. Julio enters, wearing a Marine uniform. He salutes the audience and speaks in a slight southern accent. During his speech, Charlie and Javier enter and begin removing the furniture and boxes from the house in silence.*

JULIO: Dear family. Well, folks, it's the beast again writing to you from the world of green, drabby underwear and bad food. In my last letter you got an ache-by-ache tour of Hell's Armpit also known as Parris Island but today things are even funnier. Everybody is hot to trot for the possibility of being sent to Iran to kick the Ayatollah's ass around. These bozos are actually looking forward to combat pay! What does the beast think of all this? He's looking forward to tending the Marine Corps Library as far from bullets, shells, and the criminally stupid as possible. Wait until I catch the swindler who told me it was peacetime! *(Beat)* Well that's about it from here. I'm thrilled about the sale of the house. But tell Calla that if he doesn't treat that house with respect I'm going to go there and rip his forehead off. And tell Judas—that's you Javier— that you better write to me very, incredibly soon. Or you'll have one beastly bro standing on your face when next we meet. Kisses and flowers, Julio. The beast.

*Julio salutes audience and marches off. Lights up full on the house.*

CHARLIE *(Looking around the room)*: This place. It's so different, empty. I hadn't realized how little it was.

JAVIER: Yeah? Wait'll you take a look at some of the huts out on that little paradise you're going to.

CHARLIE: I thought you said there were some things that were really nice about Puerto Rico.

JAVIER: One or two. It's great if you love polyester, food stamps, babies, mosquitos, radios . . .

CHARLIE: You're being a jerk, you promised not to be a jerk today. You could say *something* nice about Puerto Rico.

JAVIER: Yes! I don't live there. *(Laughs)* No, Charlie, I'm kidding. There were things . . . some of the smells . . . the lightning . . . the buzz of the rain forest all night long . . . some beautiful women . . . simple and direct and sweet. . . . Just remember, if you need any kind of help, call me up. All right? And keep a really close eye on those two.

*Caroline enters and stands by the doorway.*

CAROLINE: Hi!

JAVIER: Caroline . . .

CAROLINE: Oh, muchas gracias señor!

JAVIER: I didn't expect to see you.

CAROLINE: Muchas gracias, señor!

JAVIER: Oh, please . . .

*Caroline comes forward.*

CAROLINE: I almost had an accident getting here, I skidded half a mile avoiding a boy on a sled, so don't yell at me.

JAVIER: Who yelled? Did I yell?

CAROLINE: Your eyebrows are yelling at me.

*Charlie takes a box and exits through front door. Caroline crosses to Javier.*

How'd it go in Puerto Rico?

JAVIER *(Smiles)*: Well, I ran around like a chicken with its head cut off. But the people weren't so bad. What did you do for two weeks?

CAROLINE: I gave up drinking. Totally. I never drink anymore. And I don't say "frig." And I told Daddy that if he smacks my mother one more time, I'm going to have him arrested. But . . . I still get high because getting high is part of life, so fuck you.

*Charlie enters, gets box, exits.*

Are things settled?

JAVIER: Settled.

CAROLINE: Where are you staying tonight?

JAVIER: My options are simple: the Y on 92nd Street, a Central Park bench, or I can sack out here as long as I get out before Calla's brother-in-law arrives tomorrow morning.

CAROLINE: No apartment?

JAVIER: No money.

CAROLINE: Oh. Isn't that interesting. Good thing I brought this along, isn't it? *(She goes to her coat and pulls out a sizeable roll of money)* Your mother said you're broke because of your trip and you didn't get that job with the Congressman.

JAVIER: I can't take that . . .

CAROLINE: Hey stupid. Somebody sold a lot of dope this week to get this money, not to mention her savings, so turn it down, I'll cream you. *(Smiles)* This is my loan.

JAVIER: After all the—?

CAROLINE: Yes. You need some help—

JAVIER: Why are you giving me things?

CAROLINE: This money will get you a place to live, where you can live with nothing for a while. No girlfriend, no Mommy and Daddy, no Julio, nothing but your dear, depressing, judgmental, boring self. I'm giving this to you hoping your next few months are *miserable. (Beat)* You need it, you selfish . . . *(Beat)* But for now, I guess, all you need is a kiss good-bye and my best, best wishes.

*Caroline crosses to Javier, gives him a light kiss. He tries to embrace her and she pulls away.*

JAVIER: Thank you. I'm—I'll pay you back.

CAROLINE: Friggin' right you will. *(She crosses to the door, stops)* You'll forget me, won't you Javier?

*Caroline exits. Ramon enters down the stairs, with cane and suitcase, wearing his hat from the opening scene. Javier crosses to Ramon and takes suitcase.*

JAVIER: So this is the big day.

RAMON: The big day . . .

JAVIER: Goddamn, my nerves are murdering me. How's that foot feeling?

RAMON: Better. Doesn't itch now.

JAVIER: Did you clean it out today?

RAMON: I cleaned it out today.

JAVIER: Did you clean it out the way they showed you?

RAMON: Yes, exactly the way they showed me.

JAVIER: Good. Jesus, I wish my stomach would stop.

RAMON: You better take care of that.

JAVIER: You better get Mom.

*Ramon crosses to stairs, calls.*

RAMON: Mamacita? Dolores?

DOLORES *(Off)*: One minute, please.

*Charlie enters.*

CHARLIE: Me and Calla got the car all packed and the furniture's in the garage—

JAVIER: Calla and I.

*Javier holds out a pack of cigarettes. Charlie and Javier take cigarettes.*

RAMON: I want a smoke too.

*Javier gives Ramon a cigarette. Javier flicks on his lighter and the three men light up simultaneously. Dolores enters, seemingly a new woman, beautifully dressed and finally content. She smiles at Ramon and crosses to Felicia's altar to pack the pictures and icons. She lights incense and puts it on a small tray.*

JAVIER: Tickets and money, Dad?

RAMON: Everything.

JAVIER: Well, if there's nothing left . . .

RAMON: Wait, there's one thing . . .

JAVIER: . . . Calla is waiting . . .

RAMON: . . . one small thing . . .

JAVIER: . . . I don't know how you fit all that stuff in his car . . .

RAMON: . . . one thing I've been afraid to ask for, but I have to ask . . .

CHARLIE: Javier, Dad's talking to you.

JAVIER: I'm sorry . . . what is it?

RAMON: Could you do me a favor? Could you come over to me?

JAVIER: What for?

RAMON: Come over to me and give me a kiss good-bye.

JAVIER: Why?

RAMON: Because it would be nice.

*Javier crosses to Ramon and kisses him.*

JAVIER: La bendición.

RAMON: Que Dios te bendiga.

*A car's horn is heard. Charlie crosses to the front door.*

CHARLIE: We'll be right there Mr. Calla!

*Javier and Ramon break their embrace. Ramon exits through the front door. Charlie and Javier embrace.*

Oh Christ, my stomach is turning into oatmeal-diarrhea-soup.

JAVIER: What a lovely image, Charlie. Let's go, you big wimp.

CHARLIE: Turkey!

JAVIER: You have the basic mentality of a handball.

CHARLIE: Yeah—just wait—next time you see me, *I'm going to be a beast!*

*Charlie goes. Dolores crosses to center of the living room with incense.*

DOLORES *(To Javier)*: Get down. *(Javier kneels. She passes the incense over Javier's head, once)* God bless you. Get up.

*Javier stands. They embrace. Dolores leaves. Javier crosses to the window to wave goodbye. He finds Charlie's tape recorder and turns it on. Salsa plays. Javier smiles. He closes his eyes and starts to sway his hips. He stops dancing and sits in the empty living room. The lights begin to dim, throwing long shadows around Javier. The music continues. He looks around and shivers slightly.*

JAVIER: Dance for us, Javier. *(Lights continue to dim)* Salsa for us . . . Javier.

*Lights to black. Salsa music continues.*

## END OF PLAY

# Roosters

Milcha  Sanchez-Scott

# Milcha Sanchez-Scott

I was born in 1955, on the island of Bali. My mother is Indonesian, Chinese and Dutch. My father was born in Colombia, in a town called Santa Marta, and was raised there and in Mexico. My parents met in Indonesia, in the botanical gardens. My father's work as an agronomist had taken him there.

By the time I was school-age, my father was working in Europe, traveling a lot, so I was sent to Saint Agnes, a Catholic girls school near London. I learned to speak English there. I spent a lot of time with the nuns, who were so loving. They didn't *know* they were interested in theatre, but we had plenty of drama. One nun was a *fiend* for battles. She and I would spend Saturday mornings waging war with her lead soldiers.

I spent Christmas and summer holidays at the family ranch in Santa Marta, running around with my cousins. We went to a church two hours away, built by the Indians. It has a dirt floor, and indigenous paintings of the Virgin Mary, and in the rafters are milagros, which are copies of body parts. In this part of Colombia the Indians make them almost lifesize, of tin, wood or clay. If you broke your arm, prayed to a saint, and it healed, you made an arm and hung it in the church, to say thank you. My cousin Alfred, who was in military school in the United States and was considered *very* advanced, would always push me under the penises. We would sit there and giggle.

At school and at the ranch, eccentricity was so natural that I didn't know it *was* eccentricity. Of my great-grandfather, who lived to some phenomenal age, they would say, "This is the man who could not die." My cousin who freed all the birds on the ranch was called *forever* "the great bird liberator." Such nicknames brought out each person's individuality, which was in an odd way encouraged. I got my name when I was about ten—before that my father called me "Spider," because when I was born I was all arms and legs. The brother of a friend in England had a crush on me and came to Colombia for the summer. I saw him coming up the walk, slammed the door and ran away. So my father said, "Spider, you're the girl who cannot love."

When I got mad at people who of course never listened to me, I wrote their names on cardboard and put them out on the lawn. My mother could tell what kind of day I had by how many tombstones there were. My early life was sheer fantasy.

The big change came when we moved to La Jolla, California. I was about fourteen. I was so excited about going to a public high school where there were boys, and dating, and the Beach Boys, and who knew what else. The first morning I went to the bus stop and a smart-alecky boy threw a pebble at me and said, "This isn't the Mexican bus stop. You have to go to the Mexican bus stop." Then all the kids—six or seven of them—started saying that. I ran home crying, and my mother immediately put me in an Episcopalian girls school. I had never experienced racial tension, but in La Jolla we saw incredible—to *us*—prejudice.

One year I pulled a prank in school that cost a thousand dollars. My father made me pay by spending the summer picking zucchinis. In a perfect setting, right over the ocean, I worked with Hungarian refugees, Mexicans, Asians, college kids. There were tensions, but there were also resolutions. You would be a party to grown-up flirtations; to me the passion in the fields was quite wonderful. But what really mattered was seeing how people *manage*—to feed their children, to be in a good humor, to be *balanced*.

I went to the University of San Diego, a Catholic woman's college. I didn't want to leave home, because I'd spent so much time away from my parents. I had no interest in anything except reading—I majored in literature and philosophy—and theatre. I was in a lot of school plays. In the summers, and also the year after I graduated, I worked at the San Diego Zoo.

A few years later I was working with my cousin at an employment agency for maids in Beverly Hills. It was the best job I ever had. These immigrant women, who had their feet on the ground, and their eyes on the stars, and their hearts full of love, strengthened me. It was like meeting at the river.

From these women I got my material for *Latina*, my first play. I'd never tried to write. I was just collecting stories—for instance, a woman told me her child had died two years previously, and that at the mortuary she had lifted her child and put it across her face to give it a last goodbye. For two years, she said, the whole side of her face and her lips were cold. And being with my cousin again reminded me of the way we say things in Colombia: "Do you remember the summer when all the birds flew into the bedroom?" I was just writing things down.

About this time I was hired by Susan Loewenberg of L.A. Theatre Works to act in a project at the women's prison in Chino. I saw the way Doris Baizley, the writer, had put the women's stories together. When I offered Susan my notes, hoping she could make a piece out of them, she persuaded me to write it myself.

I'd found a channel to get all sorts of things flowing out. I liked controlling my own time, and *making* things—I've always admired architects. Acting seemed very airy to me because I could never take it home and show it to anybody. I had trouble being alone for long periods, but then I would go to the airport or someplace else busy to write. Doris and I used to do things like write under blankets by flashlight, which makes you feel like a little kid with a big secret.

L.A. Theatre Works got a grant and we toured *Latina* up and down the state with ten Latin actresses who were always feuding. We had one who was illegal, and wouldn't perform anyplace she thought Immigration might come, so I had to go on in her place. Then Susan commissioned me to write something else, which turned out to be *Dog Lady* and *Cuban Swimmer*. I saw the long-distance swimmer Diana Nyad on TV and I saw Salazar—the Cuban runner—and started thinking. I wanted to set a play in the water. So I put a family on a boat and a swimmer in the water and said, "Now, *what?*" I happened to be in a church and saw the most beautiful Stations of the Cross. It struck me as a good outline for anybody undertaking an endeavor—there's all this tripping and falling and rising. So that's what I used. For *Dog Lady* I just put Day One, Day Two. I figure that's the way things happen.

Susan was at a TCG conference with Max Ferra, and gave him the script. He called the very next day—he was crazy about the plays. INTAR invited me to join Irene Fornes's workshop for that year, 1984–85. I pawned some jewelry my grandmother had left me—Doris said, "That's what jewelry's for"—and went to New York. That year was the best thing that ever happened to me. I used to sit around at home and wait for Mr. Moose to call, and some days he didn't come. Irene taught me tricks to make him come, so I gained more control of my time. I met some extraordinary Hispanic writers. And I felt more accepted. I'd always been grouped as a Chicana writer, and part of me is. But a larger part is not. My roots are in South America.

*Roosters* began when a friend, Jerry Garcia, showed me a picture of relatives of his, Mexican-Americans. The woman was this *homely*, plump little thing, and the man looked like Warren Beatty. He was a rooster trainer; he'd been in and out of jail on drug charges, robbery. She was looking up at him like he was heaven on earth. During one of Irene's exercises in the lab these faces came to my mind. It was a different way of writing for me, very visual. When Jerry showed me the picture I didn't know anything about cockfights, but was immediately overwhelmed with longing to see one. I hung around a Filipino bar outside L.A. until they took me. I asked my father, "Dad, why do I have this urge to know about cockfighting? Have you ever done that?" He told me that when we were in Indonesia he took me once, because the cockfight is a religious ceremony. I didn't remember it at all.

Basically *Roosters* was written during my year in New York. It's my tearing-away-from-home play. When I finished it I remember distinctly feeling how separate I was from my parents, that I was really my own person.

# Biographical Information

Milcha Sanchez-Scott's first play, *Latina*, premiered by L.A. Theatre Works in 1980, won seven *Drama-Logue* awards. *Dog Lady* and *The Cuban Swimmer*, a pair of one-acts, were produced by INTAR in 1984, and selected for Theatre Communications Group's *Plays in Process* series. *Dog Lady* was subsequently published in *Best Short Plays of 1986*. Current works in progress include *City of Angels*, a trio of one-acts; *Evening Star*, to be produced by New York's Theatre for a New Audience in 1988; and *Stone Wedding*, a piece being created at Los Angeles Theatre Center.

Sanchez-Scott has received the Vesta Award, given each year to a West Coast woman artist, and the Le Compte du Noüy prize. She is a member of New Dramatists, and holds a First Level Award for American playwrights from the Rockefeller Foundation for 1987.

# About the Play

Originating in INTAR's Hispanic Playwrights-in-Residence Laboratory, *Roosters* was developed at INTAR and, during the summer of 1986, at Sundance Institute Playwrights Laboratory. Co-produced by the New York Shakespeare Festival, *Roosters* premiered at INTAR in 1987, under the direction of Jackson Phippin. The play opened in San Francisco at the Eureka Theatre this fall, and will be filmed for *American Playhouse* in Los Angeles in 1988. Theatre Communications Group first published *Roosters* in the September issue of *American Theatre* magazine.

# Characters

GALLO
ZAPATA
HECTOR
ANGELA
JUANA
CHATA
ADAN
SHADOW #1
SHADOW #2
SAN JUAN

# Time and Place

The present. The Southwest.

# The Play

# Roosters

## ACT ONE

### Scene 1

*Stage and house are dark. Slowly a narrow pinspot of light comes up. We hear footsteps. Enter Gallo, a very, very handsome man in his forties. He is wearing a cheap dark suit, with a white open-neck shirt. He carries a suitcase. He puts the suitcase down. He faces the audience.*

GALLO: Lord Eagle, Lord Hawk, sainted ones, spirits and winds, Santa María Aurora of the Dawn. . . . I want no resentment, I want no rancor. . . . I had an old red Cuban hen. She was squirrel-tailed and sort of slab-sided and you wouldn't have given her a second look. But she was a queen. She could be thrown with any cock and you would get a hard-kicking stag every time.

I had a vision, of a hard-kicking flyer, the ultimate bird. The Filipinos were the ones with the pedigree Bolinas, the high flyers, but they had no real kick. To see those birds fighting in the air like dark avenging angels . . . well like my father use to say, "Son nobles . . . finos. . . ." I figured to mate that old red Cuban. This particular Filipino had the best. A dark burgundy flyer named MacArthur. He wouldn't sell. I began borrowing MacArthur at night, bringing him back before dawn, no one the wiser, but one morning the Filipino's son caught me.

He pulled out his blade. I pulled out mine. I was faster. I went up on man-slaughter. . . . They never caught on . . . thought I was in the henhouse trying to steal their stags. . . . It took time—refining, inbreeding, cross-breeding, brother to sister, mother to son, adding power, rapid attack . . . but I think we got him.

*Gallo stands still for a beat, checks his watch, takes off his jacket and faces center stage. A slow, howling drumbeat begins. As it gradually goes higher in pitch and excitement mounts, we see narrow beams of light, the first light of dawn, filter-ing through chicken wire. The light reveals a heap of chicken feathers which turns out to be an actor/dancer who represents the rooster Zapata. Zapata stretches his wings, then his neck, to greet the light. He stands and struts proudly, puffs his chest and crows his salutation to the sun. Gallo stalks Zapata, as drums follow their movements.*

Ya, ya, mi lindo . . . yeah, baby . . . you're a beauty, a real beauty. Now let's see whatcha got. *(He pulls out a switchblade stiletto. It gleams in the light as he tosses it from hand to hand)* Come on baby boy. Show Daddy whatcha got.

*Gallo lunges at Zapata. The rooster parries with his beak and wings. This becomes a slow, rhythmic fight-dance, which continues until Gallo grabs Zapata by his comb, bending his head backwards until he is forced to sit. Gallo stands behind Zapata, straddling him, one hand still holding the comb, the other holding the knife against the rooster's neck.*

Oh yeah, you like to fight? Huh? You gonna kill for me baby boy? Huh?

*Gallo sticks the tip of the knife into Zapata. The rooster squawks in pain.*

Sssh! Baby boy, you gotta learn. Daddy's gotta teach you.

*Gallo sticks it to Zapata again. This time the rooster snaps back in anger.*

That's right beauty. . . . Now you got it. . . . Come on, come.

*Gallo waves his knife and hand close to Zapata's face. The rooster's head and eyes follow.*

Oh yeah . . . that's it baby, take it! Take it!

*Suddenly Zapata attacks, drawing blood. Gallo's body contracts in orgasmic pleasure/pain.*

Ay precioso! . . . Mi lindo. . . . You like that, eh? Taste good, huh? *(He waves the gleaming knife in a slow hypnotic movement which calms the rooster)* Take my blood, honey. . . . I'm in you now. . . . Morales blood, the blood of kings . . . and you're my rooster . . . a Morales rooster. *(He slowly backs away from the rooster. He picks up his suitcase, still pointing the knife at Zapata)* Kill. You're my son. Make me proud.

*Gallo exits. Zapata puffs his chest and struts upstage. Lights go up a little on upstage left area as the rooster goes into the chicken-wire henhouse. He preens and scratches. Enter Hector, a young man of about twenty. He is very handsome. He wears gray sweatpants and no shirt. On his forehead is a sweatband. His hair and body are dripping wet. He has been running. Now he is panting as he leans on the henhouse looking at Zapata.*

HECTOR: I saw what you did to those chicks. Don't look at me like you have a mind, or a soul, or feelings. You kill your young . . . and we are so proud of your horrible animal vigor. . . . But you are my inheritance . . . Abuelo's gift to me . . . to get me out. Oh, Abuelo, Grandfather . . . you should have left me your courage, your sweet pacific strength.

*A ray of light hits downstage right. In a semi-shadow, we see a miniature cemetery, with small white headstones and white crosses. We see the profile of a young angel/girl with wings and a pale dress. Angela is kneeling next to a bare desert tree with low scratchy branches. She has a Buster Brown haircut and a low tough voice. She is fifteen, but looks twelve.*

ANGELA *(Loudly)*:
Angel of God
My Guardian Dear
To whom God's love
Commits me here
Ever this day be
At my side
To light and guard
To rule and guide
Amen.
*(Her paper wings get caught in a tree branch)* Aw, shit! *(She exits)*

## Scene 2

*As the light changes we hear the clapping of women making tortillas. Lights come up full. Center stage is a faded wood-frame house, with a porch that is bare except for a table and a few chairs. The house sits in the middle of a desert agricultural valley somewhere in the Southwest. Everything is sparse. There is a feeling of blue skies and space. One might see off on the horizon tall Nopales or Century cactus. Juana, a thin, wornout-looking woman of thirty-five, comes out of the house. She is wearing a faded housedress. She goes to mid-yard, faces front and stares out.*

JUANA: It's dry. Bone dry. There's a fire in the mountains . . . up near Jacinto Pass. *(The clapping stops for a beat, then continues. She starts to go back into the house, then stops. She sniffs the air, sniffs again, and again)* Tres Rosas . . . I smell Tres Rosas. *(She hugs her body and rocks)* Tres Rosas. . . . Ay, St. Anthony let him come home. . . . Let him be back.

*The clapping stops. Chata enters from the house. She is a fleshy woman of forty, who gives new meaning to the word blowsy. She has the lumpy face of a hard boozer. She walks with a slight limp. She wears a black kimono, on the back of which is embroidered in red a dragon and the words "Korea, U.S.S. Perkins, 7th Fleet." A cigarette hangs from her lips. She carries a bowl containing balls of tortilla dough.*

I smell Tres Rosas. . . . The brilliantine for his hair. . . . He musta been here. Why did he go?

CHATA: Men are shit.

JUANA: Where could he be?

CHATA: First day out of jail! My brother never comes home first day. You should know that. Gotta sniff around . . . gotta get use to things. See his friends.

JUANA: Sí, that's right. . . . He just gotta get used to things. I'll feel better when I see him . . . I gotta keep busy.

CHATA: You been busy all morning.

JUANA: I want him to feel good, be proud of us. . . . You hear anything when you come in yesterday?

CHATA: Who's gonna know anything at the Trailways bus station?

JUANA: You ain't heard anything?

CHATA: Juanita, he knows what he's doing. If there was gonna be any trouble he'd know. Ay, mujer, he's just an old warrior coming home.

JUANA: Ain't that old.

CHATA: For a fighting man, he's getting up there.

*Juana slaps tortillas. Chata watches her.*

Who taught you to make tortillas?

JUANA: I don't remember. I never make 'em. Kids don't ask.

CHATA: Look at this. You call this a tortilla? Have some pride. Show him you're a woman.

JUANA: Chata, you've been here one day, and you already—

CHATA: Ah, you people don't know what it is to eat fresh handmade tortillas. My grandmother Hortensia, the one they used to call "La India Condenada" . . . she would start making them at five o'clock in the morning. So the men would have something to eat when they went into the fields. Hijo! She was tough. . . . Use to break her own horses . . . and her own men. Every day at five o'clock she would wake me up. "Buenos pinchi días," she would say. I was twelve or thirteen years old, still in braids. . . . "Press your hands into the dough," "Con fuerza," "Put your stamp on it." One day I woke up, tú sabes, con la sangre. "Ah! So you're a woman now. Got your own cycle like the moon. Soon you'll want a man, well this is what you do. When you see the one you want, you roll the tortilla on the inside of your thigh and then you give it to him nice and warm. Be sure you give it to him and nobody else." Well, I been rolling tortillas on my thighs, on my nalgas, and God only knows where else, but I've been giving my tortillas to the wrong men . . . and that's been the problem with my life. First there was Emilio. I gave him my first tortilla. Ay Mamacita, he use to say, these are delicious. Aye, he was handsome, a real lady-killer! After he did me the favor he didn't even have the cojones to stick around . . . took my TV set too. They're all shit . . . the Samoan bartender, what was his name . . .

JUANA: Nicky, Big Nicky.

CHATA: The guy from Pep Boys—

JUANA: Chata, you really think he'll be back?

CHATA: His son's first time in the pit? With "the" rooster? A real Morales rooster? Honey, he'll be back. Stop worrying.

JUANA: Let's put these on the griddle. Angela, Hector . . . breakfast.

## Scene 3

*Angela slides out from under the house, wearing her wings. She carries a white box which contains her cardboard tombstones, paper and crayons, a writing tablet and a pen. She too sniffs the air. She runs to the little cemetery and looks up, as Hector appears at the window behind her.*

ANGELA: Tres Rosas. . . . Did you hear? Sweet Jesus, Abuelo, Queen of Heaven, all the Saints, all the Angels. It is true. It is certain. He is coming, coming to stay forever and ever. Amen.

HECTOR: Don't count on it!

ANGELA *(To Heaven)*: Protect me from those of little faith and substance.

HECTOR: I'm warning you. You're just going to be disappointed.

ANGELA *(To Heaven)*: Guard me against the enemies of my soul.

HECTOR: Your butt's getting bigger and bigger!

ANGELA: And keep me from falling in with low companions.

HECTOR: Listen, little hummingbird woman, you gotta be tough, and grown-up today.

*Angela digs up her collection can and two dolls. Both dolls are dressed in nuns' habits. One, the St. Lucy doll, has round sunglasses. She turns a box over to make a little tea table on which she places a doll's teapot and cups.*

ANGELA: As an act of faith and to celebrate her father's homecoming, Miss Angela Ester Morales will have a tea party.

HECTOR: No more tea parties.

ANGELA: Dancing in attendance will be that charming martyr St. Lucy.

HECTOR: He will not be impressed.

ANGELA: Due to the loss of her eyes and the sensitivity of her alabaster skin, St. Lucy will sit in the shade. *(She sits St. Lucy in the shade and picks up the other doll)*

HECTOR: Who's that?

ANGELA: St. Teresa of Avignon, you will sit over here. *(She seats St. Teresa doll)*

HECTOR: Just don't let him con you Angela.

ANGELA (*Pouring pretend tea*): One lump or two, St. Lucy? St. Teresa has hyperglycemia, and only takes cream in her tea. Isn't that right St. Teresa?

HECTOR: He's not like Abuelo.

*Angela animates the dolls like puppets and uses two different voices as St. Lucy and St. Teresa.*

ANGELA (*As St. Teresa*): Shouldn't we wait for St. Luke?

HECTOR: Stop hiding. You can't be a little girl forever.

ANGELA (*As St. Lucy*): St. Luke! St. Luke! Indeed! How that man got into Heaven I'll never know. That story about putting peas in his boots and offering the discomfort up to God is pure bunk. I happen to know he boiled the peas first.

HECTOR: I don't want you hurt. It's time to grow up.

ANGELA (*As St. Teresa*): St. Lucy! I can only think that it is the loss of your eyes that makes you so disagreeable. Kindly remember that we have all suffered to be saints.

HECTOR: Are you listening to me, Angie?

ANGELA (*As St. Lucy*): Easy for you to say! They took my eyes because I wouldn't put out! They put them on a plate. A dirty, chipped one, thank you very much indeed! To this day no true effort has been made to find them.

HECTOR: Excuse me! . . . Excuse me, St. Teresa, St. Lucy, I just thought I should tell you . . . a little secret . . . your hostess, Miss Angela Ester Morales, lies in her little, white, chaste, narrow bed, underneath the crucifix, and masturbates.

ANGELA: Heretic! Liar!

HECTOR: Poor Jesus, up there on the cross, right over her bed, his head tilted down. He sees everything.

ANGELA: Lies! Horrible lies!

HECTOR: Poor saint of the month, watching from the night table.

ANGELA: I hate you! I hate you! Horrible, horrible Hector.

JUANA (*From offstage*): Breakfast!

*Hector leaves the window. Angela sits on the ground writing on a tombstone.*

ANGELA (*Lettering a tombstone*): Here lies Horrible Hector Morales. Died at age twenty, in great agony, for tormenting his little sister.

JUANA (*Offstage*): You kids . . . breakfast!

HECTOR (*Pops up at window*): Just be yourself. A normal sex-crazed fifteen-year-old girl with a big gigantic enormous butt. (*He exits*)

ANGELA (*To Heaven*):
Send me to Alaska
Let me be frozen
Send me a contraction
A shrinking antidote
Make me little again

Please make my legs
Like tiny pink Vienna sausages
Give me back my little butt.

*Juana and Chata bring breakfast out on the porch and set it on the table.*

JUANA: Angie! Hector! We ain't got all day.

*Angela goes to the breakfast table with the St. Lucy doll and the collection can.*

And take your wings off before you sit at the table. Ain't you kids got any manners?

*Angela removes her wings, sits down, bows her head in prayer. Chata stares at St. Lucy. St. Lucy stares at Chata. Juana shoos flies and stares at the distant fire.*

I hope he's on this side of the fire.

CHATA: That doll's staring at me.

ANGELA: She loves you.

*Lights fade on the women, come up on the henhouse, Adan, a young man of twenty, is talking to Zapata—now a real rooster, not the actor/dancer—and preparing his feed.*

ADAN: Hola Zapata . . . ya mi lindo . . . mi bonito. En Inglés. Tengo que hablar en English . . . pinchi English . . . verdad Zapata? En Español más romántico pero Hector say I must learned di English. *(Zapata starts squawking)* Qué te pasa? Orita vas a comer.

*Hector enters.*

HECTOR: English, Adan . . . English.

ADAN: No English . . . pinchi English.

HECTOR: Good morning, Adan.

ADAN: A que la fregada! . . . Okay this morning in the fields, I talk English pero this afternoon for fight I talk puro Español.

HECTOR: Good morning, Adan.

ADAN: Sí, sí, good morning, muy fine. . . . Hector el Filipino he say . . . *(He moves away from Zapata, so bird will not hear him)* He say to tell you que Zapata no win. Porque Filipino bird fight more y your bird first fight y your first fight y you got no ex . . . ex . . .

HECTOR: Experience.

ADAN: Sí eso, he say you sell bird to him y no fight. . . . He say is not true Morales bird porque Gallo not here. El Filipino say if you fight bird . . . bird dead. If bird still alive after Filipino bird beat him. . . . Bird still dead porque nobody pay money for bird that lose.

HECTOR: But if he wins, everybody wants him.

ADAN: I say, ay di poor, poor Hector. His abuelo leave him bird. He can no sell. El Filipino say, "Good!" Inside, in my heart I am laughing so hard porque he not know Gallo gonna be here. We win, we make much money.

HECTOR: It's my bird, I have to do it myself.

ADAN: You tonto! You stupido! You mulo! Like donkey. . . . He help you, he the king . . . he you papa. For him all birds fight.

HECTOR: No!

ADAN: Why? Why for you do this? You no even like bird. Zapata he knows this, he feel this thing in his heart. You just want money to go from the fields, to go to the other side of the mountains . . to go looking . . . to go looking for what? On the other side is only more stupid people like us.

HECTOR: How could you think I just wanted money? I want him to see me.

ADAN: Sorry. . . . I am sorry my friend. . . . I know. . . . I stay with you y we win vas a ver! Okay Zapata! We win y est a noche estamos tomando Coors, Ripple, Lucky Lager, unas Buds, Johnnie Walkers, oh sí, y las beautiful señoritas. (He gives Zapata his food) Eat Zapata! Be strong.

HECTOR: I almost forgot, look what I have for you . . . fresh, warm homemade tortillas.

ADAN: Oh, how nice.

HECTOR: Yes, how nice. Aunt Chata made them.

ADAN: Oh, much nice.

HECTOR: Today she woke up at five o'clock, spit a green booger the size of a small frog into a wad of Kleenex. She wrapped her soiled black "7th Fleet" kimono around her loose, flaccid, tortured, stretch-marked body and put her fat-toed, corned yellow hooves into a pair of pink satin slippers. She slap-padded over to the sink, where she opened her two hippo lips and looked into the mirror. She looked sad. I looked at those lips . . . those lips that had wrapped themselves warmly and lovingly around the cocks of a million campesinos, around thousands upon thousands of Mexicanos, Salvadoreños, Guatemaltecos. For the tide of brown men that flooded the fields of this country, she was there with her open hippo whore's lips, saying, "Bienvenidos," "Welcome," "Hola," "Howdy." Those are legendary lips, Adan.

ADAN: Yes . . . muy yes.

HECTOR: What a woman, what a comfort. Up and down the state in her beat-up station wagon. A '56 Chevy with wood panels on the sides, in the back a sad, abused mattress. She followed the brown army of pickers through tomatoes, green beans, zucchinis, summer squash, winter squash, oranges, and finally Castroville, the artichoke capital of the world, where her career was stopped by the fists of a sun-crazed compañero. The ingratitude broke her heart.

ADAN: Oh my gooseness!

HECTOR: She was a river to her people, she should be rewarded, honored. No justice in the world.

ADAN: Pinchi world. (He and Hector look to mountains) You look mountains. In my country I look mountains to come here. I am here and everybody still look mountains.

HECTOR: I want to fly right over them.

ADAN: No, my friend, we are here, we belong . . . la tierra.

JUANA *(From offstage)*: Hector, I ain't calling you again.

*Lights up on the porch. Juana and Chata are sitting at the table. Angela is sitting on the steps. She has her wings back on. St. Lucy and the collection can are by her side. she is writing on her tablet.*

JUANA: Oh Gallo, what's keeping you?

CHATA: Men are shit! That's all. And it's Saturday. When do they get drunk? When do they lose their money? When do they shoot each other? Saturdays, that's when the shit hits the fan.

*Enter Hector and Adan with Zapata in a traveling carrier.*

JUANA: It's because I'm so plain.

HECTOR: We're better off without him.

CHATA: Buenos días Adan. Un cafecito?

ADAN: Ah. Good morning, Mrs. Chata, no gracias, ah good morning, Mrs. Morales y Miss Angelita.

*Angela sticks out her donation can. Adan automatically drops coins in.*

JUANA: Angela!

ADAN: No, is good, is for the poor. Miss Angela, she good lady . . . eh, girl. *(He pats Angela on the head)*

JUANA: Why don't you leave the bird, so your father can see him when he gets home.

HECTOR: He's my bird. He can see it later.

JUANA: I can't believe you would do this to your own father. Birds are his life . . . and he's so proud of you.

HECTOR: This is news. How would he know, he hasn't seen me in years.

JUANA: It isn't his fault.

HECTOR: It never is.

JUANA: Your father is with us all the time, he got his eye on us, he knows everything we're going.

ANGELA: Everything!?

JUANA: I brag about you kids in my letters. . . . His friends they tell him what a smart boy you are . . . that you're good-looking like him. . . . He's proud. . . . "A real Morales," that's what he says.

HECTOR: And did he call me a winner? A champ? A prince? And did you tell him I was in the fields?

ANGELA: What did he say about me, Mama?

HECTOR: Nothing, you're a girl and a retard. What possible use could he have for you? Grow up!

CHATA: No, you grow up.

*Angela buries herself in Chata's lap.*

JUANA: Hector, please, Hector, for me.

HECTOR: No, Mother. Not even for you.

JUANA: You give him a chance.

HECTOR: What chance did he give us? Fighting his birds, in and out of trouble. He was never here for us, never a card, a little present for Angela. He forgot us.

JUANA: You don't understand him. He's different.

HECTOR: Just make it clear to him. Abuelo left the bird to me, not to him, to me.

JUANA: Me, me, me. You gonna choke on this me, me. Okay, okay, I'm not going to put my nose in the bird business. I just ask you for me, for Angie, be nice to him.

HECTOR: As long as we all understand the "bird business," I'll be nice to him even if it kills me, Mother.

JUANA: Now you're feeling sorry for yourself. Just eat. You can feel sorry for yourself later.

HECTOR: Why didn't I think of that. I'll eat now and feel sorry for myself later.

JUANA: Now, you kids gotta be nice and clean, your papa don't like dirty people.

CHATA: Me too, I hate dirty people.

JUANA: Angie, you take a bath.

HECTOR: Oh, Angela, how . . . how long has it been since you and water came together? *(Angela hits him)* Oww!

JUANA: You put on a nice clean dress, and I don't wanna see you wearing no dirty wings.

HECTOR: Right, Angie, put on the clean ones.

JUANA: You say please and excuse me . . . and you watch your table manners. . . . I don't want to see any pigs at my table.

HECTOR *(Making pig noises)*: What a delicious breakfast! Cold eggs, sunny-side up. How cheery! How uplifting! Hmm, hmmm! *(He turns so Angela can see him. He picks up eggs with his hands and stuffs them in his mouth)* Look, Angela, refried beans in a delicate pool of congealed fat. *(Still making pig noises, he picks up gobs of beans, stuffs them into his mouth)*

CHATA: A que la fregada! Hector, stop playing with your food. You're making us sick.

JUANA *(Looking at watch)*: 7:20, you got ten minutes before work.

*Hector drums his fingers on the table.*

HECTOR: Nine minutes. . . . I will now put on the same old smelly, shit-encrusted boots, I will walk to the fields. The scent of cow dung and rotting vegetation will fill the air. I will wait with the same group of beaten-down, pathetic men . . . taking their last piss against a tree, dropping hard warm turds in the bushes.

All adding to this fertile whore of a valley. At 7:30 that yellow mechanical grasshopper, the Deerfield tractor, will belch and move. At this exact moment, our foreman, John Knipe, will open his pig-sucking mouth, exposing his yellow, pointy, plaque-infested teeth. He yells, "Start picking, boys." The daily war begins . . . the intimidation of violent growth . . . the expanding melons and squashes, the hardiness of potatoes, the waxy purple succulence of eggplant, the potency of ripening tomatoes. All so smug, so rich, so ready to burst with sheer generosity and exuberance. They mock me. . . . I hear them. . . . "Hey Hector," they say, "show us whatcha got," and "Yo Hector we got bacteria out here more productive than you." . . . I look to the ground. Slugs, snails, worms slithering in the earth with such ferocious hunger they devour their own tails, flies oozing out larvae, aphids, bees, gnats, caterpillars their prolification only slightly dampened by our sprays. We still find eggsacks hiding, ready to burst forth. Their teeming life, their lust, is shameful . . . a mockery of me and my slender spirit. . . . Well it's time. . . . Bye Ma. *(He exits)*

JUANA *(Yelling)*: Hector! You gotta do something about your attitude. *(To herself)* Try to see the bright side.

*Juana and Chata exit into the house, leaving Angela on the porch steps. Adan runs up to her.*

ADAN: Pssst! Miss Angelita! . . . di . . . di cartas?
ANGELA: Oh, the letters . . . that will be one dollar.
ADAN: One dollar! Adan very poor man. . . .

*Angela sticks the donation can out and shakes it. Adan reaches into his pockets and drops coins into the can.*

Oh, sí, you are very good.

*Angela puts on glasses and pulls out a letter.*

ANGELA *(Reading letter)*: Adored Señora Acosta: The impulses of my heart are such that they encourage even the most cautious man to commit indiscretion. My soul is carried to the extreme with the love that only you could inspire. Please know that I feel a true passion for your incomparable beauty and goodness. I tremulously send this declaration and anxiously await the result. Your devoted slave, Adan.
ADAN *(Sighing)*: Ay, que beautiful.
ANGELA: P.S. With due respect Señora, if your husband should be home, do not turn on the porch light.
ADAN: Ah, thank you . . . thank you very much.

*Adan hurriedly exits. Angela gathers her St. Lucy doll and her donation can, and exits quickly. Chata enters from the house wearing "colorful" street clothes. She looks around, then swiftly exits. Hector enters, picks up Zapata, hurries off.*

*The stage darkens, as if smoke from the distant fire has covered the sun. Drum howls are heard. In the distance we hear a rooster crow and sounds of excited chickens as the henhouse comes to life. Gallo appears.*

GALLO: Easy hens, shshsh! My beauties. *(He puts his suitcase down, cups his hands to his mouth, and yells to the house)* Juana! Juana! Juana! *(Juana opens the door)* How many times, in the fever of homesickness, have I written out that name on prison walls, on bits of paper, on the skin of my arms. . . . Let me look at you . . . my enduring rock, my anchor made from the hard parts of the earth—minerals, rocks, bits of glass, ground shells, the brittle bones of dead animals.

JUANA: I never seen you so pale, so thin. . . .

GALLO: I'm home to rest, to fatten up, to breathe, to mend, to you.

JUANA: How long? How long will you stay?

GALLO: Here. Here is where I'll put my chair. . . . I will sit here basking in the sun, like a fat old iguana catching flies, and watching my grandchildren replant the little cemetery with the bones of tiny sparrows. Here. Here I will build the walks for my champions. Morales roosters. The brave and gallant red Cubans, the hard and high-kicking Irish Warhorses, the spirited high-flying Bolinas.

JUANA: Don't say nothing you don't mean . . . you really gonna stay?

GALLO *(Gently)*: Here. Here is where I'll plant a garden of herbs. Blessed laurel to cure fright, wild marjoram for the agony of lovesickness, cempasuchie flowers for the grief of loneliness.

*Gallo gently kisses Juana, picks her up and carries her into the house. The door slams shut. Angela enters, her wings drooping behind her. She trips over Gallo's suitcase. She examines it. She smells it.*

ANGELA: Tres Rosas!

*Angela looks at the house. She sits on the suitcase, crosses her arms over her chest as if she were ready to wait an eternity. The shadows of two strangers fall on her.*

ANGELA: What do you want?

SHADOW #1: Where's Gallo?

ANGELA: Nobody's home to you, rancor.

SHADOW #2: Just go in, tell him we got something for him.

ANGELA: Nobody's home to you, resentment.

SHADOW #1: Who are you supposed to be?

ANGELA *(Holding St. Lucy doll)*:
I am the angel of this yard
I am the angel of this door
I am the angel of light
I am the angel who shouts
I am the angel who thunders

SHADOW #1: She is pure crazy.

SHADOW #2: Don't play with it, it's serious.

ANGELA:

You are the shadow of resentment
You are the shadow of rancor
I am the angel of acid saliva
I will spit on you.

SHADOW #1: There's time.

SHADOW #2: Yeah, later.

*Angela spits. The shadows leave. Angela crosses her hands over her chest and looks to Heaven.*

ANGELA: Holy Father. . . . Listen, you don't want him, you want me. Please take me, claim me, launch me and I will be your shooting-star woman. I will be your comet woman. I will be your morning-star woman.

## Scene 4

*Lights become brighter. Angela exits under the house. The door opens. Gallo comes out in T-shirt and pants and goes to his suitcase. Juana comes to the door in slip and tight robe.*

GALLO: I never sent him to the fields.

JUANA: I know.

GALLO: I never said for you to put him there.

JUANA: No, you never said. . . .

GALLO: Then why is my son in the fields? *(They look at each other. He looks away)* Don't look at me. I see it in your eyes. You blame me. Just like the old man.

JUANA: Abuelo never said a word against you.

GALLO: I never let him down with the birds, nobody could match me. They were the best.

JUANA: He knew that. . . .

GALLO: So, he left the bird to Hector.

JUANA: He wanted him out of the fields. We didn't know when you would be out or maybe something would happen to you.

GALLO: He let the boy into the fields, that was his sin. He allowed a Morales into the fields.

JUANA: He was old, tired, heartbroken.

GALLO: Heartbroken, he wasn't a woman to be heartbroken.

JUANA: His only son was in jail.

GALLO: Yes, we know that, the whole valley knows that. You . . . what did you do? Didn't you lay out your hard, succulent, bitch's teat at the breakfast table? So he would have the strength to stand behind a hoe, with his back bent and his eyes on the mud for ten hours a day.

JUANA: Hard work never killed anybody.

GALLO: Ay, mujer! Can't you think what you've done, you bowed his head down.

JUANA: What was I suppose to do? There ain't no other work here. I can't see anything wrong with it for a little while.

GALLO: The difference between them and us, is we never put a foot into the fields. We stayed independent—we worked for nobody. They have to respect us, to respect our roosters.

*Hector and Adan enter. They are both very dirty. Hector has Zapata, in his carrier. Adan has a carrier containing a second rooster. Gallo and Hector stare at each other.*

Well . . . you are taller. This offshoot . . . this little bud has grown.

HECTOR: Yeah, well . . . that must be why you seem . . . smaller.

GALLO: Un abrazo!

HECTOR: I'm dirty. I'm sweaty.

GALLO: I see that.

HECTOR: I'm afraid I smell of the fields.

GALLO: Yes.

HECTOR: Of cheap abundant peon labor . . . the scent would gag you.

GALLO: It's going to kill you.

HECTOR: Mama says hard work never killed anyone . . . isn't that right, Mother?

JUANA: It's only for a little while. Your papa thinks that—

GALLO: I'll tell him what I think. Now what about those tamales you promised me?

JUANA: Ah sí, con permiso . . . I got some work in the kitchen.

ADAN: Oh sí, Mrs. Juana, los tamales . . . que rico.

JUANA *(Smiling at Adan)*: I hope they're the kind you like. *(She exits into house)*

GALLO: Hijo, you always take the bird with you into the fields?

HECTOR: No, not always.

GALLO: This bird has to look like he's got secrets . . . no one but us should be familiar with him.

HECTOR: This is Adan.

ADAN: Es un honor, Mr. El Gallo.

*Angela sticks her head out from under the house. Adan and Gallo shake hands and greet each other.*

GALLO *(Referring to Zapata)*: Let him out . . . he needs a bigger carrier . . . he's a flyer.

ADAN: Como Filipino birds?

GALLO: Yes but this baby boy he's got a surprise. He's got a kick.

ADAN: Like Cuban bird?

GALLO: He'll fight in the air, he'll fight on the ground. You can put spurs or razors on that kick and he'll cut any bird to ribbons. You can put money on that.

ADAN: Hijo! Señor . . . how you know? He never fight. Maybe he only kick in cage.

GALLO: I know because I'm his papa. . . . *(Pointing to the other carrier)* That your bird?

ADAN: Sí, pero no good . . . no fight. San Juan, he run away.

GALLO: I'll make him fight. Just let him out.

ADAN: Mr. El Gallo, you give this pendejo bird too much honor. Gracias Señor, pero this poor bird, he no can fight.

GALLO: Is it the bird, or you who will not fight?

HECTOR: The bird is too young. He doesn't want him to fight.

GALLO: I've never seen a bird that won't fight, but there are men who are cowards.

HECTOR: He is not a coward.

ADAN: This is true, pero I am not El Gallo. In my country all men who love di rooster know Mr. El Gallo. They tell of di famoso día de los muertos fight in Jacinto Park.

GALLO: Ah, you heard about that fight. You remember that fight, Hector?

HECTOR: No.

GALLO: First time you saw a real cockfight . . . Abuelo took you. . . . How could you forget your first cockfight? *(To Adan)* Go on, take your bird out. I'll make him fight.

*Gallo takes a drink from a bottle, then blows on San Juan. As he does this, lights go down almost to black. Pinspot comes up center stage, as other lights come up to a dark red. During this process, we hear Gallo's voice—"Ready," then a few beats later "Pit!" On this cue two dancer/roosters jump into the pinspot. This rooster dance is savage. The dancers wear razors on their feet. The Zapata dancer jumps very high. The poor San Juan dancer stays close to the ground. Throughout the dance, we hear drums and foot-stomping. At every hit, there is a big drum pound. During the fight, Hector appears on the porch.*

HECTOR *(To himself)*: It was in Jacinto Park . . . the crowd was a monster, made up of individual human beings stuck together by sweat and spittle. Their gaping mouths let out screams, curses, and foul gases, masticating, smacking, eager for the kill. You stood up. The monster roared. Quasimoto, your bird, in one hand. You lifted him high, "Pit!" went the call. "Pit!" roared the monster. And you threw him into the ring . . . soaring with the blades on his heels flashing I heard the mighty rage of his wings and my heart soared with him. He was a whirlwind flashing and slashing like a dark avenging angel then like some distant rainbow star exploding he was hit. The monster crowd inhaled, sucking back their hopes . . . in that vacuum he was pulled down. My heart went down the same dark shaft, my brains slammed against the earth's hard crust . . . my eyes clouded . . . my arteries gushed . . . my lungs collapsed. "Get up," said Abuelo, "up here with me, and you will see a miracle." You, Father, picked up Quasimoto, a lifeless pile of bloody feathers, holding his head oh so gently, you closed your eyes, and like a great wave receding, you drew a breath that came from deep within your ocean floor. I heard the stones rumble, the mountains shift, the topsoil move, and as your breath slammed on the beaches, Quasimoto sputtered back to life. Oh Papi, breathe on me.

*Angela appears and stands behind her brother. Her wings are spread very far out. Drums and stomping crescendo as Zapata brutally kills San Juan. Blackout.*

# ACT TWO

## Scene 1

*Early afternoon. The table is set up in the middle of the yard in a festive way, with tablecloth, flowers, a bowl of peaches, and bottles of whiskey and wine. Gallo is in the henhouse with Adan. Hector is in the bathroom, Juana and Chata are in the kitchen. Angela is by the little cemetery writing on a tombstone.*

ANGELA: Here lies Angela Ester Morales died of acute neglect. Although she is mourned by many, she goes to a far, far, better place, where they have better food.

*Angela slides under the house as Juana comes out wearing a fresh housedress and carrying a steaming pot.*

JUANA *(Yelling)*: Hector! Angela! You kids wash up, it's time to eat.

*Juana hurries back into the house, almost knocking Chata down as she comes out with a tray of tortillas. She is heavily made up, wearing tight clothes, dangling earrings, high-heeled shoes. A cigarette dangles from her mouth.*

CHATA: Why are you eating out here?
JUANA: He wants it. Says he don't wanta hide in the house.
CHATA: Begging for trouble.
JUANA: What can I do, he's the man. *(She goes into the house)*
CHATA: Ah, they're all shit! Just want trouble. Soup's on!

*Chata pours herself a quick shot of whiskey, shoots it down and makes a face. Juana comes out with another pot.*

JUANA: You better tell 'em that the food's ready. *(Chata goes to henhouse)* Hector!
HECTOR *(Coming out on porch)*: What?
JUANA: It's time to eat . . . you look real nice honey. Makes me proud to have your papa see you all dressed up.
HECTOR: Okay. Okay. Don't make a big deal about it. I just don't want him to think—
JUANA: I just feel so happy—
HECTOR: I just don't want him to think—
JUANA: Hijito! You love your papa . . . don't you?
HECTOR: Mother!
JUANA: I know you a little mad at him . . . pero when he comes home it's like the sun when it—
HECTOR: Shshshsh!

*Chata, Gallo and Adan come out of the henhouse.*

GALLO: We have to sharpen and polish those spurs. I want them to flash.
JUANA *(To Gallo)*: The food's ready . . . we fixed what you like . . . mole, rice, frijolitos . . . tamales.

GALLO: Tamales estilo Jalisco!

CHATA *(Looking Hector over)*: Ay Papi que rico estás! *(Hector quickly sits down)* Honey! You gonna have to beat all them women off with a stick, when they see you and that rooster tonight.

ADAN: No worry Hector, I be there . . . down you mujeres, women leave de Mr. Hector and me alone. . . . Ay Mama! *(He has a giggling fit)*

GALLO *(Kissing Juana)*: It's wonderful to be in love . . . to be touched by the noble fever.

CHATA: Ah, you're better off with a touch of typhoid.

JUANA: I . . . gracias al Señor que . . . my whole family is here. *(She looks around. She yells)* Angela! Angie!

HECTOR: Mom!

JUANA: Where is she? Where is your sister?

HECTOR: Talking to the saints! I don't know.

*Juana gets up, goes to the spot where Angela slides under the house, gets down on her hands and knees and yells.*

JUANA: Angela! Angela! You leave them saints alone. You hear me!

*As everybody looks at Juana, Angela comes from behind the house and tiptoes toward the henhouse. Hector is the only one to see her. Using hand signals, she pleads to him to be quiet. Juana peers under the house.*

Angie! Honey . . . your mama worked for days to fix this food and now it's getting cold. *(To Gallo)* You should see how sweet she looks when she's all dressed up. *(To under the house)* You ain't got no manners . . . ain't even said hello to your father. *(To Gallo)* She prays a lot . . . and she's got real pretty eyes.

CHATA *(To Gallo)*: She's sorta . . . the bashful type . . . you know.

JUANA *(To Gallo)*: And she ain't spoiled.

CHATA *(Taking a drink)*: Nah, all them kids smell like that.

JUANA *(To under the house)*: Angie!

GALLO: Juana leave her alone.

JUANA: Okay. Angie, I'm gonna ignore you, 'cause you spoiled my day, this day that I been looking forward to for years and years and now you making me look like a bad mama, what's your papa gonna think of us.

GALLO: Juana, she'll come out when she's ready.

*Juana goes back to the table.*

CHATA: Maybe was them roosters fighting got her scared.

ADAN: Poor San Juan.

GALLO: Adan, drink up and I'll see you get one of our famous Champion Morales birds.

HECTOR: What famous Champion Morales birds?

GALLO: The ones I paid for dearly, the ones I came home to raise . . . isn't that right mi amor?

JUANA: Yes . . . you see honey your papa's gonna stay home . . . raise birds . . . I think Abuelo would want that.

GALLO: And after they see our bird tonight . . . see first I want them to think it's just you and the bird up there. After the bets are down, I'll take over and they're gonna know we got roosters. A toast . . .

*As Gallo stands up, everybody raises a glass, except Hector. Angela tiptoes from the henhouse carrying Zapata. She goes behind and under the house. Only Hector sees her.*

To the finest fighting cocks ever to be seen. (*He slides bottle to Hector*)

HECTOR (*Sliding bottle back*): No.

*Pause.*

GALLO: Too good to drink with your old man.

HECTOR: I only drink with people I trust.

CHATA: Me . . . I drink with anybody. Maybe that's my problem.

GALLO: I am your father.

HECTOR: Yes. You are my father.

CHATA: I like it better when I drink alone. Ya meet a better class of people that way.

HECTOR: But it's my bird. Abuelo left it to me.

GALLO: Abuelo was my father, and you are my son. I see no problem. Now let's eat.

HECTOR: Mother!

JUANA: Let's eat, honey, and we can talk about it later.

ADAN: Ay the mole muy delicious . . . the mole muy rico . . . the mole muy beautiful y Mrs. Juana. Today, you look beautiful, like the mole.

GALLO: Hm, sabroso, exquisito.

JUANA: I bet you been in plenty of fancy places got better food than this.

GALLO: This is home cooking, I know that your hands made it. . . . These . . . these are the hands of a beautiful woman. . . .

HECTOR: Ha! Bullshit.

GALLO: We say your mother is beautiful and you call it bullshit? I find that very disrespectful.

JUANA: Hijo, you're right . . . it's just the way people talk, I know I ain't beautiful.

GALLO: I say you are beautiful.

ADAN: Sí, muy beautiful.

GALLO: Ya ves! . . . If your son doesn't have the eyes, the soul, the imagination to see it . . . it's his loss.

HECTOR: That's right. I just can't seem to stretch my imagination that far.

GALLO: This is an insult to your mother.

HECTOR: It's the truth. That is a plain, tired, worn-out woman.

GALLO: Shut up.

HECTOR: The hands of a beautiful woman! Those aren't hands, they're claws because she has to scratch for her living.

JUANA: Please, Hector, let him say what he wants . . . I know I ain't beautiful. It don't go to my head.

HECTOR: But it goes to your heart which is worse. Did he ever really take care of you? Did he ever go out and work to put food on the table, to buy you a dress? All he has is words, and he throws a few cheap words to you and you come to life. Don't you have any pride?

GALLO: Your mother has great courage to trust and believe in me.

HECTOR: Stupidity!

GALLO: You know nothing!

HECTOR: You don't seem to realize that it is my rooster. And that after the fight, depending on the outcome, I will sell him or eat him. I have made a deal with the Filipinos.

JUANA: Ay Hector! You've spoiled everything. All this food . . . I worked so hard . . . for this day.

GALLO: You're not selling anything to anybody. This is nothing to joke about.

HECTOR: I don't want to spend my life training chickens to be better killers. And I don't want to spend my whole life in this valley. Mother, Aunt Chata, excuse me.

CHATA: Ah? . . . O sí hijo pase . . . sometimes Hector can be a real gentleman.

*Hector starts to leave.*

GALLO: Son! . . . You have no courage, no juice . . . you are a disgrace to me.

JUANA: Ay, Gallo don't say that to him.

HECTOR: Do you think I care what you think . . . Father.

JUANA: Hijo no . . . for me just once for me. I don't wanna be alone no more.

HECTOR: What about me? You have me, you'll always have me, I'll work, I've always worked, I can take care of you. I won't leave you.

JUANA: It ain't the same, honey.

HECTOR: Yeah. . . . He comes first for you, he will always come first.

GALLO: If you sell that bird, it will be over your dead body.

HECTOR: You can't stop me.

*Exit Hector. Chata takes a plate of food and bowl of peaches to the under-the-house area and tries to tempt Angela out.*

GALLO: He doesn't seem to realize . . . coward . . . too bad.

*Gallo goes to the henhouse. Juana starts to follow him.*

JUANA: Talk to him . . . he's a good boy . . . if you just talk . . . (*Seeing Adan still eating*) Is it good? You really like it?

ADAN: Hm! Sabroso!

CHATA: Come on Angie . . . it's real good.

*Gallo returns running.*

GALLO: He's gone . . . the bird is gone. . . .

ADAN: Yo no see nada, nada.

JUANA: He'll bring it back, he's a good boy. He's just a little upset . . . you know.

GALLO: Nobody fools with my roosters. Not even this over-petted, over-pampered viper you spawned. Go and pray to your Dark Virgin. You know what I'm capable of.

*Exit Gallo. Adan stops eating and tries to comfort Juana as she puts her head down on the table and cries.*

ADAN: No cry, no cry Mrs. Juana. Di women cry y Adan, he not know what to do. *(Juana cries louder)* Ay Mrs. Juana, for sure di flowers will die . . . di trees will be torn from di ground, freshness will leave di morning, softness will leave di night . . . *(Juana's cries increase)* Ay Dios! *(From his pocket, he brings out the letter Angela wrote for him. He crosses himself)* Mrs. di Juana . . . *(Reading with great difficulty)* Di . . . impulses . . . of my . . . heart . . . are such . . . *(Throwing letter aside)* A que la fregada! Mrs. Juana, Adan have mucho amor for you. My heart break to see you cry. I will not a breathe. When you no cry then I will breathe.

*Adan takes a big breath and holds it. Slowly Juana stops crying and lifts her head. Adan, suffering some discomfort, continues to hold his breath.*

JUANA: I been dreaming. Nothing's gonna change. I gotta face facts.

*Adan lets his breath out in a great whoosh. Angela pops out from under the house and takes a peach from Chata's hand. She stares at the peach with great intensity.*

CHATA: Angie, ain't it nice to have the family all together again?

ANGELA: There is no pit in this peach. It is hollow. Instead of the pit, there is a whole little world, a little blue-green crystal-clear ocean, with little schools of tiny darting silver fish. On a tiny rock sits a mermaid with little teenie-weenie kinky yellow hair. A tiny sun is being pulled across a little china-blue sky by teenie-weenie white horses with itty-bitty wings. There is an island with tiny palm trees and tiny thatched hut. Next to the hut stand a tiny man and woman. She is wearing flowers and leaves. He is wearing one single leaf. On their heads are little bitty halos. In their arms is a little bitsy baby. He isn't wearing anything.

CHATA: Let me see . . . *(Looking at peach)* I can't see dick!

*Blackout.*

## Scene 2

*Later in the afternoon. Chata sits on the porch steps, her legs spread out, fanning herself. Juana sits on a straight-back chair, her hands folded on her lap. She rocks herself gently. She watches Angela, who is sitting on the ground drawing circles in the dirt and humming softly. The circles get deeper and deeper.*

CHATA: It's hot . . . I am waiting for a cool breeze. . . .

ANGELA: Uh ha uh ha uh ha uh haa.

CHATA: Aire fresco . . . come on cool breeze, come right over here.

ANGELA: Uh ha uh ha uh haa.

CHATA: Women! We're always waiting.

*Angela hums for a beat, then there is silence for a beat.*

JUANA: It's because I'm so plain.

CHATA: Ah, you just work too much.

JUANA: Plainness runs in my family. My mother was plain, my grandmother was plain, my great-grandmother—

CHATA: It was the hard times . . . the hard work that did it.

JUANA: My Aunt Chona was the plainest.

CHATA: I don't remember her.

JUANA: The one with the crossed eyes and the little mustache.

CHATA: Ay, Juanita, that woman had a beautiful soul, sewing those little tiny outfits for the statues of the saints. That woman was a saint.

JUANA: She's the one told on you that time you was drinking beer with them sailors at the cockfight.

CHATA: Disgusting old bitch!

*Angela hums for a beat as she continues drawing circles.*

JUANA: I get up at six, I brush my teeth, no creams, no lotions, what they gonna do for me? I work that's all. I take care of people and I work. People look at me, they know that's all I do. I ain't got no secrets. No hidden gardens. I keep busy that's what I do. Don't stop, that's what I say to myself. Don't stop, 'cause you're not pretty enough, exciting enough, smart enough to just stand there.

ANGELA: Mama, I don't wanna be plain.

CHATA: Honey, you're too colorful to be plain.

ANGELA: Yeah, that's what I thought.

CHATA: Your mama forgets . . . those years when her heart was filled with wild dreams when she use to weave little white star jasmine vines in her hair and drive all the men crazy.

JUANA: It ain't true . . . she was the one always getting me in trouble.

CHATA: I wasn't the one they called Juanita la Morenita Sabrosita.

JUANA: Oh, Chata. We was young girls together . . . in the summer, at Jacinto Park . . . cockfights, fistfights, the music. At night we would jump out of our bedroom windows in our party dresses. With our good shoes in one hand, our hearts in the other, we ran barefoot through the wet grass, above us all the stars twinkling go, go, go.

CHATA: Nothing could stop us . . . we had such a short time being girls.

JUANA: Now, all I am is an old hag.

CHATA: It ain't true.

JUANA: Sí, it's true enough. I carry burdens, I hang sheets, I scrub, I gather, I pick up, "Here sit down," "I'll wash it," "Here's fifty cents," "Have my chair," "Take my coat," "Here's a piece of my own live flesh"!

CHATA: Es la menopause, that's what it is. You getting it early. I knew this woman once, use to pull out her hair.

JUANA: I don't care, I don't want any stories, I don't care what happens to Fulano Mangano . . . I just wanna stand still, I wanna be interesting, exciting enough to stand still.

CHATA: Ay, mujer!

JUANA: And I want to look like I got secrets.

CHATA: Juana!

JUANA: Don't call me Juana. Juana is a mule's name.

CHATA: Ah, you're crazy! That new gray hen, the kids named her Juana. See, they think of you.

JUANA: A gray hen! An old gray hen, that's all I am. An old gray hen in a family of roosters. No more! I want feathers, I wanna strut, too. I wanna crow.

ANGELA: Mama!

JUANA: Don't! Don't call me Mama. I am not Mama . . . I am . . . I am that movie star, that famous dancer and heartbreaker "Morenita Sabrosita" . . . and now if my fans will excuse me I'm gonna take a bath in champagne, eat cherry bonbons and paint my toenails. *(She goes into the house)*

CHATA *(To Juana)*: We got champagne?

*Chata goes into the house as Angela goes to the little cemetery and puts up a new tombstone.*

ANGELA *(Printing on tombstone)*: Here lies Juana Morales. Beloved Wife of El Gallo, Blessed Mother to Angela and Horrible Hector. Died of acute identity crisis sustained during la menopause.

## Scene 3

*Lights go down, as Angela sits on her box/table at the little cemetery. The long shadows of men fall on Angela and the cemetery.*

SHADOW #1: There's that spooky kid. You go brother.

SHADOW #2: Ah, it's just a weird kid. Hey! You! Kid!

*Angela does not acknowledge them.*

SHADOW #1: Call her "Angel."

SHADOW #2: Hey, Angel.

*Angela looks up.*

SHADOW #1: See what I mean.

SHADOW #2: Listen kid, tell your old man, we got business to discuss.

SHADOW #1: Yeah, and you make sure he gets the message.

ANGELA: My old man, my Holy Father, my all powerful Father, sees no problems. If there are problems, I am the angel of this yard. I am the comet. I am the whirlwind. I am the shooting stars. Feel my vibrance.

SHADOW #1: I feel it, right behind my ears, like . . . like . . .

ANGELA: Locust wings.

SHADOW #1: Let's get outta here.

SHADOW #2: Tell Gallo some pals dropped by to settle an old score.

SHADOW #1: Come on!

SHADOW #2 (*Voice trailing off*): Hey! That kid don't scare me, see.

SHADOW #1 (*Voice trailing off*): I'm telling ya, my ears hurt.

*Exit shadows. Lights go back up. Angela folds her hands in prayer.*

ANGELA: Holy Father, please help me, I feel the illumination, the fever of grace slipping away. I need to know that you are with me, that you take an interest in my concerns. Send me a little demonstration, a sign. Any sign . . . I don't care. Stigmata, visions, voices, send an angel, burn a bush. . . . I am attracted to levitation . . . but you choose . . . I'll just lay here and wait.

*Angela lies on the ground waiting. After a few beats Hector enters. He slowly walks up to Angela and looks down on her for a beat.*

HECTOR: What are you doing?

ANGELA (*Sitting up*): Ohhh . . . you're no sign.

HECTOR: What is going on?

ANGELA: Weird, shady men came here looking for Gallo. Two of them. They were not polite.

HECTOR: I see. . . . So your reaction is to lay stretched out on the dirt instead of going into the house.

ANGELA: Hector, please, I am scared. . . . I wanted a sign.

*Hector sits down next to Angela.*

HECTOR: Hey, you're the shooting-star woman, you can't be scared.

ANGELA: I am scared. Really scared. If I grow up will I still be scared? Are grown-ups scared?

HECTOR: Always scared, trembling . . . cowering . . . this . . . this second, now . . . this planet that we are sitting on is wobbling precariously on its lightning path around the sun and every second the sun is exploding . . . stars are shooting at us from deep distant space, comets zoom around us, meteor rocks are being hurled through distances we measure in light . . . this very earth which we call our home, our mother, has catastrophic moods, she keeps moving mountains, receding oceans, shifting poles, bucking and reeling like an overburdened beast trying to shake us off. . . . Life is violent.

ANGELA: You're scared about the fight . . . huh?

HECTOR: No. Whatever happens, Papi will still only care about the rooster. That's his son, that's who gets it all.

ANGELA: Maybe if we gave him the rooster he'd stay here and be happy.

HECTOR: He has to stay for us not the rooster . . . Angela . . . you . . . you were great taking the rooster.

ANGELA: He kept killing the little chicks. How could he do that Hector? He's their papa.

HECTOR: Training. Look Angela, you're the angel of this yard. You keep a close guard on that rooster. Don't let anyone near him . . . promise me.

ANGELA: Yes.

HECTOR: That's a real promise now. No crossed fingers behind your back.

ANGELA: I promise already. (She spreads her hands out in front of her, then kisses the tip of her thumb) May God strike me dumb, make me a plain whiny person and take away my gift of faith. Forever and ever, throughout my mortal years on earth, and throughout the everlasting fires of hell. Amen. Satisfied?

HECTOR: Yes.

ANGELA: Gee, maybe I should have given myself a little leeway, a little room for error.

*Chata enters from the house with a bottle and glass.*

HECTOR: Too late now. Can't take it back.

CHATA: Oh, oh, look who's here. Angie, your mama needs some cheering up, a nice hug, an angel's kiss, maybe a little song.

ANGELA: Litany to the Virgin. That's her favorite. (She exits)

CHATA: Men are shit. Pure shit.

HECTOR: And you're still drinking.

CHATA: Stay outta my drinking. You hurt your mama, Hector.

HECTOR: Too bad.

CHATA: Ay Dios, what a man he is now.

HECTOR: Yeah, well what about you? Didn't you break Abuelo's heart when you became a whore?

CHATA: They called me the encyclopedia of love. You want to turn a few pages? Your Aunt Chata could show you a few things.

HECTOR: You're disgusting.

CHATA: Is that what fascinates you, honey? Is that why I always find you peeping at me, mirrors at the keyhole, your eyeballs in the cracks, spying when I'm sleeping, smelling my kimono.

HECTOR: You're drunk.

CHATA: I ain't drunk, honey.

HECTOR: You drink too much. It's not . . . good for you . . . it makes you ugly.

CHATA: Ain't none of your business. Don't tell me what to do Hector.

HECTOR: I have to, it's for your own good.

CHATA: You got nothing to say about it, you ain't my man, and you ain't your mama's man. The sooner you learn that the better . . . take your bird, leave it, eat or sell it, but get out of here. *(Hector stands alone in the yard, as she goes to the door. She turns. They look at each other)* What are you hanging around here for? Go on! Get out! It ain't your home anymore. *(She takes a broom and shoos Hector from the yard)* Shoo! Shoo! You don't belong here, it ain't your place anymore.

HECTOR: Stop it, stop it, stop it.

*Hector goes to the outside boundary of the yard, where he falls to his knees and buries his face in his hands, as Chata comes slowly up behind him.*

CHATA: I feel like I'm tearing my own flesh from my bones. . . . He's back. Honey, we got too many roosters in this yard.

HECTOR: Did you sleep with my father? Did he yearn for you as you slept in your little white, chaste, narrow bed? Did he steal you when you were dreaming?

CHATA *(Embracing him)*: Shshsh . . .

HECTOR: I'm not like him.

CHATA: You're just like him, so handsome you make my teeth ache.

HECTOR: Whore, mother, sister, saint-woman, moon-woman, give me the shelter of your darkness, fold me like a fan and take me into your stillness, submerge me beneath the water, beneath the sea, beneath the mysteries, baptize me, bear me up, give me life, breathe on me.

*Chata enfolds him as the lights fade. We hear Angela reciting the litany*

ANGELA *(Offstage)*: She is the Gate of Heaven, the Mystical Rose, the Flower of Consolation, the Fire of Transcendence, and the Queen of Love.

## Scene 4

*Lights come up to indicate that time has passed. Angela is alone in the yard. She sniffs the air.*

ANGELA: Tres Rosas!

*Angela slides under the house as Gallo enters. He sees a brief flash of Angela from the corner of his eye. He walks slowly into the yard. He stops by the little cemetery and reads the tombstones. Feeling the urge for a drink, he goes to the table and has a shot. He sits.*

GALLO: Acute neglect? . . . uh-huh . . . I thought I felt a little spirit, slight, delicate . . . yes I feel it. A little tenderness . . . a little greenness . . . *(Examining the ground)* What's this? Tracks . . . little tiny paws . . . there . . . *(Following tracks)* and there . . .

*Gallo pretends to be following tracks to the porch. Then with one great leap he jumps in the opposite direction, surprising the hell out of Angela, and pulls her from under the house by her heels.*

Ah, ha!

ANGELA: Shit! Hey! You're ripping my wings! You shithead! Put me down! Don't touch me!

*Gallo puts Angela down, throws his hands up to indicate he won't touch her. They stand and stare at each other. Angela goes to the little cemetery, never taking her eyes off Gallo. They continue to stare for a beat, then Angela looks up to Heaven, slapping her hands together in prayer.*

There is a person here trying to con me, but I don't con that easy.

GALLO *(Slapping his hands in prayer)*: There is a person here who swallows saints but defecates devils.

ANGELA *(To Heaven)*: He comes here smelling of rosas using sweet oily words . . . it's phony, it's obnoxious, it's obscene . . . I wanna throw up.

GALLO: I came here to see my baby, my little angel, my little woman of the shooting stars, my light delicate splendorous daughter. But she is as light, as delicate, as splendid as an angel's fart.

ANGELA: Angels do not fart. They do not have a digestive system. That's why they can all scrunch together on the head of a pin.

GALLO: Oh . . . I only come with my love—

ANGELA: You only came with words . . . well, where were these words on my birthday, Christmas, my saint's day? Where's my Easter outfit, my trip to Disneyland, the orthodontist. . . . You owe me.

GALLO: Sweet Jesus. . . . What a monster! I owe you . . . but Angela! Angela! Angela! How many times have I written that name on prison walls. On bits of paper, on the skin of my arms.

ANGELA *(To Heaven)*: He's hopeless! You write everybody's name on your arms.

GALLO: Women like to know that they're on your flesh.

ANGELA: I am not a woman. I'm your baby daughter. You said so yourself.

GALLO: I'm afraid . . . fathers to daughters . . . that's so delicate. I don't know . . . what to do . . . help me Angela. How do I know what to do?

ANGELA: Instinct! Ain't ya got no instinct? Don't you feel anything?

GALLO *(Moving closer to Angela)*: When you were a little baby, you were a miracle of tiny fingers and toes and dimples and you had a soft spot on the top of your head.

ANGELA: I still have it, see.

GALLO: I wanted to take you into my arms and crush you against my chest so that I could keep you forever and nobody, and nothing, could ever, ever hurt you because you would be safe . . . my little offshoot, my little bud, my little flower growing inside my chest.

ANGELA: Papi . . .

GALLO: Sí, sí, hijita. Your papi's here.

ANGELA: And Papi these men come all the—

GALLO *(Holding Angela)*: Shshsh . . . it's nothing, nothing and you thought I forgot about you . . . well it just hurt too much, do you understand?

ANGELA: You had to pull down some hard time and the only way to survive was to cut off all feelings and become an animal just like the rest of them.

GALLO: Well, something like that. Honey you know what I wish—

ANGELA: Papa, did the lights really go down when they put the people in the electric chair?

GALLO: Angela, what a. . . . Honey you know what I wish—

ANGELA: Did they force you to make license plates? Hector and I would look real close at the ones that started with a G. We thought you made them. "What craftsmanship!" Hector used to say.

GALLO: Don't you have any normal interests?

ANGELA: Like what?

GALLO: Like swimming . . . you know what I wish? That we could take a trip and see the ocean together.

ANGELA: I've never seen the ocean. When?

GALLO: Just you and me. Laying on our bellies, feeding the seagulls, riding the waves.

ANGELA: I can't swim.

GALLO: I will teach you, that's what fathers are for—

ANGELA *(To Heaven)*: Angels and saints did you hear? My father's going to teach me to swim!

GALLO: Now Angela, I didn't promise.

ANGELA: But you said—

GALLO: I want to but I have to hurry and fix things. I have to find Hector, talk to him and find that rooster fast before Hector sells him. Honey you pray to St. Anthony, your prayers are powerful . . . unless . . . St. Anthony he listen to you?

ANGELA *(Crossing her fingers)*: Hey, we're like that.

GALLO: Ask St. Anthony, Angela . . . then we can go to the ocean.

ANGELA: Truly Papi? Just you and me? And will you stay with us forever and ever?

GALLO: Wild horses couldn't drag me away.

ANGELA: Close your eyes. Tony! Tony! Look around, Zapata's lost and can't be found. *(She goes under the house, gets Zapata, and gives him to Gallo)* I found him Papi, he was—

GALLO: Ya lindo, ya. *(To bird)* Papa's got you now. Angela you keep quiet now honey, this is our secret.

ANGELA: What about Hector?

GALLO: I'm going to talk to Hector now. You go inside and get all dressed up. So I can be proud of my girl. I'll pick you up after the fight. *(He exits)*

ANGELA: Your girl! *(Singing)* We are going to the ocean, we are going to the sea, we are going to the ocean to see what we can see . . .

*Angela goes into the house. We hear cha-cha music.*

CHATA *(Offstage)*: One, two . . . not like that . . . I'm getting tired . . . what time's *Zorro* on?

JUANA (*Offstage*): No, no. . . . Just one more. (*Singing*) Cha, cha, cha, que rico, . . . cha, cha, cha. . . . Ay, I could do it all night.

*Enter Gallo running, breathing hard. He has Zapata's carrier. He goes to the door and yells.*

GALLO: Juana! Juana!

*Juana and Chata come to the door.*

I need money . . . and my stuff. I gotta leave . . . something's come up. . . . Do you hear me? I need money now.

JUANA: I hear ya . . . you ain't even been here a day and already you're gone . . . nothing's going to change with you . . . nothing. I was having fun, dancing, remembering old times, do you know how long—

GALLO: I don't have time for this, just give me the money.

JUANA: I ain't got any!

CHATA: I got some. (*She goes in the house*)

GALLO: The Filipino, somebody told him about the bird. Oh, ya, ya my little hen, don't you ruffle those pretty feathers, I'll be back.

JUANA: No, you always gonna be running.

GALLO: If it was just me, I'd stay. You know that, Juana? You know I'd stay, but I got the bird to think of, gotta hide him, breed him good, soon as I get some good stags I'll come home . . . this is just a little setback.

*Chata returns with suitcase and money.*

JUANA: You know how long it's been since I went dancing?

CHATA: Here, you're gonna need this. (*Gives him the suitcase*) And this is all the cash I got.

*Angela enters as Gallo counts the money. She is dressed in a red strapless dress made tight by large visible safety pins, high heels, and a great deal of heavy makeup and jewelry. The effect is that of a young girl dressed like a tart for a costume party. She carries a suitcase, purse and her donation can.*

GALLO: Is this all you got?

ANGELA (*Shaking the can*): Don't worry Papa, I got my donation-can money.

*They all stare at her for a beat.*

JUANA AND CHATA: Angela?!!

JUANA: Angie, you got on your mama's old party dress.

CHATA: Yeah, and all my jewelry . . . where you going?

ANGELA: Papa, didn't you hear me? I have money. (*She shakes the can*)

GALLO: Oh honey, don't you look pretty . . . now you got a little bit too much lipstick on, let your mama wipe some off.

ANGELA: Are we leaving now?

JUANA: Gallo!

GALLO: Shshsh Juana . . . Angela, I gotta talk to your mama for a few minutes. You go in the house and I'll come and get you.

ANGELA: Are you sure?

GALLO: Don't you trust me, Angie?

CHATA: Come on Angie, I'll show you how to draw eyebrows. First you draw a straight line across your forehead and then spit on your finger and rub out the middle. Let's go in and try it.

ANGELA: Really, Aunt Chata, I'm not a child, you don't have to patronize me.

CHATA: Okay, I'll give you the low-down on blow-jobs.

*Angela and Chata go into the house.*

Now, don't tell your mama . . .

GALLO: Juana, keep her in the house until I leave.

JUANA: You promised to take her with you?

GALLO: I had to get the bird. I said I would take her to the ocean.

JUANA: Ay bruto! How could you do it?

GALLO: How was I to know this would happen . . . and Juanita, it hurts me to say this but that kid is crazy . . .

JUANA: No, no Señor, she is not crazy and I ain't gonna let you call her crazy. She got the spirit they broke in me. I ain't gonna let it happen to her.

GALLO: Shshsh! Don't get so excited. It isn't important.

JUANA: It's important . . . it's her spirit, her soul and you ain't gonna stomp on it . . . you hear me.

*Adan enters running.*

ADAN: Mr. El Gallo . . . bad men! Mucho bad, y mucho ugly. Looking for you y Zapata. All ober they look for you . . . Big Nicky's, Castro Fields, Don Pancho's. . . . You leave, Mr. El Gallo. You go far away. I take you. I go for my truck.

GALLO: You are a good friend Adan, and my new partner.

ADAN: Oh, thank you Mr. El Gallo. I am proud. But is better I come back here to Mrs. Juana y Hector.

JUANA: Thank you, Adan.

GALLO: We better hurry.

ADAN: Sí, sí, I come back with truck. *(He exits)*

*Juana goes into the house. Hector enters as Gallo starts to pack his suitcase.*

HECTOR *(Seeing Zapata)*: You must have really sold her a bill of goods to get Zapata.

GALLO: Look, there's trouble . . . the Filipino send you?

HECTOR: No, how could you think I would work for him, but I came to get Zapata.

GALLO: You're the one told him about the bird.

HECTOR: Yes. I made a deal with the Filipino. He'll leave you alone if I give him the rooster.

GALLO: That's a lie and you fell for it.

HECTOR: No, he is an honorable man, we were here unprotected for seven years and he never bothered us. It's his bird, Papi.

GALLO: No, I paid seven years of my life for this baby.

HECTOR: And he lost his son. It's the right thing to do.

*A truck horn is heard. Angela comes out of the house with her suitcase, Juana and Chata follow after her.*

ANGELA: Papa? Are we leaving now, Papa?

JUANA: Angie! No!

HECTOR: So that's it . . . Angela, get back in the house.

ANGELA: I'm going with him, Hector.

HECTOR: Get back in the house, nobody's going anywhere.

ANGELA: No! I don't have to listen to you anymore. You're not my father.

JUANA: Angie . . . he's not going to the ocean . . . he can't take you.

*We hear the sound of Adan's truck. The horn is heard as Gallo starts backing away, picking up Zapata's carrier.*

ANGELA: Papi, wait for me! Papa, you promised.

GALLO: You're all grown up now, you don't need your old man.

CHATA: Hector!

*Gallo turns, tries to run out. Angela grabs him, knocking Zapata's carrier out of his hand. Hector picks up the carrier.*

ANGELA: No Papa, we need you and Mama needs you, we've been waiting, and waiting, you can't leave, you promised me.

JUANA: They'll kill you Gallo.

GALLO (*Throwing Angela off*): Stop sucking off me. I got nothing for you.

ANGELA (*Beating her fists on the ground*): No, no, Papa! You promised me! . . . Oh, Hector. . . . No, no, I promised Hector.

*Drums begin as punctuation of the pounding of Angela's fists on the ground. Lights change. A special on Angela and another on Gallo and Hector come up, as shadows appear. Angela sees them.*

Ah. . . . Holy Father, Abuelo.

GALLO (*To Hector*): Give me that bird.

ANGELA: Saints, Angels, Mama.

JUANA (*Trying to pick up Angela*): Come on Angie, get up.

GALLO (*To Hector*): What do you want?

HECTOR: You, alive, Papi.

CHATA: Careful, Hector.

ANGELA: I've lost my faith. I am splintered.

GALLO (*Imitating Hector*): You Papi. . . . Give me life. . . . Make me a man. (*He whips out his stiletto*) This is how you become a man. (*The drums get louder. We hear howling*) Come on baby boy, show Daddy whatcha got.

JUANA: Are you crazy! That's your son!

ANGELA: I am cast down! Exiled!

*Gallo stalks Hector as drums follow their movements.*

JUANA: Oh Gallo, you're killing your own children.

CHATA: Move Hector, don't think, move!

GALLO: Oh yeah, mi lindo, you like to fight . . . eh?

JUANA: No, stop them! Please, please stop this.

ANGELA: Fallen from the light, condemned to the mud, to the shadows.

GALLO: You gotta learn baby boy.

CHATA: Look at him Hector. He's getting old, his hand is shaking . . . take the knife! Stay down old warrior. Stay down.

ANGELA: Alone and diminished. This loneliness is unendurable.

JUANA: Hector!

HECTOR: Do I have it? Is this what you want me to be . . .

ANGELA (*Looking to Heaven*):
My brains are slammed against the earth's hard crust.
My eyes are clouded
My arteries gush
My lungs collapsed.

HECTOR (*Letting go of Gallo*): No! I am your son.

*Drums and cries stop.*

ANGELA: Holy Father, Abuelo, Hector, breathe on me.

*Celestial sound as a white narrow shaft of light falls on Angela. She levitates, her wings spreading. Only Chata and Juana see this.*

HECTOR (*Taking a deep breath*): Oh sweet air! (*He gets the rooster and sees Angela*) Angela!

ADAN (*Rushing in*): I am here, I have truck . . . (*Seeing Angela, he crosses himself*) Ay Dios. (*He kneels*)

JUANA (*At Gallo's side*): Gallo look!

GALLO: Did you see the hands on that kid, just like steel, never seen finer hands . . . (*Seeing Angela*) Sweet Jesus, my beautiful monster. (*He crosses himself*)

CHATA: No, it ain't true.

HECTOR (*Standing before Angela holding the rooster*): Oh sweet humming-bird woman, shooting star, my comet, you are launched.

ANGELA: Abuelo, Queen of Heaven, All the Saints, All the Angels. It is true, I am back. I am restored. I am . . . Hector, take me with you.

HECTOR: Everywhere. . . . Over the mountains, up to the stars.

very edge.

ngelita! You take Adan. *(He goes to Angela)*

Angela): Shit happens . . . been happening all my life, that's all

A *(Holding Gallo like the Pietà)*: We seen it Gallo, with our own eyes.

ANGELA *(To Hector and Adan)*: And I want my doorstep heaped with floral offer-
ings . . . and . . .

*Hector, Adan and Angela freeze. Chata removes the flower from her hair and
holds it in her hand, trying to decide what to do. She freezes.*

GALLO: Ay Juanita, I had a vision of a hard-kicking flyer . . . *(He yawns)* the ultimate
bird, noble, fino. *(He falls asleep)*

*Juana looks at Gallo, smiles, then looks out half-smiling.*

# END OF PLAY